THE AMAZING APPLEKNOCKERS

Illinois' Cinderella Basketball Team of 1964

Teri Campbell and Anne Ryman

Lusk Creek
Publishing

Makanda, IL

Lusk Creek Publishing
550 S. Rocky Comfort Rd.
Makanda, IL 62958
www.LuskCreekPublishing.com

Edited by W. Dave Yates
Front cover and page design by Matt Bliss and Kelly Drew

Printed in China

First Edition
Second Printing

Library of Congress Control Number: 2010931773

ISBN-978-0-9819382-2-2

The photographs in this book are reproduced with the generous permission of their copyright holders.

Ordering Information:
Quantity sales. Special discounts are available on quantity purchases by corporations, associations, and others. For details, contact the publisher at the address above.

"For the people of Cobden, Illinois, and Appleknocker fans everywhere."

Table of Contents

Preface

In 1964, the Cobden Appleknockers captured the hearts of basketball fans throughout Illinois as they made their historic run to the finals of the state high school basketball tournament. They played at a time before schools were divided into classes based on enrollment. Cobden was a town of 900 residents, and the school had just 147 students. The Appleknockers competed against and defeated opponents that had more people in their high schools than Cobden had in its entire town.

They were a group of boys and a coach who set a goal and worked hard to reach it. Spurred on by talent, a competitive fire, and a hatred of losing, they faced and overcame obstacles and tragedies and the realities of everyday life, but their belief in themselves, their ability, and each other never wavered. They played as a team, and they serve as a great example of what a team can achieve when its individual members don't care who gets the credit.

If nothing else, the Appleknockers gave the sports fans in Illinois a few days of escape and the chance to believe in a Cinderella-style fairytale. And they gave the villagers of Cobden a few months of exciting entertainment and a source of pride that has lasted a lifetime.

Cobden's unusual mascot, the Appleknocker, remains one of the most unique mascots in high school sports. When Cobden made its run through the playoffs, many people wondered, "What's an Appleknocker?" There are many theories as to the origin of the name and how it came to be Cobden's nickname. Its genesis lies in the community's agricultural roots.

Cobden is nestled in the heart of orchard country in southern Illinois. Apple and peach trees surround the town. When there were too many apples on the tree limbs, workers used poles to knock some of the fruit off the trees. This process of thinning apples produced better quality fruit.

Newspaper accounts claim that Cobden's athletic teams

had been labeled Appleknockers by their opponents, and the school decided to adopt the nickname.

Frank Petty, who was the mayor of Cobden when the high school basketball team went to state in 1964, told newspaper reporters that year that the mascot's name dated back to at least the 1940s before Cobden even had a gymnasium. He said the team had made it all the way to a sectional tournament at Du Quoin, Illinois. When Cobden won the game, a spectator reportedly said, "Whoever heard of a bunch of appleknockers winning such a thing?"

Sometime later, the school adopted the name officially.

Authors' Note

This book is based on the true story of the 1964 Appleknocker basketball team. The story was compiled through extensive interviews with the coaches, players, and other main parties involved as well as scorebooks and newspaper accounts written at the time in such outlets as the *Southern Illinoisan*, the Anna *Gazette-Democrat*, the Cairo *Evening Citizen*, the Evansville *Courier & Press*, and others. The information these sources provided was invaluable, and we thank everyone who shared their time and memories. Some dramatic license was taken with quotes to provide further clarity of the thoughts and feelings of those who lived this story, but every effort was made to remain as true to the original story as possible.

Prologue

February 8, 1962
Cobden, Illinois

Coach Dick Ruggles watched restlessly as his Hurst-Bush High School basketball team played the Appleknockers of Cobden High. He directed, encouraged, paced, and cajoled, but in the end, it made no difference. The Appleknockers won by a final score of 89-64. It was his squad's second defeat of the season at the hands of Cobden, and the young coach wasn't fond of losing.

The Hurst-Bush Hummers were not a bunch of slouches, but an honest appraisal of the two teams showed that the Appleknockers simply had them outmanned. Although Cobden was playing several sophomores on its varsity squad, the team still held a substantial height advantage with players hovering from 6-foot-4 to 6-foot-6. The Appleknockers were not only tall, but also very skilled and fundamentally sound.

While his players showered in the locker room after the game, Ruggles gathered his team's gear together and began to pack for the bus ride home. Cobden's small gym was still full of people and buzzing with the sounds of victory for the home team. Celebratory hugs and congratulatory handshakes were being passed around.

Distracted, Ruggles barely noticed the scene. He was disappointed in the loss and the lackluster effort some of his players had displayed in the game. He grabbed his equipment bags and was headed for the exit when a hand clasped his shoulder and stopped him. He turned around and faced a man he had never seen before. The man was tall and looked to be about 40 years old.

"How would you like to coach these boys?" he asked. The man was Dr. Charles Neal, but most everyone called him Doc or Doc Neal. He was the local dentist and the father of two of the Appleknockers' most promising young basketball players, Chuck and Jim Neal.

"I'm Charles Neal," he said, extending a hand. "I'm on the school board here. Would you be interested in coaching this team?"

Surprised by the offer, Ruggles was unsure how to respond. Out of the corner of his eye, he caught sight of Cobden's coach, John Lipe. Lipe was surrounded by a small group of well-wishers who were obviously pleased with his team's decisive win. *This guy just beat my brains out, and you're offering me his job?* Ruggles thought. *Weren't you watching the game?*

"It looks like you already have a coach," Ruggles finally said.

"We might be in the market for a new one if you're interested."

"Well, I don't know," Ruggles hesitated, still feeling off balance by the sudden turn of events.

"Just think about it, okay?" Doc Neal said.

Ruggles had unfinished business with the Hummers, and a new job was the last thing on his mind. He gave Doc Neal a noncommittal shrug and then hoisted his equipment bags over his shoulders and hustled his players out to the bus. The February night was clear and cold with no hint of the spring that was waiting just a few weeks away. As Ruggles settled into his seat for the long ride back to Hurst, he couldn't have known that his brief encounter with Doc Neal was about to change his coaching life forever.

 **Chapter 1**

The Coach

March 1955
Boston, Massachusetts

Time was running down as the Quincy Presidents and the Somerville Highlander battled for the Massachusetts state high school basketball championship. Quincy held a two-point lead, and Somerville had the ball. The Highlander moved the ball around, working to find a final shot to tie the game. A Somerville pass was deflected, and Dick Ruggles, a 5-foot-9 senior guard for the Presidents, recovered the ball. He dribbled down the court, knowing the horn was about to sound, ready to herald victory for his team. A Somerville player chased after him and grabbed for the ball, knocking him to the floor. The referees called a foul on Somerville and gave Dick two free throws with just four seconds remaining.

He stepped with confidence to the foul line. He had already made seven-of-eight free-throw attempts so there was no reason to think these would be any different. He hoisted his first shot, and it bounced around the rim and fell off. No worries. He had another one coming. He took a deep breath, dribbled a couple of times, and launched his second shot. The ball hit the iron, rolled all around, and rattled out. A Somerville player pulled down the rebound, raced toward half court, and heaved a desperation shot. It swished through the net as the buzzer sounded. Overtime!

The teams battled through the extra period and were still deadlocked as time ran out, sending the game into double overtime. At the end of the second extra frame, the score was tied again. The officials and coaches got together and decided to settle the game in sudden death, making the first team to score the victor. Somerville got the tip off the jump ball and made the first basket to win the game and the state title. The Highlander faithful erupted in a jubilant celebration. The capacity crowd at Boston Garden stood and cheered the efforts of both teams, but the players from Quincy found little solace in the applause. Victory had been at their fingertips, close enough to touch, close enough to smell before it was ripped away.

Dick felt especially bad about the loss. *You blew it*, he thought to himself, knowing if he had made just one of his two free throws at the end of regulation, his team would be raising the first-place trophy.

Despondent, Quincy's players walked to the locker room. Their coach, Munroe MacLean, knew they were disappointed, and he gathered the team around him.

"We did our best," he told them. "I'm very proud of you boys."

MacLean praised their efforts and recounted all they had accomplished during the season. Dick and his teammates appreciated the words but nothing could ease the heartache that they all felt.

After the players had showered and changed, several college coaches joined them in the locker room. The coaches had been scouting the teams at the tournament, and they came in to talk to Coach MacLean and some of the senior members of Quincy's team.

Although he was a talented guard, college didn't appear to be an option for Dick. As a freshman, he had attended Quincy High School and taken college preparatory classes. His father worked in a shipyard and was in poor health so when Dick was a sophomore, he decided to enroll in one of the school's vocational programs. That way he would be trained with a marketable skill and be ready to enter the workforce following graduation.

Television was a glamorous and growing industry so he had applied to the television and media program. He had been informed that it was full, and so was unable to get in. His second choice was wood shop, but that program was also closed. A counselor finally enrolled him in the school's electrical program, but Dick hated it. Despite his distaste for currents and circuits and all things electrical, he had stuck it out and was slated to graduate in June from Quincy High's Center for Technical Education with an electrician's certification. He was trained to work as an electrician's apprentice. The problem was he had no desire to be an electrician. Since his diploma was from a vocational program, he would be required to go to a prep school for two years before the colleges and universities in Massachusetts would accept him.

Dick watched as many of his teammates planned their futures with the college recruiters. He felt tears well up in his eyes as the finality of the situation settled like a weight on his shoulders. His basketball career was over, and he wasn't ready for it to end.

Baseball season began, and it was a welcome distraction for Dick. He loved to play the game, and it took his mind off the disheartening way his basketball career had ended. Graduation soon came, and Dick decided to forego the electrician apprenticeship. Instead, he got a job delivering mail for the railroad. He didn't mind the work. He made a decent wage and worked with some nice people, but his heart was elsewhere. He was happiest when he was playing pickup basketball games with his friends and former high school teammates, and he knew his heart belonged to basketball.

He was a big fan of the Boston Celtics, but he was too practical to think he could make a living playing basketball. Although he had grown about an inch since graduating from high school, he still stood just 5-foot-10 and possessed only a vocational school diploma, so college teams weren't knocking down his door with offers.

During a pickup game with some buddies after work, Dick realized exactly what he wanted to do with his life. It hit him almost like an epiphany, and it was so obvious, he was surprised he hadn't thought of it sooner. His future suddenly crystallized before him, and he became excited about what lay ahead. He was going to be a coach.

Realizing what he wanted to do was the first step. Now he had to figure out how to make it happen. Dick always had a good relationship with his high school coach so he decided to ask him for advice. Coach MacLean had helped some of Dick's teammates get into college, and Dick hoped MacLean would be able to help him, too. Not wanting to waste anymore time, Dick called MacLean and set up an appointment for the following afternoon.

After work the next day, Dick drove over to Quincy High School for the meeting with Coach MacLean. School had already dismissed so the parking lot was nearly deserted. Dick's footsteps echoed softly as he walked through the empty halls of his old high school. Everything looked the same, but he felt strange being there. Even though it had only been a few months since he had graduated, he had the odd sensation that he no longer belonged there, at least not as a student anyway. The school was a big part of his past, but now he was ready to face his future.

Coach MacLean's office was located by the gymnasium, and the door was cracked open. Dick knocked, and Coach MacLean looked up from some papers on his desk.

"Come in, Dick," he said, standing up. "How are you doing?"

"I'm fine, Coach. How are you?"

"Oh, I'm fine."

The two shook hands, and Coach MacLean motioned for Dick to take a seat in the chair opposite his desk.

"What can I do for you?" Coach MacLean asked, pushing his work aside. "Or is this just a social call?"

"I want to be a coach," Dick blurted out.

MacLean looked thoughtful. "To coach in a high school you have to have a degree in education, you know. You have to go to college."

"I want to go to college," Dick told him. "I'd even like to play basketball in college."

"Do you know where you want to go?"

"No. I don't have a lot of options since I went to the vocational school."

"Have you thought about going to a prep school?" MacLean asked. He knew about the prep school requirement in Massachusetts for students who graduated from the vocational track in high school. He had a current player who was highly regarded as a college prospect, but since he was in Quincy's vocational school, local colleges were keeping their distance from him.

Dick explained that paying for two years of prep school and four years of college would be a financial hardship. Besides that he said he was ready to get started in college and felt the prep school would be a waste of time.

"I'll see what I can do for you," MacLean said, pleased by Dick's determination and ambition.

Dick thanked him and left. After he was gone, Coach MacLean found himself smiling as he remembered first seeing Dick as a freshman in high school. At the time he was about 5-foot-1 and weighed a gaunt 100 pounds. His basketball uniform hung loosely on his small frame. Quincy High School's colors were blue and white, and MacLean had dubbed Dick, "Little Boy Blue."

Over the years, MacLean had watched Dick blossom as a player. He had a natural instinct for the game, great court awareness, and was a skilled passer. As a guard, he ran the team's up-tempo offense, and MacLean had given him the freedom and responsibility to make many decisions on the court. Dick was talented enough to play in college, and MacLean was fairly certain there was a college or university somewhere that would accept Dick.

In the spring of 1956, Coach MacLean was asked to coach the North All-Star high school basketball team against the South All-Stars in a tournament in Lexington, Kentucky. The tournament was held at Rupp Arena and well attended by college coaches throughout the region.

One afternoon MacLean ran into his friend Carl Erickson, who was the athletic director at Southern Illinois University in Carbondale. The two began talking, and when the subject turned to recruiting, MacLean thought of Dick and his current player, Tom Morrell.

"I have a of couple guys back home that are pretty good players," he told Erickson. He then explained that they had attended the vocational school and were facing a prep school requirement back East.

"I tell you what," Erickson said. "I can't promise you they'll play basketball, but I can get them into SIU in the fall."

"Fair enough," MacLean said. "I really appreciate this, and I'll let them know."

When he returned to Quincy, MacLean called Dick to give him the good news.

"I found a college for you," he said.

"Really? Which one?" This was the news he had been waiting for.

Coach MacLean told Dick about Carl Erickson and Southern Illinois University. "He can't help you with a scholarship or anything, but he'll get you into school."

Coach MacLean advised Dick of the admission procedures at SIU. He told him that he thought Tom Morrell would be going, too, and that Erickson would help them get settled once they got to Carbondale.

"Keep working on your game," MacLean said before

hanging up. "You never know."

At supper that evening, Dick told his family about his plans to go to Southern Illinois University.

"Where's Southern Illinois University?" his mother asked, not entirely pleased with the news.

"It's in Carbondale," Dick answered.

"Well, where's Carbondale?"

"In southern Illinois, I guess," he replied. He wasn't trying to be a wise guy, but he had only a vague notion of where Carbondale was located.

His father drug out an atlas, and he and Dick found Carbondale in the far southern end of Illinois. With the map's legend, they figured it to be more than 1,200 miles from Quincy.

"You shouldn't have to go so far away," his mother said. "We can scrape up the money for prep school, and you can stay here."

"No, Mom. I don't want you to have to do that," Dick said. "I've already been out of high school almost a year, and I want to start college as soon as possible. Let me try it for a year, and we'll see what happens."

Lawrence and Gertrude Ruggles were salt-of-the-earth people who worked hard to provide a good home for Dick and his two sisters, Hope and Linda. They loved their children and would never stand in the way of them pursuing their dreams so they finally agreed.

Dick worked the rest of that spring and summer, saving as much money as he could for his tuition. He played basketball as often as possible, just in case he got the opportunity to play for the SIU Salukis. He also grew another inch and now stood 5-foot-11.

Summer drew to a close, and it was time to go to college. Dick packed a few bags to take with him. Since he had never been to college, he had no idea what to bring. He threw in some clothes and personal necessities and figured he could get anything else he needed when he got to Illinois. One Saturday morning in early September, he said goodbye to his sisters at their home. They were a close family, and he missed them as soon as he walked out the door.

He stared out the car window at the familiar city streets as his parents drove him to the train station. He loved the Boston area. He loved the ocean and the rocky New England beaches. He had been a big fan of the Boston Braves before they left town, and he recalled all the times he and his friends had snuck into Boston Garden to watch the Celtics play. He put on a confident front for his sisters and parents, but he was apprehensive about leaving. He had no idea what to expect when he got to SIU, but he was determined to give it a try.

When they arrived at the station, Tom Morrell was already there. Tom was a strong, athletic young man who had excelled in several sports at Quincy High School. Dick said goodbye to his parents and gave them both a hug.

"Do you have enough money with you?" his father asked.

"I think so."

"Be careful," his mother told him. "If you need anything, just call. We'll figure out some way to help you out."

"I know," Dick said, smiling bravely. "I appreciate that, but I'm gonna be fine."

"I love you, son," Mrs. Ruggles said, fighting back tears. Even though Dick was 19 years old, he was still her little boy.

They said their goodbyes, and then Dick and Tom Morrell boarded the train for their trip to the Midwest. They were scheduled to stop first in Chicago. There they would board a different train that would take them south to their destination of Carbondale.

They located their seats and settled in for the journey. Dick was glad to have a familiar face joining him, but he soon realized that Tom was more unsure about leaving Quincy than he was.

"What are we doing, Dick?" Tom asked. The look on

his face told Dick that this train was the last place Tom wanted to be.

"We're going to college," Dick said. He was excited and thankful for this opportunity, and he wasn't going to let homesickness stand in the way of his goal. He was going to be a coach.

The train rattled through Massachusetts, New York, Pennsylvania, Ohio, and Indiana before reaching Illinois. Dick and Tom felt restless and travel-weary as they walked off the train in Chicago and collected their bags. It was around 3 a.m. They went to the ticket counter to purchase tickets for the trip to Carbondale.

"You want to go *where?*" the man behind the counter asked them.

"Carbondale," Tom repeated.

"Oh, *Car*-bondale," the man said, emphasizing the first syllable of the word. "I'm sorry. I didn't understand you the first time."

They paid for the tickets and located the train that would take them south.

"What did he mean by that?" Tom asked Dick. "He didn't understand me?"

"He did the second time."

Dick and Tom both had thick Boston brogues, and Tom suddenly became conscious of his accent. "Do you think he thinks we talk funny?"

"No, and don't worry about it anyway," Dick said. "We got the tickets, right?"

The train made several stops as it meandered southward, picking up and dropping off passengers at small towns along the way. It finally pulled into the Carbondale station around 2 p.m. on Sunday. Carl Erickson, SIU's athletic director, was waiting for Dick and Tom, just like Coach MacLean had told them he would be.

"Are you the boys from Boston?" Erickson asked as the two young men emerged from the train.

"That's right," Dick said, and they both introduced themselves.

"Welcome to southern Illinois," he said.

Carl Erickson helped them carry their bags to his car, and then he drove them a short distance to a motel. It was a bright sunny day, and Carbondale was still warm in early September.

"You'll stay here tonight," Erickson informed them. "I couldn't get you into a dorm this year. They were already full so you'll be staying out at Southern Acres in Carterville."

Erickson gave them their class schedules and a map of the campus. He told them to come to his office the next morning, and he would give them their room assignment at Southern Acres.

After Erickson left, Dick and Tom called home to let their families know that they had arrived at their destination. Then they went to a diner next to the motel to get something to eat. The restaurant had only a few patrons, and they took seats in a booth near the door. Soon a waitress wearing a light pink uniform with a crisp white apron approached and handed them menus. She gave them a friendly smile and said she would be right back to take their orders.

While she was gone, Dick and Tom perused their menus. They were both famished from their long journey. The waitress returned quickly and set a glass of ice water in front of each of them.

"What can I get for you?" she asked.

She made a note of what they wanted on a small pad she held in her hand, and before she left the table this time, she said to them, "You two aren't from around here, are you?"

"No," Dick told her. "We're from Quincy, Massachusetts."

"Really?" she said, flashing another grin. "I have a pretty good ear, and I didn't think you sounded like you were from this neck of the woods."

"I thought Illinois was kind of centrally located," Tom

said to Dick after their waitress was gone. "The way some of the people around here talk, it sounds like we're in the deep South."

The next day, Dick and Tom got up early and walked the few blocks from their motel to Southern Illinois University's campus. They were both struck by the small-town ambiance. There were no skyscrapers and little traffic. The campus was situated on the south side of town and spread out over several acres. With its abundance of trees and flowering bushes, it had a fresh, rural feel, and was quite different from the university campuses in the Boston area with their bustling atmospheres and many old, ivy-covered brick buildings.

With the map of the campus that Carl Erickson had given them, they located Davies Building and found his office in the men's physical education department. Erickson introduced Dick and Tom to a few people in the office and showed them around the building. He took them to a gym on the second floor where the Saluki basketball team practiced and played its games.

"Coach MacLean tells me you boys like to play basketball," Erickson said. "It's football season now, but the basketball players still come up here and practice in the evenings. It's nothing official. They just get together and play and shoot around. You're both welcome to come up here and play."

Erickson took Dick and Tom to the Student Union and showed them where they would catch the shuttle bus to Southern Acres. He explained that a bus ran periodically to bring students to campus and take them back. He gave them the keys to the room they would be sharing and told them if they needed anything to give him a call.

Dick and Tom thanked Erickson for all his help. They walked back to the motel where they had stayed the night before and retrieved their luggage. They turned in the room key and walked back to the Student Union just as a shuttle bus pulled in.

"I guess we'll go check out Southern Acres," Dick said

as they hauled their belongings onto the bus.

The shuttle carried them through Carbondale and out of town on Route 13, going east. They passed over Crab Orchard Lake and finally reached Carterville. It was more than 13 miles round trip. *Back home there are probably a dozen colleges within 13 miles of my house*, Dick thought as he rode through the rural landscape of southern Illinois, *and here I am going to college almost 1,300 miles away.*

"Are we going to make this trip everyday?" Tom asked apparently not thrilled with the commute. "I'm ready to go home right now."

"Come on," Dick said, trying to encourage both his friend and himself. "Let's give it a try."

They did give it a try, and eventually their homesickness subsided. They got busy with classes and studying and had little time to think about what they were missing back home. They grew accustomed to the wide-open spaces and slower pace of life in the rural Midwest. They met a few other students who lived at Southern Acres and made friends easily. Their East Coast accents always garnered attention, but they got used to the comments almost as quickly as they got used to the southern Illinois drawl of many of their classmates.

In the evenings, Dick regularly went up to Davies Gym to work out and shoot baskets. Tom would sometimes go, too. The scholarship players on SIU's basketball team were always there scrimmaging, and sometimes Dick would watch them play. One night the scholarship guys were short a man, and one of the players approached Dick.

"You want to join our game tonight?" the guy asked him. His name was Seymour Bryson. He was a sophomore and played forward for the Salukis. As a freshman last season, he had led the team in rebounding.

"Sure," Dick said, happy for the opportunity to play with some of the members of SIU's team. He was still hoping to play for the Salukis.

The scrimmage went well and was a lot of fun. Dick

had missed being part of a team and playing pickup games with his friends back home. He seldom shot the ball, but he had several assists. He still had his knack for finding an open team-mate and delivering a solid pass. The other players seemed to appreciate his unselfish play.

The following night at the gym, the scholarship play-ers on SIU's team asked Dick to join them again. When they finished practicing, Seymour Bryson stopped Dick before he left the gym.

"What's your name?" Seymour asked him.

"Dick Ruggles."

"I'm Seymour Bryson," he told Dick. "We practice up here nearly every evening in the off season. You ought to join us on a regular basis."

"That sounds great," Dick said.

"Where are you from, Dick?"

His accent had given him away again. "Quincy, Mas-sachusetts."

"Small world," Seymour said. "I'm from Quincy, Il-linois."

For the next few weeks, Dick practiced with the schol-arship basketball players every night. He liked the guys and enjoyed feeling like part of the team.

"You know, Dick," Seymour said to him one evening. "That's Coach Holder over there." He pointed to a man sitting on the bleachers. Lynn Holder had been the head coach of the Salukis since 1946. He had played forward for the team from 1931-35, earning all-conference honors in 1933 and 1934.

"He's put his head in the gym a few nights," Seymour continued. "We lost a couple of players from last year, and he might ask you if you're interested in walking on the team."

"Really?" Dick said hopefully.

"If he asks you, tell him no," Seymour said.

"What?"

"Tell him you're homesick or broke or whatever, just

tell him you're not going to stay."

"But why?"

"Just trust me," Seymour said.

Dick was unsure what to think. He had been hoping he would get a chance to try out. Why should he tell the coach he couldn't stay? Seymour seemed like a good guy, but Dick was puzzled about his advice. He wondered if maybe Seymour had another buddy that he wanted to play on the team, and he was afraid Dick would take his spot.

A week or so later, Coach Holder called Dick over when the players were done scrimmaging.

"I hear you're from Quincy, Massachusetts," Holder said to Dick.

"That's right."

"You're a long way from home. How do you like southern Illinois?

"Oh, I like it a lot," Dick said. "Everyone's really nice."

"Good," Holder said. "You're going to stay and play basketball, right?"

Remembering what Seymour had told him, Dick said, "Well, I'm not sure. My parents aren't in good health, and this is kind of hard on us financially. I don't know how long I'll be able to stay." It wasn't exactly a lie, Dick reasoned to himself.

"Really?" Holder asked, looking concerned. "You know, I'd like to have you on the team. I think I can help you out. So don't go anywhere until you talk to me first."

"Okay," Dick agreed and left the gym feeling hopeful.

Three nights later when the team finished practice, Coach Holder called Dick over again.

"If you stay and play basketball for me, I've got a full scholarship for you," Holder said.

A full scholarship was more than Dick had even hoped for.

"I think I can do that," he said with a smile.

As soon as he was back at his apartment at Southern Acres, Dick phoned his parents back in Quincy. "I have some great news," he told them. "I've earned a basketball scholarship. I made the team."

His parents were pleased. They weren't the sports enthusiasts that Dick was, but they knew how important it was to him and how hard he had worked to make it. They were also thankful that he was receiving a scholarship. They had already planned to help him make it through college, but this money would certainly come in handy.

The Saluki basketball team posted a record of 13 wins and 11 losses in 1956-57, Dick's first season on the team. Seymour Bryson led the team in rebounding again, pulling down nearly 14 boards per game. He was a first team selection by the Interstate Intercollegiate Athletic Conference. Larry Whitlock averaged 17.3 points per game to lead the team in scoring. Dick got less playing time than he had in high school, but he was learning the college game. He hoped that as his experience increased so would his minutes.

At the end of their freshman year, Dick and Tom Morrell took the train back home to Quincy, Massachusetts. For Dick it was just a summer break, but for Tom it was a homecoming. Tom had realized during his year in the Midwest that he was an East Coast guy at heart, and he decided not to return to SIU for his sophomore year.

Dick bought an old green Plymouth and drove the nearly 1,300 miles back to Carbondale in the fall all by himself. His sophomore year brought many changes. He had a new roommate named Skip Butler. Skip was from Venice, Illinois, and he and Dick hit it off right away. They lived in an on-campus dorm at Thompson Point, and Dick was glad he no longer had to take the bus to Southern Acres every day.

Having his own car also gave him more freedom and independence. One of his buddies back in Boston had a minor wreck in the car during the summer, and Dick never had a chance to repair the damage. With its missing fender, the green Plymouth and Dick became very well known around campus.

On the basketball court, his playing time increased and he was a solid contributor off the bench. Coach Holder was a good teacher of the game, and Dick learned a lot under his tutelage. The team finished second in the conference, but its overall record mirrored the previous season's 13-11 mark. Seymour Bryson had another outstanding year, leading the team in scoring and rebounding with 16 points and 13.3 boards per game. He again earned all-conference honors.

Changes were taking place behind the scenes that would shake things up for the 1958-59 season. Don Boydston, who had succeeded Carl Erickson as the SIU athletic director, had his sights set on a new basketball coach for the Salukis. He was interested in Harry Gallatin, a 10-year NBA veteran. Gallatin, a 6-foot-6 center/forward, played for the New York Knicks from 1948-57 and was playing his last year with the Detroit Pistons. His physical strength and tireless work ethic had earned him the nickname "Horse" from his teammates.

During his 10 seasons in the NBA, Gallatin was selected for the All-Star game seven times. A relentless rebounder, he ranked among the top 10 in rebounding six times and led the league with 1,098 boards in 1954. He was also a solid contributor offensively, averaging 13 points per game over his career.

While his playing credentials were impressive, Gallatin had no coaching experience. That was fine with Boydston. He felt that Gallatin's high profile and knowledge of the game would give him instant credibility with the players. He had also checked into Gallatin's background and knew that he had earned a bachelor's degree in physical education and hygiene while playing basketball at Northeast Missouri State Teacher's College. Boydston also learned that Gallatin had obtained a master's degree in physical education by attending the University of Iowa during summer breaks from the NBA. Boydston was sure that Harry Gallatin would be a fine addition to SIU's staff.

When the Pistons were in St. Louis for a game against the Hawks, Boydston contacted Gallatin about coaching SIU's basketball team. They began discussions, and when the 1957-58 NBA season ended, Gallatin retired from the league and accepted Boydston's offer.

In the late summer of 1958, the 31-year-old Gallatin brought his family to Carbondale. Although he had lived in the Big Apple for several years, he was originally from Roxana, Illinois, a small town near East St. Louis, so in a way it was like coming home. Not knowing exactly what to expect, he moved into an office in Davies Building and began his new career. He soon realized that he had a lot to learn, but he approached his new job with the same zeal he had during his playing career.

Although Lynn Holder had been replaced as the Salukis' coach, he remained at SIU as a faculty member in the men's physical education department. His office in Davies was located close to Coach Gallatin's, and he proved to be a valuable source of information for the new young coach. Since this was Gallatin's first coaching experience, Holder showed him the ropes of scheduling opponents and putting together a program.

When summer vacation ended, Dick returned to SIU for his junior year. He had completed his general education requirements, and now it was time to pick a course of study. This was no problem for him. He still wanted to be a coach so he chose physical education as his major and social studies as a minor. Although he still missed home, he was glad to get back to Carbondale and the new life he was creating there. He and Skip Butler had decided to room together again at Thompson

Point and quickly fell back into their old routines.

His first week back, Dick went up to Davies Gym to meet some of the other basketball players for a shoot-around and was informed that their team had a new coach.

"Who is it?" Dick wanted to know.

"It's Harry Gallatin," Seymour told him. "He's a pro. He used to play for the Knicks."

"Yeah," Dick replied. "I know who he is." He was surprised by the announcement. He had seen Harry "The Horse" Gallatin play against his Boston Celtics many times, but he never imagined that one day Gallatin would be his coach.

Coach Gallatin called a team meeting the following day. Dick gathered with the other basketball players in Davies Gym where Gallatin formally introduced himself as their new coach. Still in prime playing shape at 6-foot-6 and 225 pounds, he was impressive in looks and stature. Don Boydston had been right about Gallatin's credibility with the players. It was clear from the start that he had their attention.

Gallatin had been busy recruiting since taking the job in the summer, and he introduced two newcomers. One was Jim Gauldoni, a 6-foot-2 guard from nearby Herrin, Illinois. The second player was Charlie Vaughn, a 6-foot-2 sharp-shooting forward from the small town of Tamms, Illinois, south of Carbondale. Gallatin had heard that the team scrimmaged together in the evenings during the off season, and he asked the players to include Jim and Charlie in their games.

The players happily obliged. The team had lost Larry Whitlock and a couple other guys to graduation so there was plenty of room for the new additions. The informal scrimmages gave them the chance to get to know each other and become friends as well as teammates. They were a competitive group so while the workouts were friendly, they were often hotly contested.

Coach Gallatin began formal practices in October. He was a strong believer in fundamentals and conditioning. As a player, he felt that he could go harder and longer than anyone else on the court because he kept himself in top physical shape. In the NBA, he had played up-tempo, fast-break basketball. He knew that for his players to execute such an offense effectively, they would have to be in good condition and be fundamentally sound in all phases of the game.

Gallatin had watched some films of Coach Holder's games and knew that his teams had played a slower, more methodical brand of basketball so Gallatin was unsure how the players would adapt to a new system. Since he was unfamiliar with the players, he spent the first few days of practice evaluating them. Along with conditioning drills, each day he ran them through drills on shooting, passing, dribbling, and rebounding.

He introduced them to his faster style of play, and they were eager to learn. Gallatin was a hands-on coach. He got out on the floor with the players to show them what he wanted them to do and how he wanted them to do it. They worked hard on the things he taught them, and he became convinced that they had the skill level to run the fast break successfully. Dick took to the new offense quickly because it was very similar to the way he had played in high school under Coach MacLean. He was excited to be playing fast-break ball again and hoped his experience would help increase his playing time.

"This is going to be fun," Dick commented to Seymour after practice one day. The practices weren't long, but they were tough, and both young men were breathing heavily.

Seymour nodded his head in agreement. "This is the way the pros play."

"That's right," Dick said with a smile. "This is East Coast basketball."

As the weeks passed, Gallatin got to know the players better. The ones he had inherited from Lynn Holder were an intelligent and talented bunch. Seymour Bryson's physical abilities were obvious. He was a leader on and off the court so Gallatin named him the team's captain. Gallatin had also no-

ticed how quickly Dick picked up the fast-break offense. Dick
was hard-working, competitive, and confident, and Gallatin
tabbed him for a starting position at the guard spot.

Throughout the first part of the 1958-59 season, the
players continued to adjust to the new system and learned to
play as a team. Although Charlie Vaughn was only a freshman, he learned the college game quickly and was a scoring
machine. He had an unorthodox shot that was nearly impossible to block and could hit shots from almost anywhere on
the court, knocking down 25- and 30-footers with consistency.
Seymour blossomed offensively, as well, in the up-tempo
system. Davies Gym was packed for every game as the fans
turned out to see the exciting, new-look Salukis play.
Dick was happy to be in the starting lineup and playing significant minutes. When the fast-break opportunity was
unavailable, the team played a varied offense, consisting of
many different set plays. Dick was a very good ball handler,
and Coach Gallatin gave him the role of playmaker, entrusting
him with the responsibility to call plays that would exploit the
weaknesses of their opponents. Dick appreciated the responsibility, and he handled it well.
As exciting as things were on the court, Dick's attention
would drift to the sidelines from time to time where a pretty
new cheerleader had caught his eye. He didn't know her name,
but he found himself looking forward to each game, knowing
she would be there to cheer on the team.

The winter quarter began in January, and Dick's roommate, Skip Butler, returned to the dorm after being home for
the Christmas break. Due to the basketball schedule, Dick was
unable to go home for the holidays. The team had a conference
game at Western Illinois University on December 20 and then
competed in the Quincy Holiday Tournament on December 27-
29 so there was no time for him to go back to Massachusetts.
The campus felt empty during breaks when only the basketball

players were around, and Dick was glad to have his roommate back.

One evening while Dick was doing homework, Skip entered their room with an announcement.

"There's a girl you have to meet," he told Dick.

"What are you talking about?" Dick asked.

"My girlfriend, Bev, has a roommate, and we think the two of you should meet."

"Did Bev put you up to this?"

"Yeah," Skip confessed, settling onto his bed. "But I think it's a good idea, too."

"You mean like a blind date?"

"Yeah. What have you got to lose?"

Dick was skeptical but also curious and asked, "Who is it?"

"You may already know her. She's a cheerleader."

Now Dick's interest was piqued. "Which cheerleader?"

Skip pulled out a yearbook and thumbed through the pages until he found her picture. "Here," he said, handing the book to Dick. "This is her. Her name's Mary Woesthaus."

Dick looked at the picture. It was the same girl he had been watching cheer on the sidelines all season. Although he was apprehensive about being set up on a blind date, he wanted to meet Mary, so he agreed.

Skip and Bev made the arrangements and set up a double date for Saturday night. With Skip riding shotgun, Dick drove his green Plymouth to the house where Bev and Mary lived.

They roomed with seven other girls at the house. They were used to seeing Skip around since he had been dating Bev for awhile, but Dick was new, and the girls gave him many appraising glances as he and Skip waited in the foyer for Mary and Bev to appear. When the two girls descended the staircase from the second floor, Dick was sure that the wait had been worth it. Mary's shiny blond hair framed her pretty face, and Dick found her just as appealing without her pompons.

Bev had met Dick several times, and she introduced him to Mary. Mary gave Dick a shy smile, and the two couples left to begin their date. Dick opened the front passenger-side door for Mary when they reached his car, and Bev and Skip climbed into the backseat. Dick drove them to a casual restaurant that was also a popular hangout for SIU students.

Mary was nervous about being on a date with Dick and said little during the ride. She had been surprised when Bev had mentioned that she wanted to fix the two of them up on a date, and Mary was even more surprised that Dick had agreed to go. After all, he was a junior and a starter on the basketball team, and she was just a freshman. She had thought he was handsome when she first saw him on the basketball court, but going on a date with him had never even occurred to her.

When they arrived at the restaurant, it was just beginning to fill up with other couples and small groups of students. The students had returned to SIU for the winter quarter, and everyone was out for fun on a Saturday night. When the students were in town, the population of Carbondale nearly doubled, and the town took on a fresh, dynamic vibe.

The four of them settled into a booth, and the conversation began to flow. Dick soon put Mary's nerves to rest with his quick wit and easy-going manner. They lingered over dinner, talking and laughing and enjoying each other's company. Mary loved to listen to Dick talk. She liked his Boston accent, finding it unique and charming.

Bev and Skip had been on target in their match making, and when they could see that Dick and Mary were feeling comfortable with each other, they decided to make their exit.

"We're going to take off," Skip said, standing up and extending a hand to Bev.

Caught off guard, Dick asked, "Where are you going?"

"We have things to do," Bev said with a coy smile.

"But you don't have a car," Dick said. "I drove, remember?"

"We can walk," Skip replied.

"But it's so cold out," Mary protested.

Bev and Skip shrugged into their coats. "We'll be fine," Bev reassured her.

Dick and Mary watched as their friends disappeared through the front door of the restaurant. They sat in awkward silence for a few moments before they both burst into laughter. They knew that Bev and Skip had left to give them a chance to be alone together.

Mary was from Anna, Illinois, a small town about 25 miles south of Carbondale, home to fewer than 5,000 residents. It was a world away from Quincy, Massachusetts, but the two of them still had a lot in common. They were both Catholic and came from close-knit families. They were both middle children, each having an older and a younger sister. Although Mary was only a freshman, she was planning on studying home economics education and becoming a teacher. Since Dick played for the Salukis and Mary was a cheerleader, the basketball team provided another common ground for discussion.

Realizing that they had been monopolizing their booth for nearly two hours, Dick and Mary decided they had better head out. The curfew at Mary's house was midnight, but since it was only a little after 9 p.m., Dick wasn't ready to call it a night.

"Do you like to ice skate?" he asked Mary when they reached his car.

"I guess. Why?"

"I have an idea."

He drove them to campus and parked his car near Thompson Lake. The temperature had been below freezing for the past several days. This was unusual for Carbondale. Southern Illinois experienced all four seasons to varying degrees, depending on the year. The frigid temperatures had allowed a thick coating of ice to form on the lake, and several people were out taking advantage of the frozen lake.

"You want to give it a try?" Dick asked, motioning toward the skaters on the lake.

"We don't have any skates," Mary said skeptically.

"That's okay," Dick assured her. "Our shoes will be fine."

The night was clear and a three-quarters full moon and a billion twinkling stars helped illuminate the surface of the lake. They bundled their coats and scarves around themselves and scooted around on the ice in their street shoes. Mary was glad she had opted to wear a pair of rubber-soled shoes and not the dressier pumps she had considered.

Dick had ice skated a lot on outdoor rinks back home in Massachusetts, and Mary admired how gracefully he moved on the ice. Dick liked the fact that Mary was willing to brave the cold with him and that ice skating together gave him the chance to hold her hand, even if it was covered with a glove. They talked and laughed and slipped around on the lake until their feet were freezing.

When they could no longer take the cold, Dick drove Mary home and walked her to the door.

"I hope you had a good time tonight," Dick said.

"Well, I can't feel my toes, but other than that, I had a great time," Mary teased.

Dick laughed softly. "I'll call you sometime, okay?"

"I'd like that, and I'll see you Monday night, right?"

"Uh...Monday?" Dick stammered.

"We have a ball game, remember?"

"Oh yeah, that's right," he said. Basketball had been the furthest thing from his mind. "I guess I'll see you there."

"Thanks for everything," Mary said. She gave Dick a quick hug then slipped through the front door into the house.

As Dick drove to his dorm, he replayed the events of the evening in his mind. It was one of the best first dates he had ever been on. He had gone out with other girls at SIU, but there was something special about Mary that made her stand out from the rest. He didn't know it, but Mary was back at her rooming house thinking the same thing about him.

The two of them began dating steadily after that night.

It seemed that Mary had a positive impact on Dick's game because the Salukis rattled off a nine-game winning streak from January 8 to February 6. Dick scored in double figures in four of those games, posting his season high of 21 against conference-rival Eastern Illinois University on January 22.

The Salukis went on to finish the season with a record of 18-9. Charlie Vaughn led the team in scoring, averaging 23.8 points per game. He scored at least 30 points on five occasions. Seymour averaged more than 19 points per game and led the team in rebounding for the fourth straight year with nearly 11 per game, ending his career with a total of 1,244 boards.

When the spring quarter ended, Dick returned to Massachusetts for the summer break, but this time with conflicting emotions. It was his first visit back to Quincy since the prior summer, and he really missed his family. He wanted to see them, but he hated the thought of being away from Mary for so long. The two of them had grown very close since January and had practically become inseparable. They had said a teary goodbye when they parted, but both believed that their relationship was strong enough to survive the summer apart.

Dick worked during the day and saw his old friends while he was home for the summer. He had remained close with many of them and enjoyed the time they got to spend together, but Mary was always in his thoughts. He talked about her a lot and called her on the phone several times. His parents had known about their relationship, but they hadn't realized it was so serious. When Dick packed his car to head back to Carbondale for his senior year, his parents could see how anxious he was to return.

"She must be really something," his father said as he helped Dick with his bags.

"What?" Dick asked.

"You know who I'm talking about."

"She is, Dad," Dick said with a smile. "You and Mom would like her, too."

"I'm sure we would," his mother chimed in. "But it's what you think that matters."

He said goodbye to his parents and set out on the long drive to SIU that had become all too familiar to him.

The town of Carbondale seemed to wake up when the college students returned to begin each new year. When Dick arrived, he unloaded his car and put his things in his room at Thompson Point. Before unpacking, he called to see if Mary was at her rooming house. She was already there so he drove over to see her. She had missed him during the summer break, too, and was waiting in front of the house when he pulled up. They had a happy reunion, and it was clear to both of them that the time apart had not diminished their feelings for each other.

Dick went to Davies Gym to work out the first evening he was back on campus. He was a senior and knowing this was his last year to play basketball, he wanted to make the most of the time. Seymour Bryson had graduated in the spring and would no longer be on the team. Dick really liked Seymour and knew he would be hard to replace as a teammate and friend.

Along with Dick, the Salukis had several players returning, including their leading scorer Charlie Vaughn. Forwards Harold Bardo, Don Hepler, and Randy McClary were also back, along with center Tom McGreal and guard Jim Gualdoni. Coach Gallatin had also picked up some new recruits that included John Mees, a 6-foot-1 guard from Carbondale, Jim Lazenby, a 5-foot-11 guard from Pinckneyville, Larry Essenpreis, a 6-foot-3 forward from Highland, Illinois, and Jim Rosser, a 6-foot-3 forward from East St. Louis.

As the team's only senior, Dick took the lead in gathering the players together for the unofficial scrimmages. Playing together in the off season allowed the players to learn each other's strengths and weaknesses, which gave the team a head start when official practices began in October. Coach Gallatin liked Dick's initiative. He trusted Dick as a playmaker on the court and felt that the other players did as well so he named him the team captain.

The Salukis went on to have a fine season in 1959-60. They ran their up-tempo offense to a record of 20-9, winning the Interstate Intercollegiate Athletic Conference title. It was the first time SIU's basketball team had won 20 games since the 1949-50 campaign. Charlie Vaughn suffered no sophomore slump. He led the team in scoring and rebounding, averaging nearly 27 points and 9.6 boards per game and was named the MVP of the conference.

Dick had assumed the role of point guard again, setting up the offense, and he had been a steadying influence on the floor. He led the team in free-throw percentage, hitting almost 88 percent of his attempts. He was gratified that his final season as a player had been so successful.

Things were looking up for him off the court as well. He proposed to Mary, and she accepted. They planned to wed in August. In the spring, Dick had interviewed for a teaching and coaching position at St. Anne High School near Kankakee, Illinois. He was scheduled to start there in the fall.

After graduation in June, Dick began to tie up loose ends in Carbondale and prepare for the move to northern Illinois. Mary concentrated on their wedding plans. There were so many details to take care of. The ceremony was going to take place in her hometown of Anna, and although Dick's family was so far away, she wanted them to feel like they were part of things, too. Mary also had to find a college up north to transfer to. She had only completed two years at SIU and needed two more to finish her degree.

The transfer issue became a moot point when Dick was told of an opening for a coach and teacher at a small high school in southern Illinois called Hurst-Bush. Hurst and Bush were actually two separate, tiny communities in Williamson County whose students attended a consolidated high school.

Dick told Mary about the job possibility, and she encouraged him to check into it.

"It can't hurt to find out about it," Mary said.

"You don't want to go to Kankakee, do you?"

"No, it's not that. I'm going wherever you're going, but there's no reason not to look into it."

"I guess that's true," Dick agreed.

While he knew Mary would probably prefer to stay in southern Illinois since it was her home, she had always encouraged him to pursue his dream of becoming a coach, no matter where the path took them. She was happier for him than anyone when he had told her he got the job at St. Anne. She had even told him she was willing to move to Massachusetts if he wanted to go back home to find a job.

Dick found out that the pay at Hurst-Bush was less than he would receive at St. Anne, but something about the job appealed to him anyway. He knew it would be easier for Mary to continue school at SIU, and deep down he wasn't sure he wanted to leave southern Illinois. Although he still thought of Massachusetts as home, he had made a new home here over the past few years and was reluctant to start over up north.

After mulling over his options for a couple days, Dick finally called the principal at St. Anne and asked to be let out of his contract with the school. The principal obliged, leaving Dick free to accept the position at Hurst-Bush.

On the morning of August 20, Dick and Mary were married in St. Mary's Catholic Church in Anna. It was beautiful day. The sky was a bright, robin-egg blue with puffy white clouds, and the wedding was a splendid affair. Mary's older sister, Rita, was the maid of honor, and she and the other bridesmaids wore light blue dresses. Mary wore her mother's wedding gown. It was made of ivory-colored satin and lace and had a long train. The dress had been altered slightly to fit Mary, and she looked stunning. She was the first of her sisters to get married. Her father, Francis Woesthaus, was more sentimental than he liked to admit, and he got a little misty eyed as he walked her down the aisle to her groom.

Dick had never seen Mary look more lovely as she strode down the aisle toward him. He always thought she was beautiful, but today she took his breath away. He was handsomely decked out in a black tuxedo and was flanked by Jack Powers, an old friend from Quincy who was his best man. Two of his friends and teammates from SIU, Don Hepler and Tom McGreal, served as groomsmen. When Dick and Mary said their vows and pledged their lives to each other, both felt that they couldn't possibly be happier.

Many of Dick's family members and friends came out from Massachusetts to help the couple celebrate their special day. His parents and one of his sisters had come for his graduation in June, but for most of the others, this was their first trip to southern Illinois.

When the ceremony was over, the happy couple and their guests all climbed into their cars and drove to Mary's parents' house for a cake and punch reception. Everyone honked their horns as they drove, loudly announcing the union of Dick and Mary Ruggles. Jack Powers chauffeured the newlyweds in Dick's car. He and the other groomsmen had strung tin cans on it and painted "Just Married" on the side.

After the reception, everyone went to the Giant City State Park Lodge for dinner. Nestled in the scenic bluffs of Makanda, Illinois, the lodge provided a rustic backdrop for the festive occasion. The food was delicious, the company was good, and although the atmosphere was quite different from what the city-slickers from Massachusetts were used to, everyone seemed to have a wonderful time.

As the guests said their goodbyes and began to disperse, Jack told Dick and Mary that he wanted to drive them to Hurst.

"I want to see where you two will be living," he explained.

"You can't drive to Hurst," Dick told him. "You'll never find it."

"Part of the best man's duty is to be the chauffeur," Jack insisted. "You can give me directions from the backseat."

Jack drove the nearly 20 miles from Makanda to Hurst, taking in the rural expanses of southern Illinois. The orchards and pastureland that they passed were strikingly different from the tall buildings and concrete that he and Dick had grown up around. He couldn't put his finger on why, but for some reason he felt that Dick fit in this environment.

"You've moved to the boonies," Jack declared with a good-natured laugh as he spotted the sign that marked Hurst with its population of 200 residents. The drive had taken over 40 minutes.

Dick and Mary laughed, too, but they couldn't disagree. Like many towns in the region, Hurst was a small coal-mining community. The main drag consisted of little more than a post office and a few shops.

"Hold on," Jack said excitedly. "I've got to fix something."

"What's wrong?" Dick asked.

Jack pulled the car to the edge of the road and stopped. He retrieved the paint he had used to write "Just Married" and jumped out of the car. He ran up to the green Hurst sign and painted a white "+ 2" after the 200.

"Now," Jack said as he hopped back into the car, "everyone will know the Ruggles have come to town."

After a short honeymoon at Osage Beach in the Missouri Ozarks, Dick and Mary set up house in Hurst. As a perk for taking the job at Hurst-Bush High School, Dick was given a small house to live in rent free. Located next to the school, it was a four-room, brick house that reminded Mary of a cracker box. She immediately delved into the task of making a home. She cleaned from top to bottom and made new curtains for the kitchen and bedroom windows. Then she and Dick put a fresh coat of paint on the walls, which really spiffed up the place. One drawback to the house was that it had no heat. Since it was summer now, they figured they would just deal with that problem when the weather turned cold.

Dick began his first day of school at Hurst-Bush High in late August of 1960, and he was introduced to the students as Coach Ruggles. *Coach Ruggles*, he thought. *I like the sound of that*. Although becoming a coach was something that he had wanted and had been working toward for a long time, it was still strange to think that he had suddenly gone from being Dick to being Coach Ruggles.

It was an identity he had to get used to in a hurry, however, because along with teaching P.E., he coached basketball, baseball, and track. He started working with the track and baseball teams right away, and actually made the transition from player to coach quite easily. He liked working with the young men, and he found that he was nearly as competitive on the sidelines as he had been on the playing field.

With Hurst-Bush being such a small school, there was a limited pool from which to draw athletes for the sports, and many students participated on all three teams. Although he had a minimal number of kids to work with, Coach Ruggles was able to bring out the best in them. His players knew he had played basketball at SIU so they listened to his direction and worked hard for him. The Hummers soon became competitive with the other small schools in the area, especially in basketball.

Although most of the towns were separated by several miles, nothing in southern Illinois happened in a vacuum. The word of Hurst-Bush's success and its talented young coach began to spread. Few high school coaches in southern Illinois had Coach Ruggles' credentials of being a four-year college letterman in basketball, and now his coaching skills began to draw attention.

While his teams' accomplishments were getting noticed, it was, ironically, after one of the basketball team's worst defeats that he was approached about taking a new coaching job in the small Union County village of Cobden. While the offer seemed genuine, he didn't give it much thought since the season was still in progress.

Mary was already in bed when Coach Ruggles arrived home from the game that night. He peeked into the crib of his infant son, Randy, who was also sleeping peacefully. He and Mary had welcomed their first child into the world on June 6, 1961. He was a healthy, beautiful boy. Coach Ruggles had never experienced such a complete and immediate love as when he had held his baby in his arms for the first time.

Mary and Randy often accompanied him to the Hummers' games, but they had decided to sit this one out since the drive to and from Cobden was lengthy, and they would get home very late. Coach Ruggles didn't want to disturb their sleep so he kept the light off in the bedroom while he undressed and changed into his pajamas. He could see well enough with the light coming in through the half-open door and the red glow from the space heater they used to warm the room in the winter. As quiet as he tried to be, Mary stirred when he was climbing into bed.

"How was the game?" she asked sleepily.

"We got beat," he said as his head sank into his pillow. "You didn't miss anything."

"You'll get them next time, right?" Mary was his biggest fan and supporter. She had never stopped being his cheerleader.

"No," he responded with a short laugh. "This was the second time they beat us this season. We won't play them again this year."

"Well, there's always next year."

"That's true, but I don't know. That team from Cobden is loaded. We're going to have to play with a lot more effort than we did tonight if we're going to beat them."

"I'm sure you'll get it straightened out," she assured him.

Dick knew she was right. He took every loss hard. He

knew he probably shouldn't get so down, but it was his competitive nature. *It was just one game*, he thought as he tried to relax and fall asleep. He knew he would have a better perspective in the morning. His players were good kids, and they had worked hard for him the two years he had been coaching them. He would get after them in practice on Monday, and everything would be all right.

The 1961-62 basketball season ended in early March, and Coach Ruggles moved almost seamlessly into baseball season. He had almost forgotten about the job offer to coach at Cobden High School, when he was contacted again by Dr. Charles Neal, a member of Cobden's school board.

"Have you considered my offer to come coach at Cobden?" Doc Neal wanted to know.

"To be honest, I've been too busy to give it much thought yet," Coach Ruggles told him.

"Well, the offer stands. We've got a talented group of kids at Cobden, and we want to get them the best basketball coach we can."

"What's the matter with the coach you have?"

"There's nothing wrong with John Lipe," Doc Neal quickly pointed out. "He's a fine man. Don't misunderstand me about that. I'm just not sure he's the coach these boys need. He's a good baseball coach, but we need a top-notch basketball coach."

"I've got a pretty good situation here," Ruggles said.

"I'm sure you do, but I'm certain we could offer you a better deal. And I'm serious about these boys. They're a special group. A team like this doesn't come along very often."

"I appreciate the offer. I really do. Let me talk it over with my wife and think about it, okay?"

"That's fine," Doc Neal replied. "I'll be in touch."

While Coach Ruggles was weighing his options in

Hurst, the decision to remove John Lipe as the Appleknockers' coach was highly controversial in Cobden. Coach Lipe had worked at Cobden High School since the fall of 1957 when he had been hired to teach P.E. He also served as the assistant coach for baseball, the sport that was his forte. He and his wife, Shirley, were good people and extremely well-liked by both parents and students. On weekends, they would sometimes invite the ball players and cheerleaders up to their home for cookouts. They had no children of their own so they served as surrogate parents to many of Lipe's students.

Before Lipe, Jim Walker served as Cobden High School's principal and basketball coach. The basketball team was successful under Walker's guidance. The Appleknockers opened the 1958-59 season by winning 16 games in a row, setting a new school record.

The team's winning streak got plenty of attention in the local papers, which were always looking for a good basketball story to tell. The press even reported how the streak was nearly stopped at eight games because of a scorekeeper's error. Cobden was playing at Gorham, a small community in rural Jackson County, and one of the Appleknockers made a free throw that was inadvertently credited to one of the Gorham players. At the end of the game, the Cobden players left the floor, dejected, thinking they had lost, 53-52. The scorekeeper totaled the points after the game and found the mistake. The score was actually tied at 53. Coach Walker had to summon his players from the locker room, some of whom had already taken off their uniforms, to come back to the court and finish the game. The Appleknockers prevailed in overtime, 58-56, and the streak went on. The team remained undefeated until it lost to Steeleville later in the season.

Walker left Cobden in the spring of 1959, and graduation that year took most of the talent and experience that had made up the record-setting team. When Lipe was named principal and head basketball coach upon Walker's departure, he was unable to achieve the same on-court success that his predecessor had.

The Appleknockers struggled through two disappointing seasons, and – fair or not – Lipe received most of the blame. People in Cobden, like those in most small towns in southern Illinois, took a great interest in their high school sports teams, especially basketball and football. High school sports were a source of pride for both the school and community. Cobden was too small to field a football team so basketball was its marquee sport.

The Appleknockers showed a marked improvement in the 1961-62 basketball season. Relying heavily on underclassmen, especially a talented sophomore group, to compose the varsity squad, Cobden won the district tournament title, finishing with a record of 12-12. Even though it won 10 more games than it had the previous year, many people were unsatisfied with the team's accomplishments.

Most of the sophomores had played together throughout junior high school, and they had created great expectations among Cobden's basketball fans with their past success. They had learned the fundamentals of basketball from their grade school coach, Jack Lamer. He taught them the basics of shooting, dribbling, and passing, and they took to the game naturally. As eighth graders, they compiled a record of 24-3 and won the district championship.

As freshmen, they put together a remarkable campaign. While Cobden's varsity basketball team managed just two wins in the 1960-61 season, the freshman team posted a record of 13-2, including impressive victories over powerhouse teams such as Carbondale Community, Anna-Jonesboro, and Pinckneyville. These schools all had much larger enrollments than Cobden, and they had traditionally strong basketball programs.

Besides talent and skill, Cobden's players had another huge asset when it came to basketball: height. As they reached the end of their sophomore year, one member of the team already stood 6-foot-6, with two others coming in at 6-foot-4.

With an enrollment of only about 140 students, no one in Cobden could remember the last time there had been one boy in the high school who was that tall, much less three.

With its unprecedented ability and height, some fans and members of the school's administration thought that Cobden's basketball team had the potential for greatness. Doc Neal, the town's dentist and a member of the school board, was the most outspoken person with this belief. He also felt that if the team was going to preform to its fullest capabilities, it needed a coach whose expertise was basketball. John Lipe knew baseball, but Doc Neal was afraid that he didn't know enough about basketball. Doc had been looking around the area for a coach that he thought could lead the Appleknockers, and he was sure he had found the right man in Dick Ruggles.

Doc Neal had two sons who were talented basketball players so he had a personal interest in the basketball team. But he was far from the only person in Cobden who wanted to see the Appleknockers achieve success. Cobden had last won a regional tournament title in basketball in 1942, and the fans were hungry for a winning team to cheer for. Not even the good teams of the late 1950s had been able to win the regional tournament.

The Cobden School Board convened a special meeting on the evening of May 7, 1962, to address the basketball team's future and who should lead it. All seven members, Norbert Cerny, H.R. Clutts, Jerold Guthrie, R.E. Lence, Doc Neal, Carroll Rich, and C. Joe Thomas, gathered in a meeting room at the high school. These were practical men: farmers, businessmen, laborers. They knew John Lipe well, and they liked him. Cobden was a tight-knit community of about 900 residents where everybody knew everybody. Half the town was related by blood or by marriage so this discussion wasn't taken lightly.

Each man took a turn to voice his opinion on the matter, and there was much disagreement. A few of the members found it hard to believe that they were going to make a decision about the school based on a sports team. Basketball was an extracurricular activity, a sport the boys did for fun. Decisions about the school should be based in academia, they felt; education was the important thing.

The one thing they all agreed on was that Lipe had done a fine job as a P.E. and history teacher and as the high school's principal, so firing him was out of the question. Opinions differed greatly, however, about his status as the Appleknockers' coach. Doc Neal was convinced that the Appleknockers could be a very special basketball team with the right person in charge, and he stated his case at the meeting.

"I agree with all of you that John is a good man," he said. "I like John, but I believe that we have a group of kids here that have the talent to accomplish great things on the basketball court. I think we owe them the opportunity to play for a coach who really knows the game. We need a basketball coach that will get the best out of these boys."

Doc Neal made a motion to have John Lipe relieved of his coaching duties but retained in his other capacities at the school. Jerold Guthrie seconded the motion, and it went to the board for a vote. Each board member searched his conscience for the right thing to do. In the end, the motion carried by the slimmest of margins, four to three. Lipe was out as coach.

When Lipe was notified of the board's decision, he was understandably upset. He had worked hard and had been a loyal employee, and he felt a sense of betrayal by the board's actions. His wife Shirley's family had lived in Cobden since 1946, and although he was from Carbondale, he now considered Cobden his home as well. He had been told by the school's administration that they wanted him to stay on as principal at the high school, but he elected to leave. He tendered his resignation, effective at the end of the school year.

Once the decision to hire a new coach was made, Doc Neal and some of the other school board members were determined to bring Dick Ruggles to Cobden. One person whose help they enlisted in the recruiting process was Mary Ruggles' father, Francis Woesthaus, and that turned out to be key.

The Woesthauses were a close family, and Mr. Woesthaus was excited by the prospect of having his daughter and son-in-law living nearby, especially now that they had given him a grandson. Cobden and Anna were separated by just five miles, and that suddenly made the hour-long drive to Hurst seem much longer. Mr. Woesthaus told Dick and Mary how nice it would be to have them close by where they could see each other more often. He also pointed out that Mrs. Woesthaus could more easily help Mary with young Randy if the need ever arose. For these reasons, Mr. Woesthaus strongly encouraged Dick to give serious consideration to taking the job in Cobden.

When the 1961-62 school year ended, Doc Neal contacted Coach Ruggles again. He was now authorized to make Ruggles a legitimate offer of employment at Cobden High School.

"I haven't made it a secret that we want to have you come to Cobden," Doc Neal told him. "We're a small school district, but we're offering you the best contract for teaching and coaching that we can."

They discussed the terms of the contract so Coach Ruggles could make his decision. When he factored in the raise in salary that he was being offered by Cobden along with the opportunity to be closer to Mary's family, it really was an easy call to make. He told Doc Neal that he would take the job.

His unspoken reason for taking the new position in Cobden was the chance to coach the talented Appleknocker basketball team. He had seen firsthand how well they played, and he agreed with Doc Neal's assessment that they were a special team. The folks in Cobden had high expectations for this team, and now he was charged with seeing that vision fulfilled. A shudder of nervous excitement shot through his body as he thought about the task he had just agreed to take on. How far could he really take a team from such a small town?

He was about to find out.

Chapter 2

Moving to Cobden

The Cobden School Board officially hired Coach Ruggles on June 21, 1962. He and Mary said goodbye to their first home and packed up Randy and their belongings and moved to Cobden. In contrast to the coal-mining industry that made Hurst-Bush go, Cobden was a farming community in the rolling hills of northern Union County, about 13 miles south of Carbondale. Cobden was surrounded by apple and peach orchards and farms that grew everything from asparagus to strawberries.

Railroad tracks ran north and south through the middle of town, splitting it right down the center. This feature led the townspeople to claim that Cobden had the widest main street in the world. A large steel bridge spanned across the tracks at the north end of the street so cars were never encumbered by trains rumbling through town.

Although Cobden was small, it was more than four times the size of Hurst, and its downtown offered the Ruggles a few more conveniences. The east side of Main Street held Cobden's only bank. It was flanked by a row of small businesses, including Nebughr's Drug Store, Casper's Variety Store, a bar called Fuzzy's, a pool hall, Daniel's Grocery Store, and the Ideal Café. A Chevrolet dealership sat on the south end of the street along with Lence's Shell Gas Station and Thompson's Grocery Store. A funeral parlor and another gas station were on the north end.

The west side of Main Street was home to the fire house, the post office, a clinic where Dr. Helmut Hartmann served as a family practitioner, and Doc Neal worked as a dentist, and Flamm's Café, which was a popular after-school hangout for teenagers. It was also a place where men drank their morning coffee while armchair quarterbacking the previous night's basketball game. There was a coin-operated laundry, a barber shop, and three small grocery stores: Sitter's, Scott's, and Moreland's. So that the residents had their choice of which American-made car to buy, a Ford dealership was situated on the north end of the street.

The dominant structure on the west side of the street was undeniably Basler's Feed Store. It was a large, two-story gray building where farmers came to buy grain for their livestock and other supplies for their farms. Its size stood as a constant reminder that the town owed its existence to those who worked the land. The feed store was owned and operated by Robert Basler, who everybody called Bally, and it served as a gathering place for farmers and other men in Cobden to discuss town news.

Just off the main drag was the Tip Top Tap tavern, a lumber yard, and a box and basket factory. Several churches were sprinkled throughout the neighborhoods with almost every form of Christian worship represented. The school was at the northern edge of the town, and the cemetery lay just beyond that.

Like the farms that surrounded it, most businesses in town were small and family-owned. Cobden would never be mistaken for a booming metropolis, and its prospects for growth were limited by its lack of industry. Lately, businesses had started to disappear. The *Cobden Review*, the town's only newspaper, had folded in 1961, and the one movie theater had shut down a couple of years earlier.

Although train tracks cut through the town, passenger trains no longer stopped in Cobden. Passenger service had ceased in 1961, but there was still a small depot because freight trains stopped to pick up produce from the first of June through the end of August.

Despite the closing of some businesses, Cobden didn't exude the aura of a depressed community. The fruit and vegetable harvests brought plenty of activity each summer and fall, and the residents seemed comfortable with their agricultural roots. The smallness of the town allowed for an innocence that made people feel safe to leave their homes unlocked and their keys in their cars when unattended.

The Ruggles moved into a simple, two-story house one block off Main Street. Their new house was bigger than the previous one in Hurst, and it was a good thing. The job change and move were only two of the big events in their lives that summer. Mary had also found out that she was pregnant with their second child.

Coach Ruggles and Mary received a warm welcome in Cobden. Because Mary had grown up in nearby Anna, she already knew several people in Cobden and was glad to be living closer to her family and friends. They began attending mass at St. Joseph's, the local Catholic church, and became acquainted with many of the parishioners. Ruggles had been courted by Doc Neal and other members of the school board, who wanted him to coach the Appleknockers, so now that he had arrived in Cobden, they did their best to make him feel at home. In fact, when Ruggles agreed to take the job, some of the men on the school board had gone up to Hurst with a big truck and helped him pack.

A couple of weeks before school started, a teacher's meeting was held at the high school. Cobden was a unit school so its campus was comprised of buildings that housed the kindergarten, primary, and high school grades. The high school itself was a two-story red brick building that sat on a small hill overlooking the baseball field.

Coach Ruggles was looking forward to his new job, but he approached the meeting with trepidation. He felt bad about John Lipe leaving the school, and he was unsure how his new colleagues would receive him.

Initially, there had been some tension among the faculty at Cobden High School about John Lipe's resignation. Mr. Lipe was a friend to them as well as a co-worker, and some on the staff felt that the school board had treated him unfairly. They knew he had not been fired, but some still thought that the school board's actions had made his departure inevitable.

As the new school year approached, it seemed like time to put to rest the discussion of whether the board had made the right decision. What was done was done. Nothing was going to change it, and it was time to move forward. While Mr. Lipe still lived in Cobden, he had taken a new job as the assistant principal at Anna-Jonesboro High School. He had moved on, and though he had been disappointed by the school board's decision, he seemed to harbor no ill feelings.

Cobden High School's Superintendent Burt Casper, who had called the meeting, greeted Coach Ruggles when he arrived at the school a few minutes before the scheduled time.

"Thanks for coming," said Mr. Casper, a gray-haired man in his 50s, wearing black-rimmed glasses. He gave Coach Ruggles a sincere smile. "Welcome to Cobden High School."

"Thanks," Coach Ruggles said, and the two shook hands.

"We have a couple other new teachers here this fall as well. I'll introduce you as soon as everyone is here."

The August heat and humidity warmed the room, and the open windows provided little relief. There were plenty of empty chairs so Coach Ruggles took a seat by a woman who managed to look cool despite the temperature. Slim and attractive with dark hair, she looked like she knew her way around the school.

"I'm Dick Ruggles," he said.

She already knew who he was, of course. The news of his hiring that summer had spread quickly around town. She didn't want to make him feel uncomfortable, though, so she shook his hand and said, "I'm Merna O'Brien. It's nice to meet you."

"I'm the new history teacher and coach," he said.

Mrs. O'Brien nodded, "I teach typing, shorthand, and all the business education classes."

Two more men entered the room, and Mrs. O'Brien told

him that they were Marvin Stewart, the industrial arts teacher, and Jack Lamer, who taught high school math along with being the grade school principal and junior high basketball coach.

The second man held Coach Ruggles' attention. He was tall and slender with wavy brown hair. Ruggles had heard about Jack Lamer and knew that Lamer had been instrumental in developing the basketball skills of the players that Ruggles had been hired to coach.

Another man arrived, and Coach Ruggles recognized him immediately. He was Lee Patterson, who Ruggles had known as a fellow student at SIU. He was surprised to see Lee at the meeting but also pleased. The last time the two had seen each other was when Ruggles graduated, but they had gotten along well in college and had joked around a lot. Ruggles had a habit of giving people nicknames, and when he found out Lee's full name was Edwin Lee Patterson, he started calling Lee "Mr. Ed" after the talking horse on the popular TV show.

Coach Ruggles got Lee's attention and motioned him over.

"How are you doing?" Ruggles asked as he stood to shake Patterson's hand. "I didn't know you worked here."

"I just got hired this summer," Patterson said. "I'll be teaching driver's education and boy's P.E."

Unlike Ruggles, Patterson knew almost everyone in the room. He was born and raised in Cobden and graduated from Cobden High School in 1950. After working at a gas station in town for a few years after high school, he went into the service in 1953. When he got out of the service, his wife encouraged him to become a teacher. He followed her advice and was now beginning his teaching career back at his alma mater.

The superintendent got everyone's attention and began the meeting. He told the group he was looking forward to a very productive school year. Along with Coach Ruggles and Lee Patterson, Mr. Casper introduced a young woman named Diane Deihl, who was the new English teacher. He passed out everyone's class lists, and then he asked the returning teachers to help the newcomers get acclimated to the school.

Coach Ruggles felt himself begin to relax as the other teachers introduced themselves. There were 10 faculty members in all, and they were responsible for educating Cobden High's entire student body of around 140 pupils.

"Your classroom is upstairs," Edna Ohmart, the science teacher, informed him. "My room is up there, too. Let me show you where."

They walked up to the second floor, and Mrs. Ohmart pointed to one of the wooden doors. "That one is yours," she said. "I'm across the hall here. Just let me know if you need anything."

Coach Ruggles thanked her and opened the door to his new room. The heat was almost overwhelming as he walked inside, and a musty smell from the inactivity of the summer break hung in the air. He opened the two large windows to let in some fresh air and then turned to survey his new space. The floor was wooden and tall bookcases ran along one of the interior walls. A teacher's desk with a big, slate blackboard behind it sat at the head of the room, facing several neat rows of wooden student desks.

He sat down at his desk and looked over the names of the students on his class lists. He would be teaching U.S. history, government, and world problems. Mr. Casper had also given him the rosters of last year's basketball and baseball teams – minus the names of those who had graduated – since he was going to be coaching both sports, the only two Cobden offered. He thought he recognized some of the names and knew he would become familiar with them all very soon.

After a few minutes, he put the lists aside and walked back downstairs. He wanted to see the gymnasium. He had been in it a few times before when he had brought his Hurst-Bush teams to play Cobden. Both schools competed in the Southern Six Conference along with Shawnee, Gorham, and Trico.

The gym was deserted as he opened the door and

stepped inside. He flipped on the switches and watched the overhead lights bathe the gym in a warm glow. He felt a stir of pride. Cobden's gym was nice by any standards and was even more impressive considering the school's small enrollment. Most southern Illinois schools with fewer than 200 students had tiny gyms with low ceilings and barely enough room to walk between the basketball floor and the walls. This gym had been built in 1955 and had high ceilings complete with a stage at the west end. Wooden, pull-out bleachers ran along both sides of the floor and were set back far enough to provide ample space for people to walk around the court's boundary lines. The gym could hold from 950 to 1,000 spectators, more than the entire town's population, and Ruggles was sure the crowds would show up.

He breathed in deeply. No matter what a gym looked like, they all seemed to smell the same: a combination of rubber, sweat, and humidity. *The home of the Appleknockers,* he thought, *so this is why they brought me here.* He knew many people had high hopes for what would be happening in this gym in coming seasons, and he was among them. The expectations didn't feel like a burden. It was quite the opposite, actually; they energized him. It was time to get to work.

The first day of school reunited all the students who had been deprived of each other's company on a daily basis throughout the summer vacation. Several boys had gathered in the gym and were shooting hoops before classes started. Although the boys were just fooling around, there was still a competition going on below the surface. The basketball team had lost just two seniors to graduation, and with several talented players returning, the boys knew that earning a coveted starting spot and lots of playing time would not be easy.

Chuck Neal, a 6-foot-6 center, and Kenny Flick, a muscular 6-foot-5 forward, had been regular starters on varsity all last year as sophomores and both had averaged double figures in scoring. By the end of last season, two other sophomores, Tom Crowell and Kenny Smith, had joined them in the starting lineup. Tom was a guard and stood just over six feet tall, and while Kenny Smith was 6-foot-4, which was unusually tall for a guard, he was also primarily a back-court player.

The lone senior starter the previous season had been Jack Sensmeier, and when he suffered a broken wrist in the final regular-season contest, John Marsh, a 5-foot-10 junior guard, who had been a starter at different times during the season, replaced him in the lineup for the postseason tournament games. Because of Cobden's small enrollment, the Apple-knockers had to begin postseason play with the district tournament. Cobden and six other small schools had to play each other for the right to advance to the regional tournament that was held at Anna-Jonesboro High School.

Cobden's young quintet performed admirably. They defeated Grand Chain, 71-50, in the district semifinals and then nipped Mounds Douglass, 65-64, to win the title. The Apple-knockers then battled Cairo Sumner to the wire in the opening round of the regional before finally succumbing, 59-55.

Coach Ruggles wandered into the gym and watched the boys on the court with more than a passing curiosity. He was struck by how tall many of them were and impressed by the skill they displayed while engaged in a friendly pickup game. It was obvious that they had taken to heart the fundamentals that Coach Lamer had taught them in junior high.

During the course of play, Kenny Smith went up for a jump shot. He wasn't wearing high-top tennis shoes and when he landed awkwardly, one of his shoes fell off. He sat down at the edge of the court to put it back on. His lanky frame was sprawled on the floor, and Coach Ruggles walked over and kicked the bottom of his foot.

"Hey," Kenny yelped in surprise, staring up at the man standing over him. The man looked to be in his 20s, sporting a neat crew cut, and Kenny thought he looked familiar but was unsure who he was.

"If you're gonna play for me, you'll have to get some bigger shoes," Coach Ruggles told Kenny.

Startled, Kenny was unsure how to respond. He looked at the other players on the floor. When his eyes moved back to the stranger, Kenny found him watching the other boys play. *What the heck was that about?* Kenny thought as he slipped his shoe back on.

The warning bell rang, signaling that classes would start in five minutes. The boys abandoned their game, and students scattered from the gym to find their first-period classes.

Kenny Smith stopped Tom Crowell and pointed to the stranger, who was also leaving the gym.

"Did you see that man?" Kenny asked. "He just kicked my foot."

Tom had been playing basketball with the others and had noticed the man approach Kenny. "Really?"

"Yeah. Who does that guy think he is?"

"I may be wrong," Tom said with a grin. "But I think that's our new coach."

Kenny had just received an informal introduction, and he wondered how well things were going to work out.

Most of the boys had heard during the summer that Coach Ruggles had been hired, and a few were apprehensive about the new coach. Darrell Crimmins, a junior, was concerned about getting a new coach, but it had nothing to do with Ruggles. Darrell was especially upset about John Lipe leaving. Darrell had met Lipe when his family had relocated to Cobden the summer before he started his freshman year.

Darrell's father, Lloyd Crimmins, was a U.S. Air Force major and was stationed at Scott Air Force Base near Belleville, Illinois, which was about 100 miles north of Cobden. He and his wife, Shirley, had bought property southeast of Cobden with plans to move there when Lloyd retired from the military. The property consisted of a quaint two-story farmhouse and 40 acres that included rolling green pastureland, wooded areas, and a large pond. It was an ideal place to raise a family so Lloyd and Shirley had decided to make the move early, in the summer of 1960, with their three teenage sons: Lloyd, Dale, and Darrell.

Dale and Darrell had joined the summer league baseball team, which was being coached by Doc Neal. They met Chuck and Jim Neal and many of their other new schoolmates. John Lipe was a baseball enthusiast, and he was always around to help out the team. He also helped make the boys feel welcome in their new home, and they developed a good rapport, especially he and Darrell. Since Major Lloyd Crimmins was still in the Air Force, he stayed in Belleville during the week and was only able to live with his family in Cobden on the weekends. Over time, Lipe had come to have a fatherly influence on Darrell, and now Darrell was going to miss that.

When the players found out that the school board had hired Coach Ruggles, they were unsure what to expect. But he wasn't a complete stranger to them. Some of the boys were vaguely familiar with Ruggles from his two years of coaching at conference-rival Hurst-Bush. Other boys, like junior Jim Smith, remembered Ruggles when he played basketball at Southern Illinois University. A local dairy put the SIU basketball schedule on the back of its milk cartons each year, also listing the name of the SIU team captain, which in 1959-60 was Dick Ruggles. Jim remembered seeing that name every morning when he poured the milk on his cereal during the winter of his eighth-grade year. He never expected the man on the carton would end up being his coach.

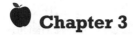 **Chapter 3**

The Games Begin

Cobden was a two-sport school, offering basketball and baseball for boys. There had been a track team in the 1950s, but it was discontinued when Coach Jim Walker left in 1959. Baseball was played in both the fall and spring, and practices were held right after school. Coach Ruggles called the initial practice during the first week of school, and 16 boys turned out to participate.

Fully half the players came from the junior class. Only three seniors joined the team, along with two sophomores and three freshmen. As was usually the case, there was no need for official tryouts. Cobden's small student body yielded only a small number of athletes to fill its roster, and Ruggles realized he would need every boy who was interested in playing if he was going to field a team.

With 11 upperclassmen on the squad, the issue of assigning positions was settled fairly easily as a lot of the boys assumed the roles they'd had in past years. Most of the boys had played baseball together, either on the school's team or in summer leagues, and they knew where they wanted to play. Many could play multiple positions with equal ability so they would switch around, and eventually everyone got to play where they wanted. The freshmen were usually relegated to the outfield, but if any of them showed a desire or talent to play a different position, he was given a chance.

Coach Ruggles used different methods and techniques than Coach Lipe so there was an adjustment period in the beginning. The boys had liked playing for Coach Lipe so it was only natural that they would make comparisons between the two men, but they soon came to feel that Ruggles was a good and competent coach. While the transition was easier for some, most all the boys got along with him fine.

Coach Ruggles tried to make the games and practices fun. He enjoyed getting to know the young men outside of the classroom. Most of the time they were an easy-going group, who got along well and displayed a sincere team camaraderie. Like the boys he had encountered at Hurst-Bush, the Cobden players were respectful, cooperative, and hard-working.

Always looking for a competitive edge, Ruggles devised a series of colors to use as signals when he wanted the players to execute a certain maneuver or play, such as laying down a bunt, stealing a base, or throwing a certain pitch. He thought that calling out a series of colors would help confuse their opponents and keep them from figuring out the meanings of the physical gestures Cobden had used in the past.

Once the boys caught on to the color scheme, they incorporated it into their games. They received more than the occasional odd look from their competitors when they started yelling out colors during the games. Coach Ruggles was unsure if the color scheme helped them win more games, but the boys seemed to have fun with the idea, and Ruggles thought they played more relaxed during games.

The practices also gave Coach Ruggles an opportunity to evaluate the players from an athletic standpoint. This was doubly beneficial as 13 of the 16 boys on the baseball team were also planning to play basketball. Although the two sports required different skills, Ruggles was able to judge the boys' speed and coordination and gain a sense of their competitive spirit. Ruggles also used the practices to get the players ready for the upcoming basketball season by having them run the bases after practice or perform other conditioning drills.

In one of his favorite drills, Coach Ruggles would put a player on each one of the bases. When he blew his whistle, the boys would have to run around the bases the number of times that Ruggles chose. If a player was caught and passed by the person who started on the base behind him, he would have to do extra running.

One day Ruggles loaded the bases and told the boys to

circle them five times. Jim Neal was on first base that day. A sophomore, he was a good athlete but wasn't known for his speed. He recently had a growth spurt and was still getting used to his 6-foot-4 frame. When the first lap was completed, he had already been caught by the boy who had started at home plate. The laps continued, and soon the player who had begun on third base had caught up to Jim. By the time they were into the fifth lap, all three boys had caught and passed him. Knowing he was beaten and that everyone was watching, Jim decided to go down in flames. He gathered a last burst of energy and sprinted to his final base, raising his arms in triumph as he reached it. The others burst out laughing, including Coach Ruggles, as Jim pretended to revel in the appreciative cheers of an imagined crowd. Then Ruggles got the last laugh when he told Jim to take a victory lap.

The boys had a good time playing baseball, but for a lot of them it was a secondary sport. In southern Illinois, baseball never generated the kind of fan support and community interest that basketball and football did, and there wasn't a great emphasis placed on winning. For many of the boys, baseball was a pastime that gave them something to do during the warm-weather months and helped fill their time while they waited for basketball season to begin.

The boys tried their best to win the baseball games. They were much too competitive to lay down for any team, and Cobden had some talented baseball players. Seniors Richard McCleland and Dale Crimmins and juniors Tom Crowell and Darrell Crimmins excelled at the sport. Juniors Chuck Neal, Jim Smith, Roy Witthoft, and Dale Yates and sophomores Jim Neal and Bob Smith were all serviceable on the diamond, so while the Appleknockers never dominated in baseball, they typically won more games than they lost.

Many of the boys, however, approached baseball with less exuberance than they did basketball. In fact, a lot of the players liked it when baseball practice or a game was rained out. On days when the field was too wet and muddy to use, the boys would trade their cleats for sneakers and play pickup basketball games in the gym. Coach Ruggles often would join in, and the boys enjoyed playing with him.

As a teacher and coach, Ruggles was an authority figure to the students. Since he was also a husband and father, he seemed like an old man to the teenagers he worked with, but he was only a few years older than them. The small age gap helped contribute to the positive relationships he developed with the players.

While most of the attention about Coach Ruggles coming to Cobden centered on sports, and basketball in particular, he was also the new history and social studies teacher, and that required a period of adjustment in the classroom. When he addressed his students on the first day of school, his New England accent was as pronounced as it had been when he first stepped off the train in Carbondale six years earlier. His brogue was decidedly different than the slow drawl that typified most speech in southern Illinois. A lot of the students thought he sounded like President John F. Kennedy, and the female students thought he was very handsome.

The students became accustomed to Coach Ruggles' accent fairly quickly, but there were times when it was difficult for them to understand some of the words he said. One day in American history class, he was explaining to the class how the early European settlers had brought horses with them when they came to America.

Not comprehending what Coach Ruggles had said, Darrell Crimmins raised his hand.

"They brought what?" Darrell asked.

"Horses," Coach Ruggles replied, but to most of his students it sounded like "hosses."

"Oh, you mean *horses*," Darrell said.

"Yes, hosses," Coach Ruggles repeated.

All the students laughed. Darrell's face reddened, and he sank down in his chair. *Oh man*, he thought. *I'm never going to get to play now.*

Coach Ruggles joined in the laughter. Darrell felt a bit of relief and hoped there would be no repercussions.

Basketball practice started on October 1, and Coach Ruggles was glad to be able to officially get in the gym and work with the players. He knew the team was stacked with talent since he had coached against most of the young men when he was at Hurst-Bush. He was now looking forward to being on their side.

The boys were also excited about basketball practice beginning, and a large group gathered in the gym after school for the first day of practice. They were shooting at the goals at both ends of the court when Coach Ruggles arrived. He blew a whistle to get their attention and asked them to have a seat on the bleachers.

"I'm glad you're all here. I think we have a chance to have a great year," Ruggles said, looking from one boy to the next. "But it's all up to you. We'll be as successful as the hard work and effort that you're willing to put in. We will be as successful as you want to be."

He paused. Although the boys were talented, he knew that talent alone would only get them so far. He wanted them to be in peak physical condition.

"Before we get started on the game, you're going to get in shape," Ruggles said. "Let's put those balls away for awhile. I see that you already have your running shoes on and that's good because you're gonna use 'em. I don't want us to play a team all year that's in better shape than we are. We aren't going to lose a game because the other team is in better condition."

The boys soon learned that Coach Ruggles was true to

his word. Each day before practice began, he had them run a trail up through the cemetery and back to the school. The route was a little over a mile long and was made strenuous by the cemetery's steep hills. This run was nothing new. Coach Lamer had required them to run the same cemetery route in junior high. Most of the players didn't mind the run, but some hated it. Bob Smith, a fun-loving sophomore with a mischievous streak, found a way to make the best of it, for himself anyway. He would occasionally hide a pack of cigarettes and matches along the route and sneak a smoke while he ran.

Once the players were back in the gym, Coach Ruggles had a host of other conditioning drills for them to do, and unlike the cemetery trail, this was a new experience. He had the boys run sprints, using the lines on the basketball court as guides. He expected the players to run at full speed, and if he caught anyone loafing, he would just make him run more. He used different versions of the sprints, depending on what he wanted to accomplish. Some were designed to work on the players' quickness, and others helped with their lateral movements so they could stay in front of their opponents on defense. The players nicknamed the sprints "killers" because the drills were so taxing. *Is Coach Ruggles trying to run us to death?* they wondered at times.

One of the drills the boys dreaded the most was running the bleachers. The first time they did it, Coach Ruggles told them to run up and down the bleachers for two minutes. At first, the boys were confident they could handle that, but after a minute of running, their legs felt heavy, and they were all gasping for air. As fatigue set in, they had to pay close attention to their footing so they wouldn't slip and hit their shins on the wooden boards. The boys decided that running the bleachers was even worse than the killer sprints, but Ruggles gave them no breaks. He had them run the bleachers every day, and before long, they could do it with much less huffing and puffing.

Coach Ruggles knew the boys probably thought he was being hard on them for no reason, but all of the drills had a purpose. Running the bleachers would build up their leg muscles and improve their jumping ability. It would also increase their endurance so they wouldn't be worn down at the end of a game. If he ever saw the boys dragging their feet, he would remind them, "I don't want you guys fading down the stretch."

While the practices were tough, most of the boys found them fun. Coach Ruggles was positive and upbeat with the players, encouraging them to try their hardest and give their best effort. A great motivator, he let the boys know he believed they could achieve anything they set their minds to. The boys couldn't argue with his methods. They had never been in better shape.

After a few weeks of arduous conditioning, Ruggles introduced shooting, ball-handling, and passing drills. He also began teaching the boys different plays he wanted them to use in the games. He knew it was important for them to learn their assignments and responsibilities so they would always know where they were supposed to be on the floor and what they were supposed to be doing. He went over the plays repeatedly until the players functioned as a unit – a team – and not individuals.

Coach Ruggles figured the boys were concerned about earning starting positions and playing time once the season was underway. Being on the starting five held a certain prestige in high school ball and gave the players a heightened status. But Ruggles wanted the boys to understand the basketball court was no place for personal glory. In practice, he emphasized the concept of team and the fact that basketball was a team sport. Every player had a role to play, and each one was important.

"The only way we're going to be successful is if we play together," he often told them.

This philosophy was well received by the players. The boys all knew each other well, and many of them had played basketball together for years. They had never been the kind of players who worried about who scored the most points or got the most rebounds in a game. They wanted to win. That was the most important thing to them. They were willing to listen to Coach Ruggles and do whatever he told them to do to make that happen. Ruggles liked that attitude. He hated to lose, and he was glad the players felt the same way.

Although they shared the same goal of winning, there was still rivalry. They were all competitive, and their scrimmages could get heated at times as they played aggressively against each other. Coach Ruggles liked the boys' passion for the game, but he was careful not to let their friendly battles escalate and cause problems. If the players were going to operate as a team, he didn't want any grudges or hurt feelings to get in the way.

Because Lee Patterson was the boys' P.E. teacher, he was in the gym a lot, and Coach Ruggles approached him one afternoon before practice.

"Hey, Lee," Coach Ruggles said. "Would you be interested in giving me a hand with the team?"

"Sure," Lee replied. "I'd be glad to help out."

Being from Cobden, Patterson knew most of the boys' families, and he enjoyed working with the young men. He began spending a lot of time with the junior varsity squad while Coach Ruggles worked with the varsity players. If Ruggles ever had to be away or leave early for some reason, Patterson would step in and run the practice. Ruggles liked having someone at school that he could discuss the team with, and Patterson took on the role of an unofficial assistant coach.

A soft-spoken man, Patterson was willing to lend a hand if Coach Ruggles or the boys needed anything, and they all appreciated his assistance. Patterson was approachable and knowledgeable about basketball. The players soon learned that they could go to him when they wanted or needed advice.

As the weeks passed, Ruggles sized up the team. *I definitely made the right decision coming here*, he thought. One of the team's biggest strengths was unquestionably the height of the players. Most high school basketball teams, especially from the smaller schools, were lucky to have one player who stood over six feet tall. Cobden had an entire roster full.

Another major asset for the Appleknockers was experience. Four seniors: John Marsh, a 5-foot-10 guard, Richard McCleland, a 6-foot-2 forward/center, Dale Crimmins, a 5-foot-11 guard, and George Boyd, a 6-foot-2 guard/forward were all seasoned veterans.

The junior class was a powerhouse of talent. While Chuck Neal, Kenny Flick, Tom Crowell, and Kenny Smith, who had grown another inch and was now 6-foot-5, had garnered the bulk of the playing time last season, there were several other capable players in that class. Jim Smith, a cousin to Kenny Smith, and Darrell Crimmins had suited up for the varsity squad as sophomores. Jim and Darrell were each over six feet tall and could play both the guard and forward positions. All of these boys had played on the junior varsity basketball team last year as well, so they had a lot of game experience. Dennis Hartsock, a 5-foot-9 guard, Dan Marsh, a 6-foot forward, and Roy Witthoft, a 6-foot-1 forward, rounded out the class.

A couple of sophomores were also promising prospects. Chuck's younger brother, Jim Neal, was already 6-foot-4 and showing great natural ability at the forward spot. Jim's best friend, Bob Smith – no relation to Kenny and Jim Smith – was a 5-foot-8 guard with good ball-handling skills.

The day before basketball practice started, Jim Neal suffered a broken thumb. He had been playing catcher in Cobden's last baseball game of the fall season, and Bob had been pitching. Jim had signaled for a fast ball, but Bob threw a curve instead. As Jim reached out to catch the ball, it hit his thumb and broke it. Because of the injury, Jim had been unable to take part in the team's shooting drills. He found sitting on the sidelines to be frustrating, so he threw every ounce of his energy into the other workouts. After the doctor removed his cast, he was able to participate fully, and his genuine love for the game shone through in his play.

"Hey, honey," Mary called to her husband when she heard him enter their home through the back door. "How was practice today?"

It was mid-November, and she had been asking him that same question nearly every day for the past several weeks. A big basketball fan, Mary truly enjoyed hearing about the practices, and her husband often shared with her his thoughts on the team's progress.

Coach Ruggles came into the kitchen where Mary was fixing dinner and gave her a kiss. He lifted the lids off a couple of pots on the stove, inspecting their contents. Then he reached down and scooped up his son, Randy, and gave him a playful hug. After depositing Randy back on the floor, Ruggles patted his wife's belly.

"How are you feeling today?"

Mary's morning sickness had never been terrible, and now that she was in the fifth month of her pregnancy, the symptoms had mostly passed, but her husband always inquired about her well-being.

"I'm fine," she said. "How was your day?"

"It was fine," he said. "Practice was good. The boys keep working hard, and they look good. Actually, they look better than good. If they play like their capable, this is going to be a great season."

"That sounds promising," Mary said.

"Yeah. These boys have a lot of promise," Ruggles said. "If things work out right, and we get lucky, I think this team can go a long way in the playoffs and even make it to state."

He was a young coach and still new in his profession, and a lot of people would consider his statement naive. There were more than 700 basketball teams in the state, and only eight made it to the state tournament each year. The teams that reached the tournament were typically from schools much larger than Cobden. Besides, it had been years since the Appleknockers had even won a regional title, and they had never qualified for the state tournament.

Perhaps it was Ruggles' youth that allowed him to dream so big. His players loved the game, and they played with an unbridled enthusiasm that was contagious. Ruggles had been around basketball his whole life, and he thought he was a pretty good judge of talent. If there was one thing he was certain of, it was that there was an abundance of talent on his squad. Not only was there talent, but there was also determination. The boys took basketball home with them every night.

Tom Crowell was one of the boys with a true zest for basketball, and his family shared his keen interest. When they were together, their conversations often centered on Tom's athletic pursuits.

When he got home from practice, his mother, Jenny, had supper already prepared. Tom carried a plate of steaming fried chicken to the table and placed it in front of his father. His younger sister, Mildred, was already digging into her mashed potatoes and gravy as Tom sat down. His mother put the lid on the potatoes to keep them warm, wiped her hands on her apron, and sat down at the table.

"How'd practice go today?" asked his father, Tom Sr., taking a sip of sweet tea.

Tom finished chewing before answering. "Coach Ruggles is tough, but he seems to know what he's doing," he said, choosing his next words carefully. "I'm kind of worried about making the starting five, though. There's a lot of good players. It's gonna to be tough."

Tom had worked his way into the starting lineup last

season, and he wanted to stay there.

His mother put down her fork. Because his father was also named Tom, to avoid confusion, the family referred to young Tom as Bill, a shortened version of his middle name.

"Bill, all you can do is work as hard as you can in practice. That's all you can do. Whether you're on the starting five or not will take care of itself. You still have another year after this."

His father nodded.

"She's right. There are a lot of good players, but you got a lot of talent. I'm sure Coach Ruggles will see that."

Tom nodded and took a bite of chicken. He wished he felt as confident as his parents. In sixth grade, he was passed over for junior high squad and ever since then, he was always pushing himself to be a better player. He remembered how he felt not to be chosen that year. He spent the summer in between his sixth- and seventh-grade years shooting baskets on the hoop in the side yard. Then he did push-ups until his arms ached. By the next year, his improvement earned him a spot on the squad.

Now, as he entered his junior year of high school, he had that same nagging feeling. With so many other good players, it was going to be hard to snag a starting position. He would have to work extra hard and pay close attention to what Coach Ruggles said in practice.

Tom got his athletic talent from his father, who had played ball during high school at the Toppingtown School near Carbondale. After he married Tom's mother, they settled on a farm owned by Charles and Pauline Lamer about five miles outside of Cobden. The farm, known to area residents as Lamer's Farm, was in the middle of the country, surrounded by thick forests and rolling hills.

Tom Sr. was the farm's foreman. Young Tom was the third of the four Crowell children and the only boy. He was born in the small four-room house that Charlie Lamer later expanded to six rooms so Tom could have his own room. Tom's mother worked hard to make the place homey. A coal stove heated the house in winter, and the house still had an outhouse at a time when many families had installed indoor plumbing.

By the time Tom was a junior, his two older sisters, Martha and Mary, were in their early 20s and living on their own. Martha was married, and Mary lived in an apartment in Cobden. Although the girls no longer lived at home, the family would gather at the farm every Wednesday night for dinner.

What the Crowells lacked in money, they made up for in love. They doted on Tom, the only boy, but he was expected to work on the farm, and the responsibility made him remarkably mature for his age.

Like many families who worked on farms, everyone pitched in during growing season. In the summer, Tom picked tomatoes, squash, cucumbers, and strawberries. The long hours of manual labor gave him a solid, sturdy build that was unusual for a 16 year old. In practice, Coach Ruggles had noticed Tom's strength and joked that he should make it mandatory for all the players to pick tomatoes in the summer.

Now Tom could only hope that his strength and his dedication would be enough to get him a place on the starting five.

● Chapter 4

1962-1963 Basketball Season Opens

Great anticipation surrounded the beginning of basketball season. Cobden's fans were anxious to see how the Appleknockers would perform under Coach Ruggles' direction. The players were tired of playing against each other in practice and were ready to face a real opponent. On November 16, they opened the season in dominating fashion, picking up a road win against Century High School, 82-37. Cobden then hosted Shawnee for its second game and won, 69-56.

The Appleknockers got their first real test of the young season when they played Carbondale Attucks on November 24. The Blue Birds were quick and athletic, and Cobden was down 13 points before coming back to win, 73-67, in overtime. The Appleknockers improved to 5-0 with lopsided victories over Hurst-Bush – Coach Ruggles' former school – and Gorham. Ruggles' emphasis on the importance of playing as a team was readily apparent in the boys' play. The Appleknockers didn't have one star player. Every boy was involved in the offense. They ran the plays that Ruggles taught them and worked hard to find good shots. Four different players led the team in scoring in the first five games with several boys reaching double figures.

Coach Ruggles experimented with various lineups for the games, using different personnel to create mismatches and prey upon the deficiencies of opposing teams. He was fortunate to have so much depth, and every boy on the roster played significant minutes. With so many talented players, the Appleknockers used an up-tempo offense, and Ruggles substituted often to keep the players fresh. On defense, they played man-to-man, zone, and a full-court press. The players had different strengths and weaknesses, but the skill level of the reserves was not much different than the starters, and Ruggles could bring players off the bench and hardly miss a beat.

The Appleknockers' schedule consisted of teams from other small towns with enrollments similar to Cobden, but most of these teams offered little competition. The Appleknockers easily overmatched them in height and talent. By halftime of most contests, Cobden had such a big lead that the outcome was not in doubt. Coach Ruggles was pleased with the victories, but he worried that the boys were not being challenged by the weak competition. The players could make mistakes, and Cobden would still come out on top. Winning was great, but Ruggles believed it was essential for the boys to learn and get better so they would be prepared when they met bigger and more skilled teams at tournament time.

Since winning was a foregone conclusion in most games, Coach Ruggles set other goals for the players. If a team had a prolific scorer, Ruggles played man-to-man defense, and told the boy guarding the opponent not to let him score. If one of the players needed to work on blocking out and rebounding, Ruggles told him not to let the man he was covering get a rebound. Sometimes Ruggles instructed the players to hold their opponent scoreless for an entire quarter. When Ruggles gave the players these extra assignments, their intensity and effort level rose. They played with the kind of effort Ruggles knew they would need when they competed against teams from bigger schools.

The players took Coach Ruggles' challenges to heart and worked hard to accomplish the goals he set. The Appleknockers racked up three more double-digit victories over Tamms, Trico, and Mounds Douglass, improving to 8-0. The local newspapers took notice of Cobden's fast start and when the Cairo *Evening Citizen* released its first basketball poll of the season on December 24, the paper ranked the Appleknockers the No. 1 team in the area.

During practice and the early games, the players' roles began to take shape. The seniors were all solid players. George Boyd and Richard McCleland were good rebounders and played hard on defense. Dale Crimmins and John Marsh were also capable defenders, and their quickness was effective when the Appleknockers applied their press.

Kenny Flick led the team in scoring the prior year, and he was again showing his offensive prowess as a consistent shooter both inside and out. Coach Ruggles considered him one of the best all-around players he had seen in his young coaching career. Kenny had a calm exterior but under the surface beat the heart of an intense competitor with a burning desire to win.

Chuck Neal was one of the team's top rebounders and defenders and also had a knack for scoring. At his height, almost no opponent could out jump him at tipoff.

Tom Crowell was a skilled ball handler who had the ability to score and get his teammates involved in the offense. He was also a solid defender who could shut down the man he guarded. The more he played, the more confident he became. Steady and calm under pressure, Coach Ruggles and the other players trusted Tom to be the playmaker on the court. On top of that, he was also a consistent free-throw shooter.

Kenny Smith was a challenge for Coach Ruggles. He wasn't the hardest working boy in practice, and he aggravated Ruggles at times with his attitude. But his talent was undeniable. He had a sweet jump shot, and Ruggles found it hard to keep him on the bench for long.

While Ruggles used different starting lineups and substituted often, he felt the team was at its best when Kenny Flick, Chuck, Tom, Kenny Smith, and Jim Neal were on the court together. The boys had a natural chemistry and a feel for each other's games that had come from playing together for so long. Their height was daunting, too, with four of the boys towering 6-foot-4 and above.

Cobden's boosters were thrilled with how the team was playing, and they flocked to the gym for the games. Even in the lean years, the Appleknockers always had fans at their games, but their following had grown this season. No matter how many people attended the games, however, Chuck and Jim Neal, Jim Smith, Bob Smith, and Tom Crowell knew they would always find their parents and relatives in the crowd. Doc and Laura Neal, Clyde and Geneva Smith, Russell and Elaine Smith, and the Crowell family were constant fixtures at the basketball games.

Doc Neal, in particular, made his presence known. He sat on the top row of the bleachers at center court, and when he got excited, he hollered so loud the boys heard him on the floor. He got so worked up during games that he was drenched in sweat by the time they were over. His wife often refused to sit with him because he got so loud.

Coach Ruggles could always count on Mary being there, too. She brought little Randy with her to almost every game, and although she couldn't hold a candle to Doc Neal, she was also a vocal fan. She found it difficult to keep her emotions in check when things got exciting. Her husband often teased her that she yelled more than he did at the games.

Whether at home or away, the team had no trouble drawing a crowd, and the boys appreciated the support from their fans. The Appleknockers hosted the Cobden Blind Draw Tournament on January 3 and 4. The other participants in the tournament were Herrin, Gorham, and Cairo Sumner. Cobden drew Gorham as its first-round opponent. The Appleknockers had already played and defeated Gorham earlier in the season, and this meeting produced a similar outcome with Cobden winning, 78-53. Cairo Sumner beat Herrin, 40-39, and would play Cobden for the title the following night.

Cairo Sumner had eliminated the Appleknockers from postseason play the previous spring by defeating them in the regional tournament. Now Cobden had a chance to avenge that loss. Shortly before the game started, though, Chuck got sick and was unable to play. Coach Ruggles moved Jim Neal from the forward to the center position. Jim performed well in Chuck's absence, scoring 15 points and grabbing several rebounds. Kenny Flick paced the Appleknockers with 23 points, and they won, 62-42.

Cobden hosted Vienna on January 8 and found itself in quite a tussle. The Vienna Eagles employed an effective full-court press, jumping out to a 13-point lead after one quarter, and they were still ahead, 38-26, at halftime. Concerned about the boys' play, Coach Ruggles had a simple message for them in the locker room.

"They aren't all going to be easy, are they?" he said. "You can't just take the floor and expect to win if you don't give it your all. Vienna wants to fight us. Now let's go out there and fight back."

Since Chuck had been sick for the previous game, Coach Ruggles let him rest the first half. He inserted Chuck into the lineup after the intermission, and the Appleknockers began to cut into Vienna's lead. Cobden only trailed by four points, 45-41, at the end of the third quarter. The game was close throughout the fourth period, but Vienna managed to hold a slim lead.

With just 20 seconds left in the game, Cobden took possession of the ball and was down by one point. The boosters for both teams stood and cheered so loudly it was hard for the players to hear Coach Ruggles call the play from the bench. Tom dribbled down the court and spotted Dale at the left hash mark. He passed him the ball, and Dale squared his shoulders and sank a 15-foot jump shot, putting the Appleknockers up, 55-54. The Eagles were unable to get another shot off, and Cobden held on for the one-point win.

The Appleknockers were now 11-0 and had shown they had the ability and determination to come from behind and win a close game over a strong adversary. Cobden was enjoying its best season since 1959, and supporters were convinced their team would have a shot at the regional title and perhaps more.

No one could have guessed what was coming next.

Kenny Flick made a decision that affected the whole team. He quit. His girlfriend, Evalena Reynolds, was pregnant, and Kenny decided the two of them should get married. At just 16 years old, it was a hard decision for him to make. Cobden had a school policy that barred married students from taking part in extracurricular activities. He had played basketball since the sixth grade when Coach Lamer selected him to play on the junior high squad. Kenny had known next to nothing about basketball back then and felt a little lost until one of Cobden's high school basketball players, Donald "Van" Vanover, took him under his wing. Van worked with Kenny one-on-one, teaching him how to shoot a proper jump shot. Van tied a rope around Kenny's ankles at practice so he would use correct form, and then made him shoot the ball over and over from 12 to 15 feet away from the basket. Kenny's dad and brothers didn't play basketball and had no use for athletics as a pastime so Kenny had never received that kind of individual instruction. Being a grade-schooler, he looked up to the older boys, especially the athletes. He had no idea why Van gave him so much attention, but he didn't question it. He worked hard and appreciated the time Van spent with him.

With Lamer's coaching and Van's extra help, Kenny's game thrived. He got an old basketball goal and hung it up in his backyard. His family thought it was a waste of time, but he ignored their discouraging comments and dubious looks, and he practiced shooting jumpers on his own until he had the technique perfected. As his skill level increased, so did his confidence. In sixth grade, he only took one shot all season. But in seventh grade, he led the team in scoring.

After devoting so much time to the game, he now found it hard to give it up. But no matter how much he loved basketball, he loved Evalena more, and he knew that marrying her was the right thing to do.

Evalena was from the neighboring town of Anna. Kenny had been introduced to her by his friend and classmate, Roger Burnett. Kenny and Evalena went to a fair together in Vienna on their first date, and they had been together ever since. It was an important relationship for Kenny. He was the youngest of four children and had come as a surprise to his parents. He had two brothers and a sister and the closest one in age was 10 years older. They weren't a particularly close family, and as his parents grew older, they showed little to no interest in his activities. Evalena provided Kenny with the unwavering love and support he needed.

In keeping with his quiet nature, Kenny didn't tell his friends or teammates of his plans. The Appleknockers were preparing for an upcoming tournament at Anna-Jonesboro, and Kenny informed Coach Ruggles he was leaving the team.

In a small town like Cobden, word spread quickly that Kenny had quit the team and planned to get married. The news upset some of the more overzealous fans. They thought Kenny was one of the team's best players and feared losing him would ruin the season. Most folks in town respected Kenny's choice, but some of the outspoken fans tried to talk him out of getting married. Kenny refused to change his mind. What he and Evalena did was their business and no one else's. When it became clear that Kenny was going ahead with his plans, those few disgruntled fans went out of their way to express their displeasure with his decision.

Kenny was hurt by their rude comments, and he felt unwanted in Cobden. He decided to drop out of school altogether. He wanted to stay in school, but he wanted to get away from the negative attitudes some people in Cobden displayed toward him.

Frustrated by the situation, Kenny went to see John and Shirley Lipe. He had been close to them when Lipe was the principal and coach at Cobden High, and Kenny felt he could talk to them. Kenny explained how he was feeling to the Lipes and said he was going to quit school. As an educator, Lipe tried to talk him out of it.

"Kenny, you're an excellent student, and you know how important getting an education is," Lipe said. "You don't want to drop out of school."

"I don't want to," Kenny said. "I have to. I don't feel right going to Cobden anymore."

"This will pass," Lipe told him. "Don't let a few hot-heads run you off."

Kenny refused to go back to Cobden High School so Lipe finally suggested that he go to Anna-Jonesboro instead of dropping out altogether. Lipe worked as the assistant principal at A-J, and he told Kenny he would help him enroll there if he wanted to go. Lipe was no expert on the Illinois High School Association's transfer rules so he also told Kenny he was un-sure if he would be eligible to play basketball at A-J this year. Kenny said it didn't matter. He needed to get a job so he would have little time to play basketball anyway.

After leaving the Lipes, Kenny thought about transfer-ring to Anna-Jonesboro. He knew he needed to get his high school diploma if he was going to get a good job and support his family. He talked things over with Evalena and decided to go to A-J.

Kenny's teammates were still reeling over his departure from the squad, and they were saddened when he left school. Everything was happening so fast it seemed surreal. The boys had been together as a unit for so long that to many of them losing Kenny felt as if someone had cut off one of their arms.

Coach Ruggles was disappointed that Kenny was gone, too. It was definitely a blow to the team. Kenny averaged about 15 points a game and while Ruggles felt other boys could pick up the scoring slack, he was concerned about replacing Kenny's rebounding and defensive play.

To top it off, Richard McCleland had left the team a couple of weeks earlier. While Richard enjoyed basketball, he played mainly to stay in shape for baseball, his favorite sport. While in first grade, he had been stricken with several child-hood diseases. He had missed so much school that he ended up repeating that year. Now he was an older senior and was going to turn 19 on January 21. That would make him ineligible to play baseball in the spring. Since baseball was no longer an option for him, he decided to pursue other interests, and he ended his high school sports career. Richard may not have been the impact basketball player that Kenny Flick was, but he was a good, experienced athlete and his leaving was a setback to the team in terms of depth.

With Richard and Kenny Flick off the team, Coach Ruggles had to make some personnel adjustments. Both boys had played forward, and now he needed someone else to fill that role. Kenny Smith had primarily played guard, but at 6-foot-5, Ruggles thought he could use his height and experience at the forward position. Cobden had many capable guards on its roster so Ruggles shifted Kenny Smith to the forward spot alongside Jim Neal and decided to start George Boyd in the back court with Tom.

Ruggles did his best to minimize the disruptions of the personnel shakeup, and he tried to keep things on an even keel with the players. He ran practice the same as always and made sure the boys were focused on their next game. There was no time to dwell on what or who they had lost. The games were coming, ready or not.

On Tuesday, January 15, play began at the Anna-Jonesboro Invitational Tournament. In the first game, Metropolis narrowly defeated Attucks, 54-53. Cobden was then set to take on Trico in the second game. The Appleknockers had already played and beaten the Trico Pioneers in December, and Coach Ruggles was glad they were playing a team they already knew. With all the turmoil off the court, Ruggles could only hope the boys had their heads in the game.

The Appleknockers got off to a slow start. It was obvious that not having Kenny Flick affected their play. They battled Trico evenly throughout the first quarter and the score was tied at 10 at the end of the period. Cobden began moving the ball better in the second quarter but held only a five-point lead at the break, 26-21.

In the dressing room, Coach Ruggles encouraged the boys.

"We can't worry about who isn't here for the game," he told them. "We have to worry about who is. Each of you has worked hard all season, and there's no reason to stop now. We're a team, and we have to stick together and play like we know how."

The Appleknockers came out strong in the third quarter, holding the Pioneers to a single field goal and only four free throws as Cobden procured a 14-point lead. George fouled out during the period, but the Appleknockers still pulled away in the final frame and won, 63-39.

Cobden's fans cheered heartily for their team's win, but the victory was bitter-sweet. Many people spotted Kenny Flick sitting in the stands with John Lipe, watching the game. A rumor had been circulating that Kenny was going to enroll at Anna-Jonesboro High School. As the news spread, the towns-people of Cobden became more troubled. They figured Lipe had enticed Kenny away from Cobden and talked him into transferring to Anna. Cobden and Anna were big rivals, and many people in Cobden became angry with Lipe. They called him a thief and other unpleasant names. Everyone was jumping to the wrong conclusion, and no one was bothering to sort out the facts.

At school the next day, Cobden's players heard that Kenny Flick was going to A-J, and they were stunned. They couldn't imagine Kenny playing for the Wildcats. Tom and Kenny Flick were best friends, and Kenny Smith was also close to him as was Chuck.

"This isn't going to work, guys," Kenny Smith said. "This isn't right."

"We've got to talk to Kenny," Tom said. "He belongs with us."

"What can we do?" Chuck asked.

"We just need to talk to him," Tom said again. "He doesn't want to play at A-J."

"We need to go get him," Kenny Smith said. "He's our friend. We'll tell him we want him to come back."

The boys agreed and when their lunch hour arrived, they piled into Kenny Smith's 1950 pea green Ford. They had no idea what they would say or do when they found Kenny Flick, but they thought they could talk him into coming back to Cobden. Things were spinning out of control, and the boys had felt powerless to stop any of it. Now that they were taking matters into their own hands, they felt optimistic for the first time as they drove the five miles to Anna. When they reached the high school, they searched for Kenny Flick. Since it was noon hour, many of the classrooms were empty, and a lot of the students were in the cafeteria, eating lunch. The boys looked all around but were unable to locate their friend.

"Where can he be?" Kenny Smith wondered.

"I don't know. We've looked everywhere," Tom said.

Disappointed, the boys abandoned their search and headed back to Cobden to avoid being late for their afternoon classes. The ride back to school was solemn. The boys had been sure they could straighten everything out with Kenny Flick. Now things seemed bleaker than ever.

On Thursday night, the Appleknockers faced Metropolis in the first semifinal tilt in the tournament. The Trojans were having a very good season and were considered one of the top teams in lower southern Illinois. A Cairo *Evening Citizen* poll ranked them No. 2 behind Cobden. Coach Ruggles knew Metropolis would be a tough test for his team. There had been little time to prepare. The boys worked hard at practice, but some of them seemed distracted. It was obvious they missed Kenny Flick and were still adjusting to the new lineup.

The Trojans got off to a fast start and with precision marksmanship shot out to a 20-14 first-quarter lead. Their accuracy continued into the second period as they missed only four of their field goal attempts in the first half and led, 39-31, at the intermission.

The Appleknockers were only down by eight points, but Coach Ruggles was more worried about the team's demeanor than the score.

"This game isn't over," he said to the players in the locker room. "We've been down in games before and come back. That's a good team we're playing tonight, but we're not going to quit."

Cobden played with better effort after the break but was unable to slow down Metropolis, who extended its lead to 55-40 at the end of the third. Coach Ruggles urged his players to tighten up on defense. Chuck fouled out early in the fourth quarter, but despite losing him, the Appleknockers staged a comeback. Using an effective press, Cobden stole the ball and forced several turnovers. Tom scored 10 of his team-high 20 points in the final period to help bring the Appleknockers within seven points, but they could get no closer. The Trojans held on for a 70-61 win. Cobden's 12-game winning streak was over.

In the dressing room, the players were dejected. They sat with their heads hanging low and their faces grim. This was the first time they had tasted defeat all season, and it was a bitter pill to swallow. Coach Ruggles was also disappointed. He was extremely competitive and hated to lose, but he didn't want the boys getting too down over the loss. The next night they were going to play the loser of the game between A-J and Shawnee, and he didn't want their play in that game to be affected by this loss. Moreover, he felt his team was at a critical juncture. The way they responded to this setback, along with how they adapted to Kenny Flick leaving, would go a long way in determining what happened the rest of the season.

"It hurts right now, but you have to learn from this and then let it go," Coach Ruggles instructed the boys. "You played hard, and you never quit. Our slow start hurt us, but I'm proud of how you fought back in the second half. We're gonna need to fight like that the whole game tomorrow night, no matter who we play."

The Appleknockers' boosters had grown accustomed to winning. This loss stung. For the fans who were already angry at John Lipe, this game added fuel to the fire. They believed that if Kenny Flick had been playing, Cobden would have won. It was a major source of contention in the small town where Lipe still lived. One disgruntled fan even threatened Lipe with physical harm, but Lipe wisely avoided the confrontation and no fight ever materialized. Lipe was a congenial man and tried to get along with everyone. The criticism hurt. He knew he had done nothing wrong, and he was not about to apologize for or feel guilty about helping Kenny Flick, one of his former students.

Kenny Flick was taken aback by the uproar that surrounded his transfer to A-J. He heard the rumor about Lipe recruiting him to play at Anna, and he wanted everyone to know that it was false. He felt bad that people were mad at Lipe for trying help him. Kenny decided the best thing to do was to drop out of school altogether. He hoped that would stop people from saying untrue things about Lipe, and he needed to get a full-time job anyway. He and Evalena planned to get married in a week or two, and he needed to make some money.

A-J had beaten Shawnee, 69-56, in the second semifinal on Thursday night, sending the Redskins into the third-place game against Cobden. When the contest tipped off on Friday night, the Appleknockers showed no ill effects of their loss to Metropolis. Coach Ruggles was gratified to see the boys play with confidence as they raced out to a 21-11 lead after one quarter. Shawnee came right back with an aggressive second period and trailed Cobden by just two points at halftime, 39-37. The game remained close through the third period with the Appleknockers maintaining a slim lead. Kenny Smith got hot in the final stanza, scoring 11 points as Cobden pulled away for a 73-66 win. Chuck bounced back from his sub-par offensive performance the previous night to lead four Appleknockers in double figures with 21 points.

The large group of Cobden supporters stood and applauded their team's effort and satisfying victory. This was the kind of game they were used to seeing from the Appleknockers. Coach Ruggles praised the team's performance in the locker room.

"You got off to a great start and finished strong," he said. "They battled you the whole way, but you didn't panic. Good things happen when you play hard and you play smart."

The players showered and changed in time to see most of the championship game between A-J and Metropolis. The Appleknockers would like to have had a crack at the Wildcats themselves, but it was almost as much fun watching them get beat by the Trojans, 73-54. Cobden now hoped to have a shot at playing against A-J in the postseason regional tournament.

With the Appleknockers back to their winning ways, the town of Cobden began to settle down. Most everyone knew that Kenny Flick was no longer attending school at A-J, and as cooler heads prevailed, they realized that they had been wrong to blame John Lipe for the situation. The people who had given Kenny a hard time needed to look at themselves and admit that it was their actions that had driven him to Anna. Those overzealous fans had to acknowledge that Kenny had made a difficult and mature decision, and they should have respected him for it or at least kept their mouths shut.

The Appleknockers scored a decisive 74-42 win over Dongola in their next game and appeared to be on track, but Coach Ruggles knew the team would have to improve to reach its full potential. His practices had always been demanding, but they became even more so in the wake of the loss to Metropolis. Some of the team's weaknesses had been exposed in that game, and Ruggles wanted to work on them. Cobden needed more than its height and natural talent to carry it past teams the caliber of Metropolis and better. Hard work and preparation were imperative. He also knew that the boys were going to have elevate their level of play to fill the void left by

Kenny Flick.

One afternoon Coach Ruggles was in the gym before practice, and he watched as the boys filed into the locker room to change into their practice clothes. Kenny Smith tagged along behind the others, walking slowly with a dour expression on his face. Ruggles had seen him earlier in the day having a disagreement with his girlfriend, Sheleigh. He knew that was the reason for Kenny's bad mood. Ruggles didn't want a puppy love quarrel interfering with practice.

"Hey, Kenny," Coach Ruggles called to him. "Do me a favor and change your attitude when you change your shoes."

If Kenny heard his coach, he made no indication and slouched into the locker room.

Practice got underway, and the team began running through some drills. Kenny was still moping around and going through the motions with little effort. He made a mistake, and Coach Ruggles called him on it.

"Hey, I know you've had a bad day, but I don't want you to ruin mine," Ruggles said. "We're trying to get something done here, and you aren't helping."

Kenny nodded toward Coach Ruggles, as if acknowledging his error, but inside he felt like Ruggles was picking on him, and he didn't appreciate him busting his chops.

Ruggles divided the players into two teams so they could scrimmage against each other. Not long into the game, Kenny missed his defensive assignment.

Coach Ruggles stopped the play, "Kenny, that was your responsibility. You have to cover that area."

"I can't be everywhere," Kenny shot back.

Ruggles had reached the end of his patience. "I tell you what," he said, his voice angry. "Why don't you just get out of the gym? Get out of the gym because you're not doing anything here anyway. Come back when you're ready to work."

Kenny looked at Coach Ruggles with a shocked expression and then walked off the court and into the locker room. He didn't want to be at practice anyway so if Coach Ruggles wanted him to leave, it was fine by him.

Out on the floor, the other players fell silent and looked at each other in disbelief. They couldn't believe Coach Ruggles had kicked Kenny out of practice. The boys knew Kenny well. He could be stubborn and hard-headed, and they were afraid he might never come back.

"Let's get going, guys," Coach Ruggles said, starting practice as if nothing had happened.

The boys did as they were told. Ruggles had their undivided attention. Whether he meant to send a message or not, he had. He made it clear when he sent Kenny Smith packing, a player integral to the team's success, that no individual was bigger than the team. When it came to basketball, Coach Ruggles was in charge.

Ruggles hid his concern from the boys, but he felt shaken by the incident. *What have I done?* he wondered. He thought Kenny's attitude was unacceptable, but he didn't want to chase him off permanently. The team had already lost too many players.

The boys finished practice, but afterwards they were concerned. They knew Kenny was mad when he left the court, and they worried he would quit the team. On the way home, Chuck and Jim Neal talked about the predicament.

"This could be big trouble," Jim said. "Coach Ruggles doesn't know Kenny the way we do. You know how Kenny can be. He may not come back."

Chuck agreed. "I know Kenny was kind of lazy today, but we need him," he said. "I hope he cools down and doesn't quit the team."

Kenny failed to show up for practice the next day, and his teammates realized how serious the situation was. They feared he was gone for good. Chuck and Tom were close friends with Kenny, and they were determined not to let another friend and teammate quit. The team was still absorbing the shock of Kenny Flick's departure. They were afraid to think about what would happen if they lost another starter.

The next day at school, Chuck and Tom talked to Kenny Smith about the incident.

"I'm done," Kenny told them. "Coach wanted me gone, well, I'm gone."

"Come on. It wasn't like that," Tom said. "We all want you on the team."

"You don't want to quit," Chuck said. "You know we need you."

Kenny knew he was being stubborn, and he had to admit that he really wanted to stay on the team. He had been angry when he left practice, but now he had a little time to think about things. He liked playing basketball, and he was good at it. If he continued to play well, there was a chance he could play in college and probably earn a scholarship to do so. He couldn't let his ego get the best of him and allow him to throw away that opportunity.

Before practice that day, Kenny stuck his head in Coach Ruggles' office. "You got a minute?" he asked.

Ruggles was seated behind his desk. He leaned back in his chair, crossed his arms, and motioned Kenny inside. "What's up?"

Kenny swallowed his pride. "I'm sorry about practice the other day, Coach," he mumbled. Humility was hard for him even though deep down he knew he was at fault.

Ruggles studied the young man in front of him. He could see that this was difficult for Kenny. "Are you ready to help us?" he asked.

Kenny nodded.

"We understand each other now, right?" Ruggles said. "We're on the same page now?"

"Yes," Kenny said, nodding again.

Ruggles leaned forward in his chair and shrugged.

"It's over then," he said. "Forget about it. Come back to the team. We need you to help us."

When Kenny left his office, Coach Ruggles sat back and sighed. He looked up at the ceiling and smiled. Like the players, he had quietly feared that Kenny would quit the team for good. He was relieved that the situation was now resolved favorably. Ruggles knew the team needed Kenny, and he thought maybe he had been a little harsh throwing him out of practice. But Kenny had been slacking off, and Ruggles wanted him and the other boys to understand that when they were at practice, they were there to work, learn, and get better. He expected them to give their best effort at all times. Ruggles believed the Appleknockers could compete with any team in the state, and if they listened to him and worked hard, they would go a long way.

The players were thrilled when they found out Kenny Smith was staying on the team. On Friday night, the Appleknockers traveled to Trico for a game. Coach Ruggles let Kenny dress for the contest, but he pulled him from the starting lineup. Ruggles was as glad as everyone else that Kenny was back, but he thought Kenny's actions at practice earlier in the week warranted a one-game suspension. Ruggles wanted the players to know that every team member was important, but no one member was more important than the team.

Cobden's fans followed the team when it played on the road, and supporters packed the fan bus. Most fans were unaware of the confrontation between Coach Ruggles and Kenny Smith that had occurred that week. Ruggles felt it was a team matter and kept the subject private. The players had talked about the situation among themselves, with some of them sharing their concerns with their parents. When the game began, the Appleknockers' boosters found it strange to see Kenny sitting on the bench.

It was an unusual position for Kenny as well. He was used to being on the floor in the middle of all the action, and it was hard for him to sit on the sidelines. When he apologized and came back to the team, Coach Ruggles hadn't said anything about benching him, and Kenny wondered how long it would last. He watched as Cobden jumped out to an early lead and was comfortably ahead at halftime, 35-19. The Appleknockers maintained their margin in the second half, and Ruggles shuffled boys in and out of the game, using every player except Kenny. *This ain't right*, Kenny thought to himself. He was frustrated at being reduced to the role of observer. Trico never threatened Cobden's lead, and the Appleknockers won, 62-46.

It was humbling for Kenny to see his teammates pull off such an easy victory without him having so much as stepped a foot on the floor. He regretted his actions in practice. *I should have kept my mouth shut*, he thought. It wasn't the first time his mouth had gotten him in trouble, and knowing himself the way he did, he doubted it would be the last. But Coach Ruggles had gotten his attention. He had learned his lesson and was anxious to get back out on the court.

After the game, Coach Ruggles told the players that he was going to a mid-winter tournament in Centralia the following day and asked if any of them wanted to go. Several big schools from the area were competing in the tournament, and Ruggles was going to scout possible future opponents that Cobden might face. He decided to invite the boys along because he thought it was a good opportunity for them to see bigger schools play. The teams in the event were different than those Cobden normally played, and Ruggles thought it was important to expose the boys to teams from larger schools so they wouldn't be intimidated when they met them on the court.

"I know it's short notice," Ruggles said. "I apologize for that, but if you are able to go, please be here at the school by noon tomorrow."

The boys were excited by the prospect of going to watch the tournament, and they told Coach Ruggles they would ask their parents' permission and let him know.

Some of the players had to work on Saturday and others had family commitments, but Chuck and Jim Neal, Tom, and

Kenny Smith managed to rearrange their schedules and obtain approval from their parents to go on the trip. They were at the school the next day before Coach Ruggles arrived.

"You boys ready for the trip?" Ruggles asked when he got there.

They all said they were. Kenny Smith had been a little worried that Coach Ruggles may not want him along because of what happened during the week. But if Ruggles had a problem with Kenny going, he said nothing. As far as Ruggles was concerned, the matter was settled, and Kenny was as welcome as any of the players.

Coach Patterson was going, too, so there were six travelers. Coach Ruggles had no idea how many players would be able to go when he extended the invitation, and he had planned for himself and Coach Patterson to each drive a carful. Since only four players were going, however, Ruggles wanted to save money and take only one car. But the boys were so big he was afraid they wouldn't all fit. Doc Neal had a Ford station wagon, and he offered its use to Ruggles, saying they would all be more comfortable if they took it.

Coach Ruggles gladly accepted. He thanked Doc Neal, and the group climbed into the car and drove the 95 miles to Centralia. When they reached Centralia High School, the tournament was in full swing. The gym was packed, and the spectators from Cobden wedged themselves onto the crowded bleachers with the other fans. The boys liked watching the games, but they had no favorites so they cheered for the good plays made by both teams on the floor.

While some of the games were exciting, the boys paid less attention than Coach Ruggles and Coach Patterson did. To Tom, Kenny, Chuck, and Jim the tournament was secondary to just having fun and hanging out together. They joked around, laughed, and talked, and ate hotdogs and popcorn for supper. It was a unique experience for them to be away from home with only their coaches to provide supervision, and they were enjoying every minute of it.

It was late by the time the championship game ended, and Coach Ruggles began searching for a hotel where he, Coach Patterson, and the boys could spend the night. He had failed to make a reservation, and as the group drove around the unfamiliar city, it became clear that there were few rooms available. The tournament had brought many fans to town, and the hotels were full. After driving for several minutes, Ruggles spotted a small hotel with a light on out front so he pulled into the parking lot.

"I'm going to go in and see if we can get a couple rooms here," he told his passengers. "I'll be right back."

Coach Ruggles entered the hotel and saw an older gentleman sitting behind a desk reading a newspaper. "Good evening," he said.

"Good evening," the man said, looking up from his paper. "How can I help you?"

"I need to rent two rooms for tonight."

"Well, I'm not sure I can help you then," the man said slowly.

"Why not?"

"I've only got one room open," he explained. "It is a double, though, with two beds."

Ruggles thought about it for a moment. He was skeptical that one room would be enough for six people, especially with the size of the boys, but it was so late and all the other establishments they had passed were booked solid.

"Two beds, huh?" Ruggles said.

"That's right," the gentleman said.

"I guess I'll take it. How much is it?"

"There's one other thing about the room," the man said. "The heat hasn't been working too well in there so it may not be that warm."

"No heat?!"

"I didn't say *no* heat, maybe just not a lot."

It was a cold January night, and Coach Ruggles had been entrusted with the welfare of four young men. He wondered what their parents would think if they spent the night in a room without heat, but he was out of options. Always quick to try to save a dollar, he decided to turn the situation to his advantage.

"Well, you can't charge me full price if the heat doesn't work," Coach Ruggles told the hotel man.

The two men negotiated a discount, and after settling on a reduced rate, the hotel man gave Ruggles the key to the room.

"It's number 12," he said. "Make a left as you go out the door. It's the unit on the end."

Coach Ruggles walked back to the car and announced, "We have a room. Get your things."

The coaches and boys had brought a change of clothing with them so they grabbed their bags out of the car and followed Coach Ruggles down the rickety walkway to Room 12.

"Here we are," Ruggles said when they reached the room. He unlocked the door and held it open for the others.

The boys walked in and flipped on the light, which dimly illuminated the room.

"I could only get one room," Ruggles told them. "We're all staying in here."

The group surveyed their surroundings in silence. The room was small and contained little more than two double beds.

"Where are we all gonna sleep?" Jim finally asked.

Coach Ruggles grinned and motioned to one of the beds. "Coach Patterson and I will take this bed," he said. "You boys can have that one."

The four boys looked at each other. They were large boys, and they knew there was no chance that they would all fit in one bed. No one moved for a long moment.

"I have an idea," Jim said. "Let's take the mattress off the bed and put it on the floor. Then two of us can sleep on that, and two can sleep on the box springs."

It was a good plan so the boys pushed both beds and the nightstand against the walls and created enough space to put one of the mattresses on the floor between the beds. Tom and Kenny claimed the mattress and flopped down so Chuck and Jim settled on the box springs. Coach Ruggles and Coach Patterson climbed into the other bed. The room was crowded, but with six people together in such a small space, they generated enough body heat that they barely noticed the heater being broken.

Although it was late, the boys were too wound up to sleep. Jim had a genuine admiration and affection for Coach Ruggles, as did most of his teammates. They knew he had a standout basketball career in high school and at SIU, and Jim decided to take this opportunity to find out more.

"Coach Ruggles," Jim said. "Did you go on trips like this with your high school and college teams?"

"Sometimes," Ruggles replied. "We had to do a lot of traveling to games in college, and we went a few places in high school, too."

Tom rolled over and propped himself up on his elbows. "Where were some places you went?" he asked.

Ruggles was a natural storyteller, and it took little encouragement to get him talking. He related stories of the escapades he and friends and teammates had when he was playing basketball. His words painted vivid pictures of a time, not so long ago, that was obviously very special to him. His anecdotes had the boys laughing, and they hung on every word, realizing that Coach Ruggles' experiences were similar to their own.

Ruggles enjoyed reminiscing as much as the players liked hearing his tales. Coach Patterson had known Ruggles at SIU so he had plenty to add, and they talked long into the night. What had begun as a simple trip to a tournament had turned into a real bonding experience for the coaches and players. On that winter night in that chilly hotel room, even Kenny Smith felt the icy relationship he'd had with Coach Ruggles beginning to thaw.

The Appleknockers' next game at University High School – the school on the campus of SIU in Carbondale – was postponed from January 29 to the 31st due to icy roads. Cobden's players were ready to get back on the hardwood, especially Kenny Smith who had sat on the bench during the last game. Coach Ruggles put Kenny back in the starting lineup. Playing as if he wanted to show that he had learned his lesson, he turned in one of his finest games of the year, pouring in a team-high 24 points while being a force in rebounding and defense. Cobden won an easy decision, 87-55.

Two nights later, the Appleknockers hooked up with Shawnee. Thanks to strong performances from Jim Neal and Tom, who scored 16 and 14 points, respectively, Cobden managed a four-point win, 54-50. It was the team's 17th victory in 18 tries, and it clinched the conference title for the Appleknockers. Cobden's fans were ecstatic and continued to attend the games in record numbers. It had been a long time since the Appleknockers won a conference championship, and they were proud of their team.

While the Appleknockers moved on with the basketball season, Kenny Flick moved on with his life away from basketball. He and Evalena got married in a small, private ceremony in Jackson, Missouri, on January 25. Kenny's mother and father stood up with them as they said their vows, and even though it was a simple affair, Kenny thought Evalena looked beautiful. He was proud to be taking her as his wife.

After the wedding, Kenny and Evalena went on a short honeymoon in Kentucky. It was nice for them to get away from Cobden and spend time together, just the two of them. The controversy over Kenny dropping out of Cobden High School and briefly attending A-J had been stressful. Everyone had an opinion on the subject, and Kenny and Evalena relished the privacy this trip afforded them. Despite the cold temperatures, they took long walks around a lake and shared with each other their hopes and dreams for their future.

When they returned from their honeymoon, it was time to face the real world. Although they were only teenagers, they had responsibilities that most people only face when they reached adulthood. They moved in with Evalena's parents, deciding to stay there until they could save enough money to get a place of their own. Evalena's mom and dad had always liked Kenny, and they were glad that he and Evalena had gotten married. They told them they could stay with them as long as they wanted, and Kenny and Evalena appreciated that, but Kenny didn't plan to stay there too long. Now that Evalena was his wife, he wanted to be the one who supported her and their impending family.

Elvis "Bud" Pearson, a Cobden resident, heard Kenny was looking for a job, and he wanted to help him out. Bud was several years older than Kenny but had known his family for years, and he really liked Kenny. Bud was a big basketball fan, and he had watched Kenny and his classmates play since they were in junior high. Bud was a salesman for Spires Wholesale Grocery in Carbondale and knew the company was looking for someone to do deliveries. He told Kenny about the job and recommended that he apply.

Kenny was thankful for the tip, and he went to Carbondale the next day to find out about the job. The manager at Spires was impressed with Kenny's intelligence and eagerness to work. He hired him on the spot. Kenny was happy to have the job. Evalena had gotten a full-time position at the glove factory in Carbondale, and Kenny figured they would soon be able to afford a home of their own.

Cobden's basketball team continued to roll through the month of February. The Appleknockers posted decisive victories over Gorham and Hurst-Bush and won relatively close contests with Tamms and Attucks. No matter what the score, the boys played hard, and the games were entertaining to watch. On February 22, Cobden hosted University High School for its last regular-season game. It was senior night for Dale Crimmins, George Boyd, and John Marsh, and the fans gave them a standing ovation when they were introduced prior to the game. The Appleknockers were enjoying their best season since 1959, and these boys were a big reason why.

The game was never close. Cobden grabbed an early lead and never looked back. The three seniors played well. George led the team in scoring with 17 points while John chipped in 16, and all three were solid on the defensive side of the ball. The victory was a team effort as Coach Ruggles worked every player into the rotation. Eleven boys marked in the scoring column, and the Appleknockers secured an 88-60 win. Cobden ended the season riding a 10-game winning streak and had a stellar record of 22-1.

Basketball consumed much of the players' time but like normal teenagers, they had interests outside the sport. Some of them decided to show off their other talents – or at least their senses of humor – in the talent contest the school was holding. Tom's girlfriend, Toni Flamm, and Kenny Smith's girlfriend, Sheleigh Clutts, were best friends, and they talked Tom and Kenny into participating in the show. The girls thought it would be funny if the boys dressed up like ballerinas and performed a dance to classical music, and somehow they convinced the boys to do it. Once Tom and Kenny were onboard, Toni and Sheleigh decided to ask Chuck and Jim Neal to join them. Since Chuck and Jim were so tall, the girls knew they would make hilarious looking ballerinas. Jim was always ready to do anything for a laugh so he immediately signed on. Chuck was more reserved than the other boys so it took more effort to get him to agree, but he finally did.

The boys went to Toni's house in the evening to get ready for the show. Toni and Sheleigh choreographed a simple routine for them and showed them the steps.

"What are we supposed to wear in the show?" Tom

wanted to know. "Don't ballet dancers wear tights? I don't have any tights."

"Me either," the other boys chimed in.

"Don't worry. We've figured out your costumes," Sheleigh said. "We think you should wear long underwear, and we're making tutus for you to wear over it."

Toni had bought pink netting, and she brought the sheer material into the living room where the boys were gathered. "We're making the tutus out of this."

The boys started having second thoughts about the show, but Toni and Sheleigh persuaded them to stay in it.

"It's gonna be fun," Toni told them. "Everyone will love it."

She pinned pieces of the netting around the boys' waists and fashioned tutus to fit each of them. The boys looked ridiculous, but with lots of encouragement from the girls, they started getting into character. They learned the dance routine and practiced the steps until they had them memorized. Toni and Sheleigh could hardly contain their laughter as they watched the boys work on their dance moves.

The talent contest was the next night and students, parents, and townspeople filled the gym to watch the show. The acts were performed on the stage at the west end of the gym, and Tom, Kenny, Chuck, and Jim stood backstage, waiting for their turn. They had played dozens of basketball games in this gym over the years and had never felt as apprehensive as they did now.

"I can't believe we're doing this," Chuck finally admitted, looking down at his tutu.

"It's gonna be fun, remember?" Jim said. "That's what Toni and Sheleigh said."

"Yeah, keep reminding me," Chuck said.

The host of the show announced their names, and the boys took their places on the stage. The curtain rose, and Tom, Kenny, Chuck, and Jim were standing center stage, wearing long underwear with pink tutus. The music of *Swan Lake* started, and the boys struck a balletic pose and then began to dance. The audience howled with laughter. Watching those big boys pirouetting awkwardly, but in unison, around the stage in tutus cracked everybody up. While the spectators were in stitches, the boys somehow managed to keep straight faces as they performed their routine. The boys' serious expressions made the audience laugh even harder. By the time the routine was finished, people's sides ached from laughing and happy tears streamed down their cheeks.

The host took the stage at the end of the show to give out the awards to the best acts. Prizes would go to the entries that won first, second, and third places. Toni and Sheleigh were sure the boys would to win the top prize. Their act had been original, and the crowd had loved it. But when the winners were announced, Tom, Kenny, Chuck, and Jim had to settle for second place. First prize went to a group of grade school children who called themselves the Fifth Grade Music Makers.

Toni and Sheleigh took the loss harder than the boys. They were disappointed and thought the judges had made a mistake. Admittedly, the Music Makers were a cute and talented little group, but no act had gotten as big a response from the audience. To make matters worse, Toni's little sister, Diane, was the clarinetist for the Music Makers.

Tom, Kenny, Chuck, and Jim were competitive, but they took their second-place finish in stride. Everyone had enjoyed their routine, and the players had fun doing it; that was good enough for them. If the talent show had been a sporting event, they would have taken the loss more seriously and not been as willing to accept second place.

Coach Ruggles had been in the audience, watching the show. He was as amused as everyone else with the boys' ballet routine. He was thankful that they were better ball players than ballerinas. The Appleknockers were about to start postseason play, and he knew the team wouldn't get far if they were pinning their hopes on the boys' dancing ability.

Chapter 5

1963 Postseason Basketball Tournament

Once the regular season was in the books, the Apple-knockers, like the other high school basketball teams in the state, turned their focus to the postseason Illinois State High School Basketball Tournament sponsored by the Illinois High School Association. As usual, the IHSA tournament trail began with district play where the smallest schools battled each other for the right to advance to regional competition. For the second year in a row, Cobden was hosting a district tournament.

The Appleknockers had won the district title last year. This season they were the top-seeded team and heavily favored to repeat as champions. Dongola was the No. 2 seed, and both Cobden and Dongola received byes into the semifinals. The other teams competing in the district were Goreville (No. 3 seed), Mounds Douglass (No. 4 seed), Thebes (No. 5 seed), and Alto Pass (No. 6 seed). The champion would move on to the Anna-Jonesboro Regional Tournament.

Cobden opened play on Thursday, February 28, against Mounds Douglass, who had defeated Thebes the previous evening. The Appleknockers had already played the Tornados earlier in the season and won handily, 75-31. When the game tipped off, Mounds Douglass tried to hold the ball in an effort to control play, but on back-to-back possessions Cobden stole the ball and drove down the court for easy scores. The Tornados had trouble shooting over the towering Appleknockers and were unable to put a point on the board until four minutes had elapsed in the first quarter. Coach Ruggles used his bench freely, and nine players scored for Cobden in the first period as the Appleknockers took a convincing 17-5 lead.

Cobden continued its balanced offensive attack in the second period. The Appleknockers also yanked down nearly every rebound, and their defensive pressure stifled Mounds

Douglass again, allowing Cobden to go ahead, 35-13, at half-time.

Although the Tornados picked up their scoring in the second half, the Appleknockers extended their advantage to over 30 points and were up, 60-29, at the end of the third. Coach Ruggles used his reserves during the final frame, and Cobden coasted to a 79-53 win.

In the second semifinal game of the night, Dongola took on Goreville, who had dispatched of Alto Pass in the first round. There were some tense moments in the contest when a few of the players fell as they hit slick spots on the court. The roof of Cobden's gym had cracked during the cold winter, and rain from the night before dripped from the rafters. The officials stopped play occasionally to wipe up water and keep the floor as dry as possible.

Dongola was up, 9-8, after the first period, but Goreville came back in the second quarter and held a 10-point edge at the break. Bill Parrish, Goreville's ace and the leading scorer in the area, dropped in 30 points in the second half to secure the Black Cats' victory, 74-44, and help them earn a spot against the Appleknockers in the finals the next evening.

Cobden hadn't played Goreville during the regular season, but it was apparent to everyone that Bill Parrish was the Black Cats' main threat. Coach Ruggles knew Parrish would be difficult to contain, and he didn't want the boys to get too caught up in trying to stop him. Ruggles believed that if the Appleknockers played their game, they had enough fire power to take down Goreville even if Parrish got his 30 points.

"Play the team not just one man," Coach Ruggles reminded the boys before the game. "If we play our game, we'll be fine."

Cobden got off to a fast start in the game as Chuck hit a basket just 10 seconds after tipoff. The Appleknockers increased their lead to eight points, before Bill Parrish knocked down two free throws for Goreville to make the score, 8-2.

Cobden used its decided height advantage to control the re-bounding and opened up a 21-14 gap at the end of the quarter.

The Appleknockers moved in front, 27-18, early in the second quarter, but Parrish spearheaded a drive that brought the Black Cats within four points, 27-23, with five minutes remaining in the stanza. Cobden put an end to Goreville's rally when it kicked its fast-break offense into high gear. Paced by Tom's 13 points, the Appleknockers scored 21 in the last four minutes of the period and entered halftime leading, 48-31.

Cobden overpowered the Black Cats in the second half, and Coach Ruggles was able to use his reserves a good portion of the time as the Appleknockers continued to pull away. Parrish generated nearly all of Goreville's offense, scoring 35 points before fouling out late in the game. But he was unable to single-handedly stop Cobden as it notched an easy 91-52 win.

The Appleknockers' fans cheered loudly. They had been on their feet for the last few minutes, hoping their team would reach the century mark, but even though the boys came up nine points short, the crowd gave them a hearty ovation for their impressive victory.

The players celebrated along with their fans. They were happy to have defended their district title and were looking forward to playing in the regional tournament. Local newspaper reporters and photographers were at the game, and they took pictures of Coach Ruggles and the boys as they were presented with the district championship trophy.

Regional Tournament

The Anna-Jonesboro Regional Tournament featured eight teams and was scheduled to tipoff on Tuesday, March 5. Local sportswriters considered Cobden a favorite to win the tournament with its 24-1 record and the district championship already in its pocket. A-J was the defending region champion and No. 1 seed so many basketball experts tabbed it as a strong contender for the title.

Cobden and A-J were on the same side of the draw, meaning if both teams won their first-round games, they would meet each other in the semifinals. It was a matchup that the players and fans had been yearning for all season. Located just five miles apart, the close proximity fueled a heated rivalry between Cobden and Anna. The teams were in different conferences and never played each other during the regular season unless they met in a tournament, which hadn't happened this year. Anna was four times larger than Cobden and the biggest town in Union County. Being a larger school, especially once consolidated with Jonesboro, A-J often came out on top in its battles with the Appleknockers. This year Cobden's players and fans were optimistic they could turn the tables. The players in Cobden's junior class had beaten Anna when they played each other as freshmen, and they were confident they could beat them again.

Coach Ruggles knew about the Cobden-Anna rivalry, but he didn't want the boys thinking about it yet. Cairo Sumner was the Appleknockers' first-round opponent in the regional, and the players needed to concentrate on the Red Devils.

"We have to take care of business against Cairo Sumner before we get to Anna," Coach Ruggles said to the boys at practice. "Remember this is the tournament now. One loss and we're done. Let's take it one game at a time."

The prior season, Cairo Sumner beat Cobden in the quarter-finals of the regional tournament, but this season when the teams met at the Cobden Blind Draw Tournament, the Appleknockers had come out on top, 62-42. Coach Ruggles thought the recent victory would be beneficial because his players would have an idea of what to expect in the game. With so little time to prepare for teams on the tournament trail, it was a bonus to play a familiar foe.

A near-capacity crowd was on hand when play opened at the Anna-Jonesboro Regional Tournament on Tuesday night. A-J defeated Mounds, 67-44, in the first game to easily reach the semifinals where it awaited the winner between Cobden and Cairo Sumner.

When the second game tipped off, the Red Devils were hot, making several shots from long range and jumping out to a 10-5 lead. The Appleknockers looked static on offense, and their defense was ineffective as they trailed, 18-12, at the end of the period.

Coach Ruggles was steamed when the players came to the bench. "Where was our defense?" he barked. "We can't just stand there and watch them shoot. We've got to get after them!"

Cobden used a swarming defense in the second quarter, and the Red Devils managed just two field goals. Cairo Sumner's center, Jerome Johnson, was called for his fourth foul and was taken out the game. His absence gave Chuck and Jim Neal more room to work inside, and their offense enabled the Appleknockers to jump in front and take a one-point lead at the intermission, 24-23.

Cobden started the third period with a bang. The Appleknockers went on a 13-0 run to break the game wide open. Coach Ruggles used his reserves throughout, running different players into the game in a rapid substitution pattern. Cobden's defense remained stout and seemed to fluster Cairo Sumner. The Appleknockers increased their margin to 15 points by the end of the quarter and were ahead, 44-29. The Red Devils were never able to mount a charge in the final period, and Cobden posted a 69-51 win.

A loud, sincere applause rang out in the gym. It had been a number of years since Cobden had won a game in the regional tournament, and the fans wanted the players to know that they were proud of their accomplishment. Cairo Sumner had thrown a scare into the Cobden faithful during the early stages of the game, but they never doubted that their Appleknockers would persevere.

The stage was now set for the showdown with A-J. Coach Ruggles and the players had seen most of the Wildcats' impressive win over Mounds. Ruggles knew they were a talented team and would be a tough opponent. He wished they had more than one day to prepare.

At practice the next day, Ruggles found the players eager to work. They had been wound up all day, happy about their win from the previous night and anxious about their game with A-J. They listened attentively as Coach Ruggles spelled out the game plan for their bout with the Wildcats, and they executed the plays over and over until they knew them thoroughly. None of the boys grew weary from the strenuous practice. The A-J game was a big deal to them, and they were leaving nothing to chance.

Anna-Jonesboro's gym brimmed with expectant fans, and the atmosphere was charged with electricity on Thursday night when the Appleknockers and Wildcats tipped off their semifinal game. A-J scored first by hitting a shot from the outside, but Cobden answered right back with two fast field goals, making the score, 4-2. The Appleknockers maintained the lead throughout the quarter and were up, 20-15, at the end of the first.

Cobden continued to play well in the second quarter. The Appleknockers were focused on defeating A-J but were unable to put much distance between themselves and the Wildcats thanks mostly to A-J's Gary Goforth. He came off the bench and fired in two long-range bombs from about 30 feet. The Appleknockers played unselfishly on offense, passing the ball efficiently and finding their teammates when open. Whenever they needed a basket, one of the boys would deliver, and Cobden held a six-point lead at halftime, 34-28.

The Appleknockers got into foul trouble during the third period with Chuck picking up two fouls within moments, giving him four for the game. Coach Ruggles took him out and put John Marsh in. A-J made a strong surge, tying the game at 37 with three minutes to play in the quarter, but Cobden responded. John scored eight straight points as the Appleknock-ers closed the frame on a 10-3 run and led, 47-40.

The fans shouted encouragement to their respective teams. The gym was so loud it was hard for the players to hear what Coach Ruggles was saying to them in the huddle. Cobden's supporters had wanted this game all season, and now they were engrossed in the play. Adults and students alike were on the edges of their seats. They were glad that the Appleknock-ers were leading, but the margin was too narrow to allow them to relax. Most felt that Cobden would win, but with another quarter to play, they knew there was still work to do.

The Appleknockers scored two baskets to start the fourth quarter and opened up their largest lead of the game, 51-40. Jim Neal, who was having an excellent game offensively, was called for his fifth foul and had to go to the bench. The Wildcats lost Goforth on fouls late in the period as they were making a push, but the Appleknockers held them off and won, 64-58.

Cobden's fans sprang to their feet, releasing their pent-up energy as they cheered for their team. The victory over A-J meant almost as much to the fans as it did to the players, and they showered Coach Ruggles and the boys with applause. On the sideline, the boys hugged each other and their coach, throwing their fists in the air in triumph.

In the locker room, the boys reveled in their win. Beat-ing a big rival like Anna made the victory even sweeter than normal. Coach Ruggles watched the boys celebrate, enjoying the moment with them. He knew there was more work to do. While this game was important, it was only the semifinals. The boys still had the championship to play for the next night.

When the noise level in the room finally lowered, Coach Ruggles spoke up, "You played a good team tonight and got a great win. I'm proud of the way you played, and you should be proud of yourselves. It was a true team effort."

"Just remember," he continued. "We haven't won anything yet. We have another game tomorrow night to decide the regional championship. I know you wanted to beat Anna, but beating Anna wasn't the goal. We want to win this regional tournament and move on to the sectional. Enjoy this now, but don't forget we have an important game tomorrow night and more to come."

After the players showered and changed, they found seats on the bleachers and watched the end of the second semifinal game to see who their opponent in the final would be. Tamms got 34 points from Teddy Gleghorn and used a fast-break style of play to run past Shawnee, 74-57. The Appleknockers would tangle with Tamms for the title.

Coach Ruggles had told the boys to start thinking about their next game, but most of them were still savoring their win over A-J. Beating A-J was special, and they weren't ready to abandon the feeling of pride the victory gave them. They could worry about Tamms tomorrow; there was plenty of time to think about that game. They had just beaten their arch rival, and even though it was just the semifinals, for tonight that was enough.

Coach Ruggles and the players had a pretty good idea of what to expect in the final the following night. Cobden had already played Tamms twice this season. The Appleknockers had won both games, but the second one was close. The Eagles were extremely quick with several weapons on offense, and they could be a dangerous team when they got on a roll. Cobden had depth and a significant height advantage on its side. Coach Ruggles stressed to the boys that rebounding and defense would be keys in the game.

Although Anna-Jonesboro was out of the tournament, its gym was packed Friday night for the regional final, and the spectators were expecting a good game. Cobden won the opening tip and scored first when Jim Neal made a layup. The Appleknockers' teamwork and unselfish play on offense was evident as they scored four more field goals, one by each of the other four starters – Tom, Kenny Smith, George, and Chuck – to take an early 10-point lead. Cobden also managed to hold Teddy Gleghorn scoreless in the first quarter and led, 22-13, after one.

The Appleknockers committed several fouls in the second quarter, and the Eagles made their free throws, cutting into Cobden's lead. Chuck and George had three fouls each so Coach Ruggles took them out of the game and put John and Dale in. Teddy Gleghorn managed his first basket in the second period, but the Appleknockers remained in front, 39-32, at the half.

Cobden sustained the lead in the third quarter, but like A-J the night before, Tamms refused to go down quietly. The Eagles' Benny Moore and Floyd Boyd were having great games, and Teddy Gleghorn began to heat up offensively to bring Tamms within five points of the Appleknockers, 57-52, at the end of the third.

Chuck was called for his fifth foul early in the fourth period and was sent to the sideline. The Eagles made both free throws to close the gap with Cobden to three points. John, who had replaced Chuck when he fouled out, hit a jump shot to restore the Appleknockers' five-point lead. Moments later, George picked up his fifth foul and was also forced to the bench. Coach Ruggles signaled for a timeout.

"Let's stop playing around with these guys," he said. "We need to block out and move our feet on defense. Stay in front of them and stop the unnecessary fouls. Let's just play our game."

Cobden's fans started getting nervous now that two starters were on the bench, but the Appleknockers' reserves were experienced and able to hold their own. Cobden outscored Tamms 17-10 over the remainder of the quarter and won, 76-64, to earn the school's first regional basketball title since 1942.

The anxious feelings the Appleknockers' fans felt during the game now gave way to a delirious happiness, and they gave the team a standing ovation. The players jumped high in the air and slapped each other on the backs as they realized they were regional champions.

While the boys celebrated their victory on the court, they had no idea their friend and former teammate, Kenny Flick, watched from a seat high in the rafters. It wasn't the first time since leaving school that he had been to one of the Appleknockers' games without the fans or players knowing, not even his good buddy, Tom. Kenny was unsure how well he would be received as a spectator, and not a player, so he had snuck in quietly and usually sat on the opposing team's side of the gym.

As busy as Kenny was with his marriage and work, he missed playing basketball with his friends. He loved the game and had played for so long that it was like second nature. He had been playing pickup games with a lot of older guys since he had left school, but it wasn't the same as being part of the team he had grown up with. Although he was no longer playing for Cobden, he wanted the team to do well. He watched as the Appleknockers were presented with the regional championship plaque, and in his heart, he was cheering as loud as anyone in the gym.

● Chapter 6

Preparing for Sectionals

The townspeople of Cobden had been supporting the team all season, but after the regional, interest went into overdrive. It seemed as if every conversation at the feed store or Flamm's Café centered around basketball. The boys were having an extraordinary season, and the fans were enjoying every victory. They were especially proud that after more than 20 years, the Appleknockers had brought the regional crown back to Cobden.

More than just the local community members were taking note of the Appleknockers' success. After winning the regional title, Cobden became known in the press as a "Little David" team. The term was used for a team that had progressed through a district tournament, won a regional, and then moved into the tough sectional round of the state tournament.

With an enrollment of about 140 students, Cobden was the smallest school still in the event, and reporters from many newspapers began paying closer attention to the Appleknockers. The team had lost only one time in 28 games and was riding a 15-game winning streak. Coach Ruggles started getting phone calls and interview requests from sportswriters all over southern Illinois. Now that Cobden had advanced to sectional play, people began wondering just how far the team could go.

The Appleknockers were set to meet McLeansboro on Wednesday, March 13, in the Harrisburg Sectional Tournament. Despite Cobden's outstanding record, basketball experts considered the Appleknockers an underdog in its sectional game. McLeansboro was a veteran-laden squad that had finished fourth in the state tournament last year and was seeking a return trip to Champaign. The Foxes had compiled a 25-2 record this season and were ranked fourth in the state in the Associated Press's final regular-season poll.

Coach Ruggles had scouted McLeansboro at a holiday tournament earlier in the season in the event that Cobden would play the Foxes down the road. He knew McLeansboro would offer formidable competition. McLeansboro was paced by All-State performer Jim Burns, a do-it-all guard who stood over 6-foot-3. He was a gifted offensive player who had been the leading scorer at the state tournament a year ago. He was joined on the team by his twin brother, John, and a host of other skilled ball players. Ruggles knew the Foxes were experienced and talented, but he still thought that if the Appleknockers played to their potential, they could beat them.

The Appleknockers had two good practices after school on Monday and Tuesday. Coach Ruggles tried to push the distractions and preoccupations of the increased media attention aside and focus the boys' attention on the game. He went over the game plan for McLeansboro and tried to keep the practices as routine as possible. He tried not to make the players nervous by overemphasizing the importance of the game.

On Wednesday, a special energy could be felt throughout Cobden High School. In every classroom, schoolwork took a backseat to discussions of that night's game. This was one of the most exciting things to happen at the school in years. A pep rally was held in the gym during the last period of the day. The cheerleaders performed cheers and a dance routine to the school's fight song, and the students were on their feet as the players were introduced, giving each one a loud round of applause.

"On behalf of the players, I want say thank you for the support you have given us all year," Coach Ruggles said to the assembled group. "Cobden has the best fans any team could ask for, and we appreciate you coming to the games and filling the gym. You have been a huge help to us all season."

When the pep rally ended, the players headed home to grab a bite to eat. The game wasn't until 8 p.m., but Coach Ruggles asked the boys to be back at the school before 6 p.m. to catch the bus to the game.

Harrisburg was more than an hour's drive from Cobden. The players chatted freely and easily as the trip began, but as the miles ticked by, their conversations quieted, and their thoughts turned to the game. The boys were well aware of the Foxes' reputation and their stature in the rankings. Being a bigger school, McLeansboro cast an intimidating shadow, and while the Appleknockers were confident in their abilities, many of the boys felt more than the usual case of pre-game jitters.

When the Appleknockers took the court to warm up, the Cobden contingent cheered enthusiastically. Cobden's boosters had gobbled up all of the tickets the school had requested in advance, and those fans without advance tickets drove to Harrisburg and bought tickets at the door. They had been following the team all year and were eager to see Cobden play in its first sectional in 21 years. Many spectators from other towns also cheered for the Appleknockers. Cobden was the underdog after all, and folks from other small towns in lower southern Illinois were rooting for the team.

The Appleknockers appreciated the crowd's support as they tried to get acclimated to Harrisburg's Davenport Gym. The boys were used to playing in different venues. They had played lots of games on the road, but this gym floor was the largest they had ever played on. It was also one of the largest crowds they had played in front of so they were glad to hear familiar voices and cheers as they adjusted to the new setting.

McLeansboro's fans had also turned out en masse to watch the sectional, and the gym was at capacity when the game tipped off. The Foxes took control early and scored four buckets to gain an 8-0 lead. Cobden appeared tense and uncertain, and Coach Ruggles called a timeout to talk to his guys.

"What's happening out there?" Ruggles asked. "We came here to play, didn't we? So let's play. We can't just stand around and watch."

The Appleknockers settled down after the timeout and moved the ball better on offense. Their zone defense was effective in holding McLeansboro to just one more field goal in the quarter, and Cobden only trailed by two points, 10-8, at the end of the first period.

The Foxes struck first in the second quarter, getting a bucket and a free throw to go ahead by five, but then Cobden reeled off six consecutive points to lead, 14-13. Two quick baskets by Ron Farlow put McLeansboro back in front, 17-14. Jim Burns got on a roll offensively for the Foxes, and Chuck was called for two fouls as he tried to defend Jim when he drove to the hoop. Jim was deadly from the free-throw line, making all four shots. He made three more free throws in the period, and McLeansboro increased its margin to seven points at halftime, 27-20.

The teams exchanged baskets early in the third quarter, and the Foxes maintained their advantage. Jim Neal and Tom hit back-to-back shots for the Appleknockers as they got within five points, 34-29, midway through the quarter. Chuck picked up his fourth foul, and Coach Ruggles took him out and put John in. The Foxes' tough man-to-man defense held Cobden without a field goal the rest of the period. The Appleknockers managed only one free throw and were down 11 points, 41-30, after three quarters.

Cobden was never able to threaten McLeansboro's lead in the fourth quarter. Chuck fouled out soon after the period started and had to go to the bench. The Appleknockers missed his height and rebounding prowess as the Foxes grabbed several offensive rebounds and stuck them back through the hoop. Cobden made several bad passes when it attempted to fast break, and its turnovers led to baskets by McLeansboro. Coach Ruggles called timeouts to try to get his players back on track, but nothing seemed to help. The Appleknockers even missed their free throws.

Cobden's fans watched in dismay. They were unaccustomed to seeing their team play so poorly this season. Kenny Flick was at the game, sitting on McLeansboro's side of the gym, unbeknownst to the Appleknockers and their boosters.

He grew frustrated watching Cobden play. He knew the Foxes were good, but he felt if the Appleknockers played to their full potential, they would win. For some reason, that wasn't happening tonight. *Come on*, Kenny thought, mentally encouraging Cobden's players. *You can beat these guys.*

But it was not to be. Cobden was effective on defense, but its high-powered offense that had averaged nearly 73 points per game never got started. McLeansboro pulled away for a 59-39 win.

The game's outcome was a foregone conclusion several minutes before the final horn sounded. McLeansboro's fans were on their feet cheering. Their team was moving on. The Appleknockers were going home; their season was over.

Cobden's dressing room was an unpleasant place to be after the game. The team had underperformed in the game, and Coach Ruggles told them so. His criticism stung as it mixed with their own feelings of disappointment about the loss. They had such a good season. They were having so much fun, and they weren't ready for it to end, especially not on such a down note. Losing by 20 points was embarrassing. They knew they could have played better, but to lose by so much left a bitter taste in their mouths. The boys soaked in the showers extra long, drowning their disappointment, before they climbed back on the bus to head home.

Just as the bus ride to Harrisburg had allowed for ample time to think about the game, the ride home gave as much time to reflect on the loss. The boys rode mostly in silence. Some tried to sleep, while others just stared out the windows. For the three seniors, Dale, George, and John, the loss not only ended their seasons, but also their basketball careers. They were going to miss playing together.

Tom closed his eyes and laid his head on the back of his seat, but rest eluded him. The game kept running through his mind. He was not only a competitive player but also a cerebral one. He tried to figure out what went wrong. He had to give the Foxes some credit. They were a great team, but it was more about the mistakes Cobden had made than the way McLeansboro had played. On some level at least, he felt the Appleknockers had beaten themselves.

Coach Ruggles had been critical of the boys immediately after the game, but it was only because he knew they were capable of playing better than what they had shown tonight. It may have seemed farfetched to some people since Cobden had just won its first regional title in 21 years, but Ruggles believed the Appleknockers had the talent to make it through the sectional and super-sectional and qualify for the state tournament. It was a lofty aspiration for a team from such a small school, but one he thought was attainable.

Now he wondered if the boys believed it was possible. Were they satisfied being regional champions, or did they realize they had the ability to achieve so much more? Bigger didn't always mean better. Did they know they could compete with any team in the state, no matter its size?

Ultimately, Ruggles took responsibility for the team's sub-par performance. He should have foreseen that the players would be more nervous than usual playing in the sectional for the first time and that the pressure they felt could adversely affect their play. He had tried to keep everything "business as usual," and maybe that had been a mistake. He wished he had done more to prepare them for such an important game. If the boys had a better idea of what to expect at the sectional, they may have played with more confidence. He knew this was idle speculation now, of course, since the Appleknockers' season was over.

The cheerleaders, students, and supporters were waiting for the players when they arrived back at Cobden High School. Although Cobden had lost, the fans cheered the boys when they exited the bus. The Appleknockers had a great season, and regardless of how it ended, the fans were extremely proud.

The boys were a little surprised by the reception. The cheers from their friends, classmates, and families helped ease the pain they were feeling from the loss, but the disappointment did not completely disappear. It was too fresh. Only time would fully heal their wounds.

Tom's parents and his sisters, Mary and Mildred, had been at the game as they had every game during the season. They were waiting for him when he got off the bus. The disappointment was written all over his face, and they knew their words would do little to make him feel better.

"You gave it a good effort, son," Tom Sr. said, putting an arm around his son's shoulder to comfort him. "It just wasn't your night."

It should have been our night, Tom thought to himself. Then he said, "Wait 'til next year. We're going all the way."

The boys soon learned that the new-found fame and extra press coverage they garnered after winning the regional was a double-edged sword. Several area newspapers reported their exploits against McLeansboro with unflattering commentary. The morning after the game, the players were still feeling down about their lackluster play and their season being over, and the local media chimed in, adding insult to injury.

Sportswriter Merle Jones of the *Southern Illinoisan* wrote: "The Cobden Appleknockers, the little school with the 27-1 record, folded up in the heat of sectional basketball tourney competition at Harrisburg Wednesday and were an easy 59-39 victim of the McLeansboro Foxes. Coach Gene Haile of McLeansboro did not even bother to scout Cobden as he had his chief worries over such potential regional foes as Carrier Mills and Harrisburg. So another 'Little David' met defeat... For some reason the boys from the small schools never seem to play up to their capabilities when they meet the big boys."

 **Chapter 7**

A New Arrival and a Taste of
State Tournament Play

Coach Ruggles had little time to dwell on the disappointment. Mary was due to deliver their second child any day. There was nothing like the creation of a new human life, especially one that he was responsible for, to put things in perspective.

On Tuesday, March 19, Coach Ruggles drove to West Frankfort to watch the super-sectional game. After McLeansboro beat Cobden, the Foxes lost in the sectional finals, 62-59, to the Metropolis Trojans, the only other team to beat Cobden during the season. Metropolis and Herrin were now battling each other for the chance to go to the state tournament in Champaign.

The game was a good one. Metropolis built a three-point advantage at halftime and pushed that margin to six points at the end of the third period. Herrin stormed back in the fourth quarter, scoring 17 points, but its rally fell short by a point. The Trojans held on to win, 53-52.

While Coach Ruggles watched an exciting game in West Frankfort, Mary was at home in Cobden, experiencing some excitement of her own. She started into labor, and her contractions were coming with increasing intensity. She had no way of reaching her husband so she called her mom and dad who lived in Anna. She told them that she was in labor and asked them to come and get Randy. He was just 20 months old, and they had already decided that her parents would keep him while she delivered her second baby.

Coach Ruggles got home about the same time Mr. and Mrs. Woesthaus arrived to pick up Randy. It was around 11 p.m., and they found Mary standing in the bathtub.

"My water just broke," she informed them. "Hurry!

We've got to go to the hospital."

Coach Ruggles called Memorial Hospital in Carbondale to let the doctor know that Mary was in labor and that they were on their way. Then he grabbed the bag that Mary had already prepared with a change of clothing, a nightgown, and a few other personal items and helped her out to their car. He sped quickly but carefully through the crisp, early-spring night up Route 51 to Carbondale. When they reached the hospital, Mary was admitted immediately but then was told that her regular obstetrician, Dr. Maloney, was unavailable to deliver her baby. A different doctor, Dr. Baysinger, was summoned.

The unexpected news caught Mary off guard. She had formed a close doctor-patient relationship with Dr. Maloney, and she had assumed he would be with her for the delivery. Coach Ruggles held her hand and assured her that everything was going to be fine. She tried to relax, but that was easier said than done as her labor pains grew more intense. Now all they could do was wait.

When Dr. Baysinger arrived at the hospital, he examined Mary and found that her labor was progressing quickly so he had her transferred to a delivery room. As she was wheeled down the hallway, the doctor spotted Coach Ruggles and recognized him as the Appleknockers' coach.

"You were at that game tonight in West Frankfort, right?" Dr. Baysinger asked him. "Wasn't that something?"

The doctor had also attended the super-sectional game, and the two of them rehashed the thrilling, one-point victory by Metropolis, going over the key plays and miscues by the members of each team.

Mary could hear them talking from inside the delivery room. She knew how long her husband was capable of discussing basketball and wondered if the nurse was going to have to deliver her baby. The labor pains came faster and harder, and she knew the baby would arrive soon.

Her instincts were correct about the baby's imminent arrival, and Dr. Baysinger didn't let her down. He delivered a beautiful baby girl at 12:30 a.m. on March 20.

After the delivery, Mary was wheeled back to her room, and the baby was taken to the nursery. Coach Ruggles and Mary were thankful that their new little girl was healthy and that there had been no complications. Since they already had a son, they were pleased to have a daughter.

"She's beautiful, isn't she?" Mary said.

"Of course," Coach Ruggles agreed, smiling proudly. "She looks just like her mother."

Mary was exhausted after giving birth and soon drifted off to sleep. With Mary and the baby tucked in for the night, Coach Ruggles went home to get a few hours of sleep.

The next morning he called Mary's parents and told them that Mary had a girl and everything had gone well. Mr. and Mrs. Woesthaus were delighted to hear that they had a granddaughter, and they told him that Randy was doing fine. Coach Ruggles called his family in Massachusetts and gave them the good news, and then he went back to the hospital to be with his wife and baby daughter.

Mary had rested well during the night, and she had just finished feeding the baby when Coach Ruggles entered her room.

"How are my girls?" he asked, feeling almost over-whelmed with emotion at the sight of them together.

"We're doing fine," Mary answered. "In fact, she just finished her breakfast."

"You gave us a little scare last night," Coach Ruggles said to his baby daughter. "I was afraid I was going to have to pull over in Boskeydell and deliver you myself."

"Oh, thank heaven we made it here," Mary said and then asked, "What are we going to name her?"

"I thought we were naming her Debbie," he said.

They had been referring to the baby as "Debbie" for the last several months of the pregnancy. They preferred to call the baby by a name because they thought it sounded more personal then just saying "it" or "the baby." They had done the same

thing when Mary was pregnant with Randy. They had called
him "Skeeter."

They hadn't known that their baby was going to be a
girl, but now that she had arrived, Debbie seemed like the logi-
cal choice for her name.

"I'm not sure she looks like a Debbie," Mary said.

"Well, what does she look like?"

"I don't know."

Coach Ruggles leaned in closer so he could get a better look. They both scrutinized the baby's tiny features and
smooth skin. To Coach Ruggles, she looked like a sweet baby.
She could be a Debbie as far as he could tell, but he figured his
wife probably knew best when it came this sort of thing. Mary
finally came up with Kathleen. They filled out her birth certifi-
cate with Kathleen Marie and decided to call her Kathy.

Coach Ruggles had planned to go to Champaign to
watch the Elite Eight at the state tournament on Friday and
Saturday. Now that Mary had Kathy and was going to be in the
hospital for a few days, she wanted him to stay with her. But
knowing how important basketball was to him and his career,
she didn't try to stop him.

With a twinge of regret about leaving Mary so soon
after she had given birth, Coach Ruggles decided he would
go ahead and take Lee Patterson and juniors Chuck Neal, Roy
Witthoft, and Darrell Crimmins to Champaign as scheduled.
Although Cobden had lost in the first round of the sectional,
Ruggles still believed his team had the ability to play at the
state level. He wanted to expose some of his players to the
atmosphere of the state basketball tournament and plant a seed
in their minds that they belonged there.

The team was losing three solid contributors in George
Boyd, Dale Crimmins, and John Marsh, but several experi-
enced, talented players would be returning next year. The
Appleknockers had never qualified for the state tournament.
Small schools like Cobden rarely seemed to have the ability to
beat teams from the much bigger schools. There were excep-

tions, of course, like Hebron and Braidwood, so maybe 1964 would be Cobden's year.

Coach Ruggles and his four passengers met at the high school at 6 a.m. on Friday, March 23. They had a 220-mile trek ahead of them, and they wanted to make sure they made it to Champaign for the full slate of games that began at noon. Metropolis was scheduled to play the Centralia Orphans, who were ranked No. 1 in the state in the final Associated Press poll, in the first quarter-final game.

Coach Patterson rode shotgun, and the three boys piled into the back of Ruggles' car. With Chuck standing 6-foot-6 and Roy and Darrell both over six feet tall as well, the backseat appeared to be a mass of arms and legs as they jockeyed with each other for elbow and leg room. Once everyone was settled, Coach Ruggles eased his car through the rolling hills of southern Illinois and out onto the flat stretch of highway that would carry them to the state tournament. Plains and cornfields dominated the landscape, and it was easy to see how Illinois got its moniker: the Prairie State.

For the first time, the state tournament was being contested at the University of Illinois' new Assembly Hall. The arena had cost approximately $8.4 million and taken nearly four years to build. It was an impressive architectural achievement. With seating for more than 16,000 people, it was considerably larger than Huff Hall, the previous site for the state tournament's final games.

It seemed that the whole world had converged upon Champaign for the state tournament. March Madness it was called. Henry V. Porter, a former assistant executive secretary of the Illinois High School Association, had coined the term in 1939. In an article called "March Madness" that was published in the IHSA's magazine, *Illinois Interscholastic*, Porter commemorated the spectacle of the annual state boy's basketball tournament that routinely drew sellout crowds, bringing together teams and basketball fans from all over the state. Basketball fever had spread throughout Illinois, and it was alive and well.

Ruggles and his passengers found themselves in a traffic jam with all the other basketball fans going into the city. As they sat idling in traffic, they noticed some girls in the car behind them. The girls waved to get their attention, so Roy hopped out of the car and ran back to see what they wanted.

"What's going on?" he asked, bending down to peer in the driver's side window.

The girls said they were from Springfield and wanted to make sure they were headed in the right direction. They were going to the state tournament to cheer for their high school, Springfield Lanphier.

"As far as I know, you're going the right way," he said.

Noticing his letter jacket, the driver of the car asked him, "Where are you from?"

"Cobden."

The girls looked at each other then asked almost in unison, "Where's Cobden?"

"Wait 'til next year," Roy told them. "Cobden is going to be up here." He surprised himself a little when he realized he actually meant it.

When Coach Ruggles pulled into the parking lot at Assembly Hall, the kids from Cobden were awestruck by the building's size. Coach Ruggles had been to Boston Garden and Yankee Stadium, but Assembly Hall with its 400-foot-wide folded, concrete dome was easily the biggest sporting arena his players had ever seen. The boys filed into the cavernous hall with the other basketball fans and were still marveling at its size as they found their seats and settled in for the tournament tipoff.

Metropolis was no match for Centralia on the opening afternoon of the event. The Orphans, proving worthy of the copious praise that had been heaped on them all season by the downstate media, raced out to an 18-10 lead after the first quarter and led, 38-19, at halftime. The Trojans never mounted a serious threat after the break and bowed out of the tournament with a 74-45 loss.

The second game of the day turned out to be a much more entertaining affair. Close throughout the first half, the Springfield Lanphier Lions held a three-point advantage at the intermission over the Knights of Rockford Auburn, 29-26. The Knights erupted in the third quarter, scoring 21 points and holding Springfield to just 10, to take an eight-point lead, 47-39, at the end of the period. In the fourth quarter, it was the Lions' turn to roar as Lanphier caught fire, erasing the deficit to claim a two-point win, 58-56.

The first game of the evening session featured defending champion Stephen Decatur High School, the Runnin' Reds, and the Peoria High School Lions, the first Illinois high school boys basketball champions in 1908. Both teams had storied histories in basketball with numerous appearances in the state finals. On this night, Peoria's Craig Alexander nearly knocked off the defending champs single-handedly. He scored 30 points, including 12-of-15 from the free-throw line as Peoria won, 60-45.

The 1962 state runner-up, Chicago Carver, played the Geneva Knights in the last quarter-final game. Faring better than the team that topped it a year ago, Chicago Carver led virtually the entire game and won, 57-50.

On Saturday, the five spectators from Cobden returned to Assembly Hall and joined the throngs of basketball fans for the semifinal contests. Mighty Centralia survived a scare in the first game. Springfield Lanphier jumped out to 31-24 halftime lead before the Orphans rallied to tie the score at 39 going into the final frame. Centralia outscored the Lions 11-7 in the fourth quarter to earn a spot in the championship game with a 50-46 victory.

The second semifinal game pitted Chicago Carver against Peoria. Craig Alexander had another big game offensively, scoring 23 points for Peoria, but Chicago Carver's balanced scoring prevailed in the end as it posted a thrilling 40-37 overtime win. Unranked at the end of the regular season, Carver had earned a place in the state finals for the second straight year.

During the break between the afternoon and evening sessions, Coach Ruggles and the group drove into Champaign for a quick supper. The restaurants teemed with basketball fans and sports reporters from all over the state. Everyone talked about the matchup between Centralia and Chicago Carver in the championship game. Most people favored Centralia. Many of Carver's players had played in the state title game the year before, and that experience could not be dismissed; Carver appeared to be a worthy foe.

Back at Assembly Hall, Springfield Lanphier and Peoria began the evening's action with the third-place game. The score was tied at 20 at the intermission, but Springfield pulled away in the second half. Mike Rodgerson knocked down all 13 of his free-throw attempts and scored 23 points as Springfield prevailed, 60-47.

In the championship game, Chicago Carver grabbed a four-point halftime lead and held that advantage going into the fourth quarter. Centralia battled back throughout the final period and had a one-point lead with just seconds remaining on the clock. Chicago Carver worked to get a final shot, and the crowd at Assembly Hall watched anxiously as reserve guard Anthony Smedley lofted his only shot of the game. It went in, giving Chicago Carver an improbable 53-52 victory and its first state championship. Joe Allen and Ken Maxey both had big games for Carver, scoring 18 points apiece, but Smedley made the shot of the tournament.

The following morning the gang from Cobden left Champaign and headed for home. Coach Ruggles was ready to get back to Mary and Randy and to spend time with his new baby girl. The boys were overdosed on basketball but still energized by the excitement of the state tournament. They couldn't wait to tell their friends and family members about the experience.

At school on Monday, Chuck, Roy, and Darrell told

their teammates about the trip to Champaign. Many of the boys had watched the final game on television so they had seen Centralia fall to unranked Chicago Carver.

"You wouldn't believe how big that place was. It was huge," Chuck told Tom and Kenny Smith as they changed in the locker room before baseball practice.

"The teams up there were really good," Kenny said. "But from what I saw on TV, I think we could play with any of them."

"I do, too," Tom said. "Especially if we had Flick back with us."

The boys were confident in their basketball ability. Their self-assurance came from their past successes on the basketball court. They had played together for so many years that they instinctively knew each other's moves on the floor. They trusted each other as teammates and friends. They had won so many games together that they simply expected to win. Losing wasn't in their vocabulary. While the loss to McLeansboro was a blow to their egos, they had already begun to put the disappointment behind them.

"It would be great just to get to play one game up there," Chuck said.

"Why just one game?" Coach Ruggles asked. He had entered the locker room unnoticed by the boys and had overheard their conversation. "If you win the first game, you get to play two the next day. That should be your goal."

The boys thought about his statement for a moment then Kenny spoke up confidently, "That is our goal."

The three boys looked at each other and nodded in agreement. They turned to their coach, and he could see the resolve and determination in their eyes. Together they made a pact that they would go all the way the next year. They vowed that their team would be playing ball on the last day of the Illinois state high school basketball tournament.

Their pact would be in jeopardy less than two months later.

 **Chapter 8**

Unexpected Peril

March slid into April, and April drifted into May, and the sting of Cobden's loss to McLeansboro in the sectional tournament receded. The Appleknockers had beaten long-time rival Anna-Jonesboro and won the regional championship, and though unsatisfied, the players were proud of those accomplishments. The weather warmed up, and most the boys got busy with baseball season and the other distractions of high school.

Although the loss to McLeansboro had faded with the changing season, some disappointment remained. Talk began circulating around Cobden that the Cobden School Board was considering changing the policy that barred married students from participating in athletics and other extracurricular activities.

It's hard to say where the rumor got started because everyone wanted the rule changed. Cobden had a team of exceptionally talented ball players, and many people considered Kenny Flick to be the best all-around player. They wanted him back in an Appleknocker uniform. Most fans believed that if the Appleknockers were going to reach their full potential and compete with the bigger schools, they needed Kenny Flick.

The players wanted Kenny back on the team, too. They were an extremely close group of boys, and Kenny had been a friend and teammate for many years. They missed having him around, and as much as they wanted him back on the basketball team, they wanted him back in school even more. He was a good student with near-perfect grades in his classes.

The school board members also wanted Kenny back on the team. This was the same group of men who had scoured southern Illinois to find the right coach to lead their basketball team. They had recognized the potential for greatness in this team, and it seemed like they were shooting themselves in the foot by sidelining one of its best players, especially when they had the authority to change the rule.

When the rumor about the possible policy change filtered down to the players, they hoped it was true, and Tom was eager to tell Kenny the news. The two had stayed in touch and seen each other as often as they could after Kenny dropped out, but school was never the same for Tom without Kenny being there. Tom wanted him back in school for their senior year.

Kenny and Evalena lived in a mobile home on the outskirts of Anna, and after baseball practice, Tom drove to Kenny's house.

"I have some good news," Tom announced after Kenny greeted him at the door.

"What is it?"

"You better get ready to start studying again," Tom said.

The sun was still high in the May sky, warming the late afternoon as the two friends settled in chairs on Kenny's small lawn.

"What are you talking about?" Kenny asked.

Tom was going to try to be coy and string his buddy along, but he found he was too excited so he just blurted out, "They're going to change the rule at school, and you're going to be able to play basketball."

"What?"

"You heard me," Tom said. "They're going to change the rule, and it won't matter if you're married. You can still play ball."

"Where'd you hear that?"

"Everybody's talking about it," Tom told him. "Doc Neal and some of the other school board members are saying they're going to change the rule."

"So it hasn't been changed yet?"

"Not officially I don't guess, but it's in the works. And then you can come back to school, and we can play basketball together again like we're supposed to."

Kenny was skeptical, but he told Tom with a laugh,

"Okay. When they do change it, then I'll come back."

"I'm gonna hold you to that," Tom said.

The two friends talked awhile longer, catching up on what was happening in their lives. Tom told Kenny about how the baseball team was doing and about taking his girlfriend, Toni, to the prom, saying that they had double dated with Kenny Smith and his girlfriend, Sheleigh, and had a really good time. Before he left, Tom steered the conversation back to the purpose of his visit.

"I'm glad you're coming back," he said.

"Yeah. That's if they change the rule," Kenny reminded him.

"They will. Trust me."

"If you say so."

After Tom left, Kenny thought about going back to school. He had been thinking about it a lot. He wanted to go back. He needed to get his high school diploma if he was going to get a good job and be able to support his family. Right now, he and Evalena both worked full time to make ends meet. Kenny knew that even if he went back to school, he would still have to work, at least part time. He had no idea whether the Cobden School Board would change the rule, and he wasn't holding his breath. Deep down he hoped it all worked out.

Tuesday, May 14, was an unseasonably warm and humid spring day in southern Illinois. For the second day in a row, the temperature had risen well into the 80s, several degrees above the average high. Coach Ruggles had canceled baseball practice after school, and the boys were eager to take advantage of the summer-like weather so some of them decided to go swimming at Little Grassy Lake, a man-made lake about 15 miles north of Cobden.

"I gotta ask my dad if I can go," Chuck told his friends.

He asked Kenny Smith and Tom to go with him to see his dad because he knew his dad would say yes if his friends were there. The three boys went down to the clinic and found

Doc Neal in his office.

"Hey, Dad," Chuck said to his father. "How's it going?"

Doc Neal saw the three boys standing in the doorway of his office. "What's going on?"

"We don't have practice today, and since it's so hot, some of the guys are going swimming," Chuck said. "Is it okay if I go with them?"

Chuck knew his dad wouldn't let him go if he knew they were going to Little Grassy. The boys rarely swam there, and for some reason, Doc Neal didn't like that lake, so Chuck conveniently left out that detail. Because Tom was there, Chuck knew his dad probably thought they were going to Lamer's Pond, the pond on the property where Tom lived, and Chuck decided not to correct that assumption.

Doc Neal was no fool, and he knew that Chuck had brought Tom and Kenny along as reinforcements in order to get his approval, but he saw no harm in letting his son go swimming with his friends.

"Sure. Go ahead," he said. "But don't come home late. It might feel like summer today, but you still have school tomorrow."

Chuck thanked his dad, and the boys piled into Chuck's car. Their spirits were high as they cruised northward on the winding road toward the lake. They only had about two weeks of school left before summer vacation, and they were looking forward to the break. Like most teenagers in Cobden, the boys worked on the farms and orchards that surrounded the town in the summer. The work was hard and the hours long, but it enabled them to earn money to spend on their girlfriends and put gas in their cars.

As they approached Little Grassy, the road straightened and led into the parking area for the public campgrounds and boat dock. The expansive 1,200-acre lake was aptly named because its greenish surface blanketed a muddy bottom pockmarked with jagged holes. A series of fingerlike coves jutted off from the main body of the lake. The boys were expecting some of their other classmates to come, but since they were the first to arrive, they picked one of the coves near the boat dock and waded into the chilly water. Despite the afternoon heat, the water remained cool. Ignoring the temperature, the boys plunged in up to their waists and splashed each other relentlessly.

While they goofed around and waited for the others, Chuck and Kenny decided to swim across the lake. Not being a strong swimmer, Tom doubted he could make it the distance they were going so he told Chuck and Kenny he would wait for them near the shore. Chuck and Kenny took off, heading for the opposite bank. Being the competitors they were, they soon turned the swim into a race to see who could make it across first.

They matched each other stroke for stroke, their arms cutting through the water, and soon Chuck began to pull ahead. They were about halfway across the cove when something made Kenny turn and look back. He stopped cold at what he saw. Tom was in water over his head, flailing and thrashing about.

"Chuck," Kenny hollered. "Tom's in trouble! Go get help!"

Chuck was closer to the other side of the lake so he continued in that direction. Kenny started swimming back toward Tom. Fear rose in Kenny's chest as he saw Tom sputtering and sinking below the water. Kenny was swimming as fast as he could, but he felt like he was moving in slow motion. He couldn't get there fast enough.

Kenny finally got close enough to grab his friend, but in a fit of panic, Tom knocked his arm away. Tom choked and wrestled with the water. His head kept going under. Kenny tried to grab him again. He wanted to pull Tom out of the water, but he slipped from his grip. Tom disappeared in the murky water.

Kenny went under, trying to find his friend, but he

couldn't see him anywhere. Kenny dove down again, searching until his lungs burned from a lack of oxygen and his muscles were numb with fatigue. Out of breath and barely able to stay afloat, he finally struggled to the shore. As he hauled himself from the water, he saw a man standing under a tree on the bank.

"Help! We need help," Kenny yelled. "You've got to help my friend!"

"I can't swim," the man yelled back.

"What?!" Kenny shrieked, frantic and dazed. There was no time to waste. He needed someone to help Tom now.

"I'm going to get help," the man said.

Kenny pulled himself to a standing position. His knees buckled, but he managed to stay on his feet. His breaths came in short, shallow rasps as he strained to get air. His heart pounded in his ears, and he felt dizzy and disoriented. All he could think about was Tom. He scrambled up the bank toward the parking lot and practically ran into Jim Smith. Jim had gone home after school to tell his parents he was going swimming and grab a pair of shorts, and he had just made it to the lake.

"Hey!" Kenny shouted. "You gotta help me."

"What's wrong?" Jim asked.

"Tom drowned!" Kenny didn't recognize his own voice as he spit out the words.

"No way!" Jim said. He couldn't believe it, but he saw how distressed Kenny was so he didn't want to argue.

They rushed back to the shore, but there was no sign of Tom. A light breeze rippled the lake's surface, giving no hint of the tragedy that had just taken place.

"Oh, God," Kenny groaned. "Oh, no." An overwhelming sense of dread spread through him. He dropped to his knees. A bitter-tasting bile rose in his throat and filled his mouth as he began to cry.

"What happened?" Jim asked.

"I don't know. It happened so fast." Kenny's eyes were

wild and unfocused. "Me and Chuck were swimming across the lake and something happened to Tom, and he got out in the deep water and got in trouble." Kenny's words were coming fast now as he tried to explain something he didn't understand himself. He took a deep breath. "Chuck went for help, and I tried to save him, but I couldn't. He was fighting. I tried to help him. I tried to save him. I tried to pull him out of the water, but he kept going under...he drowned."

"Oh no, Kenny," Jim said, in shock at what he had just heard. "What do we do?"

"Get help. Go get someone to help us."

Jim ran to his car and headed back to Cobden. Tears flooded his face, blurring his vision as he raced along the curvy country road, and he fought to keep control. He couldn't believe this was happening, and he wasn't sure where to go for help. *I've got to tell my dad*, he thought and drove straight home.

His mother, Geneva, was outside on the patio when he pulled into the driveway. Jim jumped out of the car.

"Where's Dad?" he hollered.

Geneva immediately noticed his red eyes and tear-stained face and knew something was very wrong. She got up from her chair. "What's the matter, son?"

"Tom drowned," he blurted out.

He told his mom what had happened.

"I gotta tell Dad."

She told him his dad was working at the gas station in town, and Jim got back in his car and drove directly there.

"Hey, Dad!" he called as he burst into the filling station. "Something terrible happened. I need your help."

"Calm down," Clyde Smith said to his son. "What happened?"

Jim told his dad about the events that had just transpired at Little Grassy.

Clyde grabbed the phone, his hand shaking as he dialed the operator. He asked to be connected to the police station in

Carbondale and was quickly passed through. He explained the situation to the voice on the other end of the line and then hung up and called Kenny Smith's dad, Cecil, and Doc Neal. Both men said they were going up to Little Grassy, and Clyde told them he would meet them there.

Before going to the lake, Doc Neal stopped at Lamer's Farm. He had told Clyde he would talk to Tom's dad, and he thought it was best done in person. Pauline Lamer, the lady who owned the farm, met him at the door when he arrived and informed him that Tom Sr. was still out in the field.

"Please call him in," Doc Neal said. "It's very important that I see him now."

Pauline noted Doc's grim expression.

"I'll get him right now," she said.

There was a large wrought-iron bell on the farm that was used to summon the workers from the field. Pauline grabbed the rope and started ringing it. When Tom Sr. and Pauline's grown son, Roy Glenn Lamer, heard the bell tolling, they left their work and headed for the main house. Tom Sr. had an uneasy feeling in his stomach as he walked in from the field. In his experience, the bell was only used when there was an emergency, and he feared bad news was coming.

Doc Neal and Pauline waited in the yard, and soon Tom Sr. and Roy Glenn emerged from the back field. Tom's mother, Jenny, was at home ironing clothes when she heard the bell clanging, and she wandered up to Lamer's house to see what was going on.

"Hello, Doc," Roy Glenn said. "What brings you out here?"

Doc Neal swallowed. His mouth had gone as dry as sandpaper. He looked from Tom Sr. to Jenny and back again. He met Tom Sr.'s eyes and held them for a moment, trying to find the right words. What he was about to say was going to crush them. Tom was such a good boy. He was their only son, and Doc knew how proud they were of him.

"You know the boys went swimming at Little Grassy," Doc said. "Well, something happened, some kind of accident. I don't know what it was, but Tom got in trouble...and he drowned."

"What?!" Pauline cried.

"No." Roy Glenn shook his head. "No, sir. Not Bill."

Jenny staggered backward a few steps, the weight of the words pushing her off balance. "No," she said, more as a plea than an assertion.

Tom Sr. grabbed his wife and gently pulled her to his side as much to steady himself as her. *Had they heard Doc correctly?* he wondered. He wanted to believe it was a horrible misunderstanding. Doc's tone and disposition told him otherwise. Tom Sr.'s face had turned an ashen white when he looked at Doc.

"What happened?" he asked.

Doc gave him the information he had received from Clyde Smith.

Tom Sr. wrapped his arms around Jenny as if trying to protect her from the pain of Doc's words.

"Have they found him yet?" he asked, his voice barely above a whisper.

Doc shrugged. "I'm sorry. That's all I know. I'm going up there now," he paused and added, "I'm so sorry."

Tom Sr. nodded. "I'm going up, too."

He looked down at his wife. Her body was slack against his, and her eyes were swimming in tears. "I have to go... I have to see what happened," he said.

Jenny didn't want him to leave, but she knew he was right. He had to go. Tom Sr. held her a moment longer. Their world had just been turned upside down, and he was almost afraid to let her go. Then Pauline took Jenny's hand.

"I'll stay with you, honey," she said. "I'm here whatever you need."

I need Bill, Jenny wanted to yell. *I need my son.* Instead she buried her face in Pauline's chest and began to sob.

Roy Glenn didn't want Tom Sr. behind the wheel so he offered to drive to Little Grassy. Tom Sr.'s mind was spinning as they wound through back roads to the lake. He stared out the window. Generous clumps of blue, purple, and gold wild flowers dotted the verdant hillsides, but he hardly noticed the scenery. Since hearing the news about his son, his world had become as void of color as a black and white movie. *Bill was dead. How could that possibly be true? He was so young and so alive.* Just yesterday they had sat together in their backyard and shared a pitcher of iced tea. Tom Sr. had been working out in the field for 12 hours and was dreading going home to a yard that needed mowing. When he arrived at the house, Bill was sitting in the backyard waiting for him. He had already poured a glass of tea for each of them. Baseball practice had been canceled for the day, and Bill had come straight home after school and mowed the grass for his dad. The two of them had sat in the yard and talked for over an hour. Tom Sr. could almost taste the refreshing, cold liquid now as he savored that moment with his son.

The lake was a flurry of activity when they arrived. Rescue units from Carbondale, Carterville, Du Quoin, and Pinckneyville had responded to the calls for help, and their crews were on the scene, searching for Tom's body. The area had been cordoned off with rope to hold back the onlookers, and Kenny Smith and Chuck were standing just inside the protective barrier.

When Cecil Smith got to Little Grassy, he went immediately to Kenny's side. "What happened here, son?" he asked.

"I don't know, Dad," Kenny said in a weak voice. "We were just here to swim, and Tom got in over his head..."

Kenny's voice trailed off. He was on the verge of tears and couldn't repeat the story again. It hurt too much. Officials had already questioned the boys about Tom's drowning, and they had done the best they could to explain what had happened while still in shock that it had actually occurred. Neither

Chuck nor Kenny knew how Tom had gotten into the deep water. The lake was full of abrupt drop-offs, and Tom may have accidently stepped off into one of those. Or it was possible he had changed his mind and decided to try to swim across the cove with his friends. Everyone wanted to know how and why such a horrible thing could happen. There was no definitive answer. That was a secret the lake would keep.

Cecil could see that Kenny and Chuck were upset and exhausted, and he decided it would be best to get them away from the lake. Cecil told Doc Neal he was going to take the boys home. Doc agreed that was a good idea, but Doc chose to stay at the lake. Roy Glenn and Tom Sr. had just arrived, and Doc decided to stay and lend what moral support he could while the divers searched for Tom's body.

Back in Cobden, the news of Tom's drowning began to spread, and everyone who heard about the tragedy reacted with shock and sadness. At first, many of his friends and classmates refused to believe it. They thought it had to be some kind of mistake or a sick practical joke. A lot of students went to Flamm's Café, a popular after-school hangout, to try to get more information and find out what had really happened. When confirmation came that what they had heard about Tom was true, the impact hit them like a ton of bricks. Tom was such a nice, easy-going guy, and he was extremely popular. He was handsome, smart, athletically gifted, and down to earth. He never flaunted his talents, and everyone liked him.

He was especially close to many of his teammates, and they were deeply affected by the news. Tom was more than just a friend. On the basketball court, he was their leader, someone they could always count on when they went into battle. Off the court, he was their buddy, a regular guy with a great sense of humor and the heart of a lion. It was hard for them to imagine that he was really gone.

Jim Neal had gone to Marion after school with his girl-friend, Patti Sanders, and when he got home, his mother told him what happened. A gregarious young man, it was one of the rare times when he was at a loss for words, and his tears flowed freely. He was struck with a deep sense of regret. He had planned to go swimming with the boys, but had changed his mind when Patti called and asked him to run errands with her. Now he wished he had gone to the lake. He knew he never would have tried to swim across the cove with Chuck and Kenny Smith. If he had been there, he would have stayed near the shore with Tom. And when Tom got in trouble, he would have been there to help him.

I should have been there, he thought. It was too late to change things now, but Jim would have given anything to have had a chance to help his friend.

Martha Flamm, Toni's mother, had taken Toni's younger sister, Diane, into town for a 4-H meeting. When they arrived at the American Legion Hall where the meeting was being held, Mrs. Billie Reeves, the girls' P.E. teacher at Cobden High, met them at the door.

"Martha," Mrs. Reeves said, her voice shaking. "Have you heard the news?"

"What news?" Martha asked.

"Oh, there was a terrible accident at Little Grassy Lake," Mrs. Reeves said, lowering her voice to a whisper so Diane couldn't hear. "Some boys were swimming up there, and Tom Crowell drowned."

"Lord, no," Martha said. "Heavens no!"

"I know. It's awful. It's hard to believe, but I heard about it up at school. It just happened a little while ago."

"Are you *sure*?" Martha asked.

"I'm afraid so. I thought I better tell you right away because I knew you'd want to know. I know how close he and

Toni are."

Close? Martha thought. Toni and Tom had started dating at the beginning of Toni's junior year of high school. They had been inseparable for nearly two years, and she knew how much Toni loved him.

"Toni," Martha said. "I've got to tell her." She didn't want her daughter to get this kind of news in a phone call, and she couldn't imagine how she would take it. She knew it would break her heart. "You're sure it was Tom?"

Mrs. Reeves nodded sadly.

"Can you keep an eye on Diane during the meeting? Bob or I'll be back to get her soon. I've got to get home to Toni."

Mrs. Reeves said she would take care of Diane, and Martha rushed back to her car. Her head was in a fog as she drove home to the farm. She sat in the driveway in her car for a few moments, collecting herself before going into the house. The screen door swung shut behind her and banged against the doorframe as she walked into the kitchen. Toni was sitting at the table doing homework and looked up when she heard the noise. She saw her mom standing in the doorway. The afternoon sun glowed behind her, casting her in silhouette with shadows obscuring her face. Toni hadn't expected her mother to return from town so soon and wondered why she was back.

"You forget something?" Toni asked with a grin.

"I'm going to tell you something that's going to kill you," Martha said, her voice raw with emotion. "That boy is dead. Tom's dead."

The words seemed to travel across the space between them in slow motion then stung like fire when their meaning finally registered.

"No!" Toni heard herself scream.

No one had ever spoken a more unbelievable statement to her before, and while she couldn't fully comprehend it, she knew instantly that it was true.

"Noooo!" she yelled again. She stood up and shook her

head violently, hoping her protests could change what was.

Martha went to her daughter's side and took her in her arms. Toni hugged her mom tightly as tears spilled from her eyes and rolled warm and wet down her cheeks. Her heart ached with a physical pain, and she thought she might be sick. She wanted to say "no" again, to scream it, but she couldn't find her voice.

The two of them clung to each other in the middle of the kitchen. Although Toni was 17 years old and almost a grown woman, at that moment she felt like a small child in her mother's arms. Martha knew how badly Toni was hurting and wished she could make it stop, but there was nothing she could do. Martha also kept thinking about Tom's parents. *That poor family*, she thought. She couldn't conceive of the pain they must be feeling at the loss of their son. It was so unfair. She had gotten to know Tom well while he and Toni dated, and she knew him to be a fine young man.

After several moments, Toni pulled away from the embrace. Her mother's words came back to her. *Tom's dead.* The finality of those two little words stirred her denial. *It's a mistake*, she thought. *It's not possible.*

"Are you sure, Mom?" Her voice was pleading as she choked back tears. "Who told you that? Maybe they're wrong."

"I'm sure. Mrs. Reeves was at school and--"

Toni cut her off. "*What* happened?"

"He drowned," Martha told her. There was no way to say it gently. "There was an accident at Little Grassy."

Toni remembered Tom telling her he and some friends were going swimming after school. It was the kind of thing they did all the time and had sounded so harmless. How did it go so wrong?

Toni brushed her mom's arm off of her shoulder. She didn't want to be consoled right now. She wanted to be with Tom. She ran out of the kitchen, up the stairs, and into her bedroom, slamming the door shut behind her. She picked up a picture of Tom off her nightstand and looked at his handsome face. She ran her fingers over the smooth glass, trying to touch his smile, his eyes. She thought of how happy she was the day he gave her that picture, how happy they always were when they were together. *Will I really never see you again?* she thought.

She felt a wave of nausea sweep over her, and her brain seemed to shut down. It was too much to process, and she couldn't think straight. She threw herself on her bed and clutched Tom's picture to her chest. She cried tears that sprang from a well deep within her, a well that seemed to have no limit to its supply.

Kenny Flick was at work at Spires Wholesale Grocery in Carbondale when the accident happened. As soon as he found out about it, he drove to Little Grassy. He was familiar with the area near the boat dock where his friends had been swimming. Several emergency vehicles were there when he arrived. He ducked under the makeshift barricades that had been erected to keep people away from that section of the lake and ignored a rescue official who told him to stay back.

Kenny saw Tom's father, Doc Neal, Roy Glenn Lamer, Clyde Smith, and a few other men from Cobden down by the lake, but he didn't approach them. Instead, he stood alone at the top of the path that led down to the dock. There were several men in the water, searching for Tom's body. Kenny's chest felt tight and heavy, making it difficult to breathe in the dense, humid air. It was hard to watch as the men dove into the water and then resurfaced after several moments, but Kenny felt like he needed to be there. He thought about the time he had taught Tom to swim at Goober Jorham's pond when they were kids. He knew Tom wasn't a great swimmer, but he was strong, and Kenny never thought Tom would have drowned. He didn't understand how it could have happened.

Tom was his best friend, as close to him as a brother, and Kenny missed him already. The two of them were country kids, with both of their families living and working on farms owned by other people. Their similar backgrounds and a love of basketball had drawn them together, and they had shared a special, unbreakable bond. Kenny could depend on Tom if he ever needed anything, and he knew Tom felt the same way.

For a long time, Kenny gazed in silence at the placid water, feeling hollow and empty inside. Sunlight sprinkled through the leaves, and a kaleidoscopic pattern of color danced across the surface of the lake. He wondered how something that looked so benign and peaceful could have committed such a vicious and cruel act, and he wondered if he would ever feel completely whole again.

While Tom Sr. was at the lake, Tom's older sisters, Martha and Mary, went out to the farm to be with their mother and younger sister, Mildred. Martha's husband, Kenneth, had also come, and they all sat together in the small living room, holding each other and crying. None of them could believe that Bill was really gone. As the only boy, he occupied a special place in their family, and they knew their lives would never be the same without him.

Jenny was thankful to have her daughters with her, but without Bill there, the house still felt empty. She thought of how just two days earlier, the whole family had been together at the house to celebrate Mother's Day. Mary had given her a beautiful new dress as a gift, and when she opened it, Bill urged her to try it on. She went in her bedroom and put it on and then went back out to the kitchen.

"How do I look?" she asked as she danced around the room, doing the Charleston and showing off her new dress.

Everyone laughed, but Bill pretended not to be amused and teased her saying, "I don't know about you, Mom. I was going to say you look really sharp. But after that dance, I'm not so sure."

"Come on, little squirt," she had said to Bill. "Come dance with your momma. It's Mother's Day."

Bill had refused, but Jenny wouldn't take no for an answer. She took him by the hands and pulled him through the house, dancing the Jitterbug. Bill had tried to pull away but Jenny persisted, and Bill finally relented and danced a few steps with her. The two of them were always doing silly things like that, and for a moment she smiled at the memory. Then her heart broke as she realized it was the last time she would ever dance with her son.

Mary Ruggles was at home with Randy and Kathy when Laura Neal called and told her about Tom. Like everyone who heard, she was stunned and filled with sorrow. In the short time she had known Tom, he had always been outgoing and friendly, and she liked him very much. Her thoughts turned immediately to the Crowell family, and her heart ached for them. They were such good people. Tom's parents and sisters attended all of his basketball games so she had seen firsthand what a close and supportive family they were. She knew they must be devastated by this tragic loss. As a new mother, she couldn't imagine the agony of losing a child.

Mary lifted Kathy out of her crib and held her snug against her chest. Then she gathered up Randy and hugged him tightly. Tom's sudden and unimaginable death had made her feel vulnerable, and she needed to hold her children close and know that they were safe.

Coach Ruggles was taking evening classes at Southern Illinois University, working on his master's degree and had been in class when Tom's accident occurred. When Ruggles got home, he found Mary on the couch, holding Kathy in her arms.

"How're my favorite girls?" he asked. He bent to give Mary a kiss and then stopped when he saw she was upset. "What's the matter?"

Mary hesitated. She could see the concern in his face. "It's terrible, honey."

"What is?"

"Some of the boys went swimming after school, and something awful happened, and Tom Crowell didn't make it. He drowned."

The words hit him like a punch in the gut. His legs felt rubbery, and he sank down on the couch beside her. "Oh, Mary," he said. "No."

"I know," she said. "It's so terrible. When Mrs. Neal called me, I didn't know what to think."

"What'd she tell you?"

Mary recounted the few details in their short conversation. Coach Ruggles listened to the story in disbelief, continually shaking his head. Tom was such a wonderful boy, so intelligent and hard-working. *How could something like this happen?* he thought. *And why?* It just didn't make sense.

Coach Ruggles cared for all of his students, and he was particularly fond of Tom. Tom's role as the team's point guard required a great deal of communication between the two of them, and they had developed a good rapport. Ruggles admired Tom's leadership qualities and playmaking ability and often thought of him as a coach on the court. He also knew how much Tom's teammates liked and respected him. He had never known a group of boys to be such good friends and get along with each other so well. They were more like family than teammates, and he knew what a crushing blow this would be to them.

Ruggles leaned back and laid his head on the back of the sofa. He covered his face with his hands. He wept for Tom's family and friends and for the loss of a young life that had touched so many people but still had so much more to do.

Back at Little Grassy Lake, Tom Sr. waited while the divers searched for his son. He knew they were doing their best, but it seemed to be taking forever. The wait was excruciating. On the outside, he maintained a calm demeanor, but inside, he was a bundle of nerves. He paced in small circles on the bank. He tried to avoid looking at the water but was unable to stop himself. He wouldn't wish such an agonizing ordeal on anyone.

When the rescuers finally recovered Tom's body and brought him out of the lake, the sight was almost too much for Tom Sr. to handle. His stoic façade crumbled. A floodgate of emotions burst open, and he broke down in tears. Roy Glenn, Doc Neal, and Clyde Smith had stayed at the lake with him so he wouldn't be alone. They knew there was nothing they could do or say to make the situation easier, but sometimes just being there was enough.

Roy Glenn drove Tom Sr. home, and when they got to Lamer's Farm, grief hung so thickly in the air it seemed to turn the sunny sky to gray. Tom Sr. went inside and found his family huddled together in the living room. He gave Jenny and each of his girls a hug and told them that Bill had been found. He sat down on the couch, but the walls seemed to be closing in on him so he got up and walked back outside. He was gone for a long time. Mary began to get worried. She went to look for him, and she found him lying in the backyard, weeping.

Mary bent down and put her hand gently on his shoulder. She had never seen him cry before.

"Daddy," she said softly. "I'm here."

Slowly, he turned to face her. He took her hand, allowing her to comfort him while knowing she was in great pain herself. He took several deep breaths, trying to compose himself.

"I'm nothing," he said almost apologetically when his tears subsided enough for him to speak.

"That's not true," Mary said quickly.

"I'm just an old laborer, a farmer, but Bill was going places," Tom Sr. went on. "Bill had plans. He was going to college. He was going to make a good life for himself."

Mary felt her heart clinch, and the pain was so acute that she couldn't hold back her own tears. She and her father embraced, and they held each other for a long time, mourning the loss of their beloved Bill and the promise of his life that would never be fulfilled.

Kenny Smith and Chuck spent the night at Kenny's house. They were traumatized by Tom's death, and their parents tried to keep them secluded and away from all the phone calls and people stopping by to find out what happened.

The two boys sat in Kenny's bedroom, talking and crying late into the night. They were still in shock that they had lost their close friend. The whole thing seemed unreal. It felt like they were living a terrible nightmare, and they wanted someone to wake them up. They loved Tom like a brother, and they were consumed by the tragedy and overcome with sorrow and guilt over being unable to save him. They rehashed the events at the lake over and over, wishing they could change what happened.

"We never should've tried to swim across the cove," Chuck said.

"I know. That was stupid," Kenny said. "We should've all stayed together. We should've stayed with Tom."

They lapsed into a sad silence as they realized their words and their regrets would never bring Tom back. He was gone, and they felt like it was their fault. Their parents had told them they weren't to blame, but that's not how they felt.

Kenny stretched out on the floor and lay flat on his back, staring up at the ceiling. His mind raced, and his thoughts were hazy and jumbled. Most of the afternoon and evening were a blur. He didn't even remember how he got home from the lake. He was exhausted, but he knew sleep was impossible. Every time he closed his eyes, he saw Tom go under the water and disappear. The disturbing image was seared into his conscience, and he shivered, feeling the cold water of the lake all around him. Even then he knew there were some wounds that time would not heal.

Tom's funeral was held in the Cobden High School Gymnasium on Friday, May 17. The outpouring of support was tremendous as mourners packed the bleachers and filled the folding chairs that were set up in rows across the gym floor. High school and junior high classes were canceled for the afternoon so all of the students could attend. Tom's death had been like a dark cloud over the whole town. He was well-known and well-liked in the community and now hundreds of people had come to pay their respects in the same place where they had cheered his athletic feats.

His friends and teammates – Kenny Flick, Kenny Smith, Chuck, Jim Smith, and Jim Neal – served as pallbearers. They carried in the casket, looking solemn and forlorn. Losing their friend had taken an obvious toll. Chuck and Kenny Smith looked especially wan. The strain and lack of sleep from the past few days was clearly etched on their faces.

The cheerleaders followed behind the boys and placed small bouquets of flowers on the casket. Although Toni was a cheerleader, she didn't participate with the others in the funeral. She was too upset. She and her mom, Martha, sat with Tom's family in the front row during the service.

Tom's mom and dad held hands, trying to draw strength from one another. The shock of their son's death had begun to wear off, but it had been replaced with a deep sense of loss and longing. This wasn't the way it was supposed to be. Parents weren't supposed to bury their children. They were supposed to watch them grow up and become adults and start families of their own. They missed their son, and it was hard to let him go.

The emotions Tom's parents were feeling were being echoed through all of his family and friends who were gathered in the gym. These people all loved Tom, and none of them wanted to say goodbye. There wasn't a dry eye in the place when the preacher eulogized the life of the young man who had meant so much to so many, the young man who had been taken from them too soon.

 **Chapter 9**

Trying to Move On

The lazy, hazy days of summer arrived, and despite the loss of their dear friend, Tom, life went on for the folks in Cobden. In an agricultural-laden area like southern Illinois, summer days were anything but lazy for most residents, and the Appleknocker basketball players were no exception. Roy Witthoft got a job on a farm in rural Randolph County. It was about 45 miles northwest of Cobden and close to where his family had lived before moving to Cobden the summer before his sophomore year.

Chuck and Jim Neal, Kenny Smith, Jim Smith, Darrell Crimmins, and Bob Smith all worked at Flamm Orchards, a sprawling farm on Highway 51 on the northern outskirts of Cobden. A family operation founded in 1888, the farm grew apples, peaches, and a variety of vegetables that were shipped throughout the Midwest. Flamm's was owned by Toni's father, Bob, and four of his nephews: Eddie, Albert, Bill, and Leonard, who almost everyone called "Slim."

The boys worked in the packing shed and in the fields and orchards, hoeing and picking fruits and vegetables. The days were long, hot, and humid, but the boys were used to that. Nearly everyone in Cobden worked on a farm at some point in their lives so the labor was nothing new. Because most of their friends also worked there, it seemed like the thing to do and the place to be. Although they were there to work, they managed to have as much fun as possible.

Always competitive, the boys would often challenge each other to see who could pick the most fruit. Since they were paid by the bushel, the winner enjoyed a double victory. During lunch breaks, they would pitch nickels at a target, wagering on who could achieve the highest level of accuracy. At quitting time, they raced each other in from the fields to see who was the fastest. To make all of these activities more fun and interesting, they would bet small amounts of money on the outcomes.

One day, Albert Flamm took several of the boys to his house to pick up equipment that was needed at the packing shed. Albert and his wife, Carolyn, had recently moved to a home on Jamestown Road near Skyline Drive, the road that led to the neighboring town of Alto Pass. The boys loaded the equipment into the back of Albert's truck and hopped in to ride back to the farm.

"How long do you think it would take to run back to Flamm's from here?" Chuck asked the other boys.

"I don't know," Kenny Smith said. "How fast do you think you could do it?"

"I don't know, but I could probably do it faster than you," Chuck said.

Kenny knew it was a challenge from Chuck, but he refused take the bait. It was 90 degrees, and Kenny wasn't about to run all the way back to Flamm's in the sweltering heat and humidity.

"Well, we're not gonna find out today," Kenny said. "It's too hot to run that far."

None of the other boys would take Chuck up on his offer, either. They had more work waiting for them when they got back to the farm, and they knew it was unwise to waste their energy on a race.

"Why don't you just run it yourself, and we'll see how fast you can do it?" Darrell suggested.

The other boys thought that sounded like a good idea.

"How long will you give me?" Chuck asked.

The boys knew it was about three miles so they figured it would take Chuck about 25 minutes.

"I think I can do it faster than that," Chuck said. He did the math in his head. If it was three miles, and he ran each mile in seven minutes, he could be there in 21 minutes.

"You think you can do it in less than 25 minutes?" Darrell asked. "How about 20?"

Chuck thought for a moment, knowing he would have to run each mile in less than seven minutes. He felt he was in pretty good shape.

"Yeah, I can do it in 20 minutes," he said.

"No way," Darrell said, shaking his head.

The other boys doubted it, too, but Chuck remained confident. Each boy bet him a dollar, high stakes for these young men, that he couldn't make it in 20 minutes, and he accepted the wagers. Albert was ready to drive the boys back to the farm, and Chuck told him about the bet. He asked Albert if it would be okay if he ran back to the shed.

Albert was in his early 30s and had known the boys for years. He had watched most of them grow up and was fond of them, never missing a basketball games, not even a road one.

After hearing Chuck's story, he shook his head and said, "You think you can make it in 20 minutes? I'm with these boys. You can't run it that fast. I'll take the bet, too."

Everyone looked at their watches to make sure they were synchronized, and then Chuck jumped out of the truck bed and started running. Albert cranked over the truck's engine and motored off down the road. The boys waved at Chuck as they passed him. He watched them until the vehicle disappeared from view. At 6-foot-6, Chuck had long legs and was able to cover ground quickly, but the hot sun was beating down on him, and he soon began to feel its effects. The glaring rays bounced off the black asphalt, causing everything to appear wavy. His strides began to shorten, and his breathing grew heavy. He was starting to think this run may not have been such a good idea when Bill Flamm pulled alongside him.

"What are you doing out here, Chuck?" Bill said, slowing his truck to match Chuck's pace.

"I'm running back to the shed," he said, huffing slightly. "I bet the guys I could do it in 20 minutes."

Bill chuckled. "Get in, and I'll give you a ride back, and you'll be sure to make it on time."

"Really?" Chuck asked. "That'll be great."

He climbed into the passenger side of Bill's truck, and Bill drove toward the farm. When they got to a hill on the southern end of the orchard that overlooked the packing shed, Chuck asked Bill to let him out.

"Thanks. This is far enough," Chuck said. "You won't say anything to the guys, right?"

"It's our secret," Bill said grinning, then drove on down the road.

Chuck sat down among the peach trees at the top of the hill, making sure he kept out of sight. He could see some of the boys down below. They had unloaded the equipment from Albert's truck and had carried it into the shed. He checked his watch. He knew if he made it to the shed too quickly, the boys would know he had cheated so he stayed where he was. He waited until 19 minutes had passed from the time he began his run and then took off running down the hill. He arrived at the packing shed with 20 seconds to spare.

The boys were shocked Chuck had made such good time.

"You surprised me, Chuck," Darrell admitted. "I didn't think you'd make it."

Chuck was bent over at the waist with his hands on his knees, breathing heavily. He feigned exhaustion. "Well, I did," he said.

"Are you sure you didn't find a shortcut?" Jim Neal asked skeptically.

"How could I take a shortcut?" Chuck pretended to be offended by his brother's accusation. "I made it in 20 minutes so everybody pay up."

The boys reluctantly got out their wallets. Everyone who had bet, including Albert, forked over a dollar. He accepted the money graciously, feeling only a twinge of guilt as he pocketed his "winnings."

"Show's over," Albert said and ordered the boys back to work.

While they spent their days on the farms, their evenings were filled with more leisurely pursuits. They went on dates with their girlfriends and hung out with each other at the drive-in movie theater in Anna. Some of the boys played baseball in the summer leagues, and they would also get together at each other's homes to play pickup basketball games on their backyard dirt courts. Whenever possible, they snuck into the school's gym to play basketball there. All the time they spent together at work and at play helped them form an even stronger bond of friendship.

The weeks passed quickly, August arrived, and in Cobden, August meant one thing – peach season. Work in the orchards increased dramatically during peach season, and orchard owners brought in dozens more workers to help with the harvest. There was no cold storage so all the peaches that were picked had to be packed and shipped the same day so they would arrive at market still fresh.

Flamm's hired a crew of boys from Hurst-Bush High School to help pick the peaches, and they worked side-by-side with the Cobden boys in the orchard and shed. The boys knew each other in passing because they played against one another in basketball and baseball. The young men from Hurst-Bush had been coached by Ruggles before he had moved to Cobden. The boys enjoyed trading stories and experiences with each other about their mutual mentor.

During the two to three weeks that the peach harvest lasted, the boys worked at Flamm's seven days a week. On some days, they worked until 10 p.m. or later. The volume of peaches that was picked, hauled from the orchard, packed, and loaded onto trucks was immense. They were fuzzy little fruits, and their fuzz would stick to the boys' sweaty skin and cause them to itch like crazy. Weeks after the harvest ended, the boys would find themselves still scratching from a residual itch.

As autumn approached, the students' thoughts turned to the new school year. Toni was glad that she was going to college. It would have been difficult and painful to go back to high school without Tom. He was a big part of her life, and she missed him terribly. In her senior yearbook, he had written the words: "Don't ever forget me whatever happens between us. Promise." That was a promise she could easily keep. He was in her heart forever. She was excited about starting a new phase in her life, but thoughts of Tom were always close. She took his picture with her went she went to SIU.

Most of Tom's other good friends returned to Cobden High School, and it seemed strange and sad not to have Tom there. The members of the Class of 1964 were extremely close, and Tom's absence left a void. However, one unexpected bright spot occurred on the first day of school: Kenny Flick returned. He hadn't told his classmates he was coming back to school, and they were thrilled to see him.

During the summer, Doc Neal talked to Kenny Flick and told him that the school board had changed the policy that barred married students from participating in extracurricular activities.

"Of course, we all want you playing basketball again, but we want you back in school, too," Doc Neal said. "Education is important, and you've always been a good student. You have to think about your future. Getting your high school diploma can open up a lot of opportunities for you."

Doc Neal had been a good athlete himself back in high school, and his intellect and athletic ability had afforded him the chance to attend Saint Louis University where he played basketball. He knew Kenny was full of promise as a student and athlete, and he didn't want to see those talents go to waste.

Kenny told Doc Neal he would consider going back. He remembered the deal he had made with Tom shortly before he drowned. Kenny had told Tom he would go back to school if the rule was changed. He wanted to keep his promise, but he had family responsibilities to think about.

Kenny had to work, and he knew it would be impossible to keep his full-time job at Spires Wholesale Grocery and attend school at the same time, especially if he was going to play basketball, too. He told Evalena about his conversation with Doc Neal. She was happy that he had the chance to return to school in Cobden, and that he would be allowed to play basketball again. Evalena's parents lived in Cobden now, and she told Kenny if he wanted to go back to school, they could move back in with them.

Kenny hesitated at first. He wanted to be the bread winner and not have to rely on others for support. But he also knew Doc Neal was right about the importance of getting a diploma. He had a lot to figure out if he was going to go back to school.

A couple of days after Kenny had talked to Doc Neal, Bud Pearson, the man who had helped him get the job at Spires, contacted him. Nothing in Cobden was a secret for long, and Bud had heard that the school board had changed its policy, and Kenny would be able to play basketball again. Like all the other avid basketball fans in town, Bud wanted Kenny back on the team, and he thought he could help. Bud no longer worked at Spires. He had taken a job at Bunny Bread, a large regional bread manufacturer and bakery, in Anna, and he thought he could get Kenny a job there.

"Kenny, are you planning to go back to school?" Bud asked, telling him he had heard about the board's decision.

"I'm thinking about it," he said. "Trying to work things out."

"Well, I think I can help you with a job."

"What do you mean?" Kenny asked. "You already helped me."

"I'm talking about a job at Bunny Bread," Bud explained. "You can't work at Spires and go to school, but there's a job at Bunny Bread you can do on Sundays and go to school at the same time."

Bud told Kenny he would put in a good word for him if he was interested in the job, and Kenny thanked him for his help. Kenny really appreciated what Bud was doing for him. Just a few months ago, Kenny had felt unwelcome in Cobden, and now people like Bud and Doc Neal were doing everything they could to get him back in school. Kenny knew their ulterior motive to get him back was so he could play basketball, but he felt they had his best interests at heart as well.

The next day, he called Bunny Bread to inquire about the position. It was a part-time job delivering bread and baked goods to stores throughout southern Illinois on Sundays. His shift would start at 4 a.m. and end around 5 p.m. It would be a long day, but he found out that he would make almost as much money in one shift as Evalena made working full-time at the glove factory. Also, because he worked on Sunday, the schedule wouldn't interfere with any basketball games.

He discussed the opportunity with Evalena, and they decided he should take the new job. They also decided to move back in with her parents. Evalena was going to have their baby soon, and she said it would be easier on her to have her parents close by if she needed any help. She also wanted Kenny to go back to school. They knew these changes would make that possible.

The teachers and student body welcomed Kenny Flick with open arms, and he was glad to be back. He soon found going back was tougher than he thought. He was required to double up on classes during the first semester to catch up on what he had missed last year. It was an extremely full load, but he had always been a good student, and he continued to excel in the classroom.

The other thing that made returning to school difficult was that Tom was no longer there; school felt wrong without his best friend.

Kenny Flick was not the only one who felt Tom's loss deeply. Kenny Smith was having a hard time. He was still dealing with Tom's death and the guilt he felt over being unable to save him. Sometimes at school he would sit alone and cry and think to himself, *What would Tom and I be doing today?* Kenny also missed his girlfriend, Sheleigh. She was a student at SIU, and although they were still dating, he didn't get to see her every day. He passed on joining the baseball team that fall. His heart just wasn't in it, and he decided he was going to concentrate on basketball.

All of Tom's friends and family members had to come to terms with his death in their own way and time. The grieving process was different for everyone, but it was something they all had to go through.

Kenny Flick had just settled into the hectic routine of his new job and being back in school, when his life got a lot more complicated...in a good way. In the early morning hours of September 27, Evalena woke him up.

"I think this is it, Kenny," she said. "It's time to go."

Kenny dressed quickly and grabbed the bag that Evalena had packed for the hospital. Evalena's mom, Mrs. Reynolds, also got up so she could accompany them to the hospital. Dawn was just breaking. The dew was still heavy on the grass, making their shoes damp as the three of them crossed the lawn and climbed into the car. Kenny used the wipers to remove moisture from the windshield and headed to Union County Hospital in Anna. The dark blue sky brightened as he drove, showing the promise of a pleasant early fall day. Kenny and Evalena were nervous and excited, not knowing for sure what lay ahead but that their lives were about to change forever.

When they reached the hospital, Evalena was taken to a room and her doctor was called. Kenny sat by her bed, holding her hand as her contractions became harder and came with increasing frequency. He found it difficult to watch his wife in pain, but the nurse assured him that everything was all right. Her labor was progressing normally. After what seemed like an eternity to Kenny, and probably even longer to Evalena, her obstetrician, Dr. Rife, arrived to examine her.

"You're doing just fine," the doctor told Evalena. "I'll

be taking you to the delivery room soon."

A few minutes later, a nurse came in with a wheel-chair to transport Evalena down the hall to the delivery room. Kenny followed them, but when they reached the doorway, the nurse stopped him.

"I'm sorry," she said. "Only the patient is allowed in here. You can wait in her room or the waiting room."

The nurse saw the hesitation in Kenny's eyes and added in a kind voice, "Don't worry. We'll take very good care of her."

Kenny gave his wife a kiss and squeezed her hand then watched helplessly as she was wheeled into the delivery room, and the door fell shut behind her. He and Mrs. Reynolds went back to Evalena's room and sat down, but they were too anxious to stay there very long. They got up and walked down to the waiting room and took seats in hard plastic chairs where they could see the door to the delivery room and a clock on the wall. It was a small hospital with very little activity going on at that time of the morning. Kenny could feel each minute as it crawled by quietly. He prayed that Evalena was okay and that their baby would be healthy. He had little experience with babies and had seldom been around children, and he wondered what kind of father he would be. He hoped he would be a good one.

He wondered how things were going inside the delivery room and how long it would take. He and Evalena had been waiting for this day for months, and it was hard to believe the moment was finally here.

His wait was soon over.

The door to the delivery room opened, and the nurse stepped out, wearing a light green surgical gown and cap over her nurse uniform. She removed the protective mask that was covering the lower half of her face, smiled, and said, "Congratulations. It's a boy. You have a son."

Kenny's heart leapt. He was unable to hide his excitement. He was thrilled to have a boy. "Can I see them?"

"Of course." The nurse led him into the delivery room.

Evalena was tired from the delivery, but to Kenny she had never looked more radiant. She was propped up on a couple of pillows, holding their son, who was wrapped in a soft white blanket. Kenny peered into his son's tiny face. The emotion he felt was instant and overwhelming.

"This is your son, Kevin," Evalena said.

The two of them had talked about names while Evalena was pregnant and decided if they had a boy, they would name him Kevin. They chose Wayne for a middle name because it was Kenny's middle name.

"Do you want to hold him?" Evalena asked.

Kenny took the baby into his hands. Kevin was so small, and Kenny's hands were so big, but when he cradled his son in his arms, it was a perfect fit. Even at just 17 years old, Kenny knew with complete certainty that he would love Evalena and their child for as long as he drew breath.

🍎 Chapter 10

Back to the Court

Several boys showed up when basketball practice began the first week of October. Cobden's historic season a year ago had sparked great interest in the sport, and boys who never played basketball came out for the team.

Coach Ruggles started practice with conditioning. He wanted his players in tip-top shape. For two weeks, no one even picked up a basketball. The boys ran up and down the bleachers to increase their leg strength and improve their stamina. They also ran the infamous sprints known as "killers" and "suicides" to help with their quickness.

The boys who had been through the trenches with Coach Ruggles last year were used to this grueling conditioning. The practices were an eye-opening experience for the others. After a few days of nonstop running, some of the newcomers quit. They decided they would support the team as fans.

One young man who had never played on the basketball team before but was undaunted by the tough conditioning was Ralph Rich. A junior, he had never played organized sports because a doctor had diagnosed him with a heart murmur when he was very young. Growing up, he always worked with his father on their farm, which required a great deal of physical exertion. Now 6-foot-2 and in good shape, he figured if he could work, then he could play basketball, too. He went to see the town doctor, Helmut Hartmann, during the summer vacation, and after a thorough examination, the doctor reluctantly gave him the go ahead to participate in sports. Ralph's parents were concerned about his health. But they knew how much he wanted to play, so they agreed to let him.

After seeing Dr. Hartmann, Ralph had played pickup basketball games that summer with the guys on the team and really enjoyed it. He knew he was far behind the other players in terms of development and skill, but he practiced a lot on his own and was determined to make the team.

While Ralph and the other boys were enduring the rigorous workouts, Chuck was sidelined. He had recently injured his knee while playing football during the lunch hour. A couple of boys had tackled him, and he had twisted his leg. He wrapped his swollen knee and tried to ignore the pain. At a baseball game the following day, he stepped up to bat, and felt something pop as he swung at the ball. This time there was no ignoring the pain. He limped home, and when his mom saw his knee, she made an appointment with Dr. Hartmann.

The doctor drained the fluid off Chuck's knee to relieve the swelling and put a cast on his leg from his foot up to his thigh.

"You'll need to wear that to keep your knee immobilized," the doctor explained. "I'll check it again in six weeks."

"Six weeks?!" Chuck asked in disbelief. Basketball practice would be starting in a few days, and he hated to miss a day.

"This is a serious injury," Dr. Hartmann told him. "It will take time to heal. You have to be careful or you may not play ball again."

The words hit Chuck like a freight train. *Not play ball again?* he thought. That possibility had never crossed his mind. He had just been horsing around with his friends at lunch. He had no idea he had hurt his knee so badly. He vowed to be the model patient and do exactly what Dr. Hartmann told him. He wanted to make sure his knee healed properly and as quickly as possible.

Even though Chuck missed the workouts, he was still part of the team and attended practice every day. He watched from the bleachers as Coach Ruggles put the boys through their paces. People looking in from the outside probably would think he was crazy if they knew how much he wished he was on the floor working and sweating alongside his teammates.

Two weeks of conditioning weeded out the boys not truly committed to playing basketball. When the dust settled, Coach Ruggles had 12 players on his varsity squad, and the team included plenty of height. Seniors Kenny Flick and Kenny Smith and junior Jim Neal all stood 6-foot-5. When Chuck's knee healed, his 6-foot-6 presence would be back in the lineup. Four other seniors, Jim Smith, Roy Witthoft, and Darrell Crimmins, all 6-foot-1, and Dan Marsh, an even 6-feet, added more size and depth. Juniors Bob Smith, 5-foot-8, and Ralph Rich, 6-foot-2, were also on the roster along with two sophomores, Rodney Clutts and Roger Garner, who both stood 5-foot-8.

Now that the team was set, Coach Ruggles decided to break out the balls and get busy playing basketball. He had been watching the players closely and knew his team was once again loaded with talent. He hoped he could bring out the best in them. When the players showed up for practice that afternoon, Ruggles asked them all to gather on the bleachers before the session started.

"You've been working very hard, and there's a good reason for that," he said. "Gentlemen, with continued hard work and a little luck, you have the talent to go to the state tournament and be playing ball on the last day of basketball season next spring."

Kenny Smith and Chuck looked at each other, remembering the pact the two of them and Tom had made with Coach Ruggles when the season ended last spring.

"I know we've all been thinking about Tom," Coach Ruggles continued in a lower voice. "We know Tom should be here, and we miss him. Let's do the best we can this season and make him proud."

The boys sat quietly, digesting their coach's words. As a team, they decided to dedicate the season to Tom.

After a few moments, Ruggles looked at Roger Peterman, the team manager, and said, "Roger, help me get some balls out." Then he turned to the players. "Line up on both sides of the lane," he told them. "We're going to do some shooting drills."

The players were happy to finally be doing something besides running, and they came to practice each day with a renewed energy. Although there was less conditioning, practices were far from easy. Coach Ruggles was just as demanding when teaching them different offensive plays and important defensive principles. He wanted the boys to enjoy the game of basketball, but he also expected them to always give their best effort.

While the boys were perfecting their skills, their image was about to get an upgrade. Amos Newlin, a salesman from a sporting goods store in Carbondale, came to the school to see Coach Ruggles. The school board had offered to buy new uniforms for the team, and Newlin brought several examples for Ruggles to look at.

Practice had just ended when Newlin arrived, and some of the players were still hanging around the gym. They saw a stranger talking with Ruggles and wondered what was going on.

"Who's that?" Roy asked Chuck.

"I have no idea," Chuck answered. "I've never seen him before."

"What do you think they're doing?" Roy said, noticing the large pack the man was toting.

"We could go find out," Jim Neal said. He was very respectful of authority figures, but he was also never shy about involving himself in situations that interested him.

Before the boys could speculate further, Coach Ruggles called to them, "Could one of you come here and help this gentleman with his bag?"

All three boys practically raced to the man's aid. Chuck got to the bag first and asked, "Where would you like me to take it?"

"We're getting new uniforms," Ruggles said to the players. "Let's go into the locker room and see what he brought us."

Newlin opened his bag and started laying out different jerseys and warm-up jackets on the benches. "I've got many styles to choose from," he said.

The garments he showed were okay, but they resembled the uniforms the players already had. Coach Ruggles looked at the boys. All three shook their heads no.

The salesman could see they were unimpressed.

"Let me show you something else," he said.

He pulled out another uniform that had intricate stitching around the numbers. "This is a new line we just started carrying," he told them. "It's the same style the St. Louis Hawks are wearing and comes with this warm-up jacket and these pants." He laid all the pieces out together. The warm-up jacket and pants had elaborate detailing and trim.

The boys' eyes lit up when they saw the striking ensemble. They thought it would be fun to have uniforms like a professional NBA team, and they told Coach Ruggles that was the uniform they wanted.

Ruggles agreed. It was a sharp-looking uniform, and he liked it, too. The only downside was the price. It was the most expensive style Newlin carried. Small schools like Cobden kept the same uniforms for four or five years. Ruggles wondered what the team would do next year after Chuck, Kenny Smith, and Kenny Flick graduated. Those boys were so tall, and there were no underclassmen coming up who would wear their sizes.

"Let me make a phone call," Coach Ruggles said to Newlin. "I'm going to check this out with the school board."

Ruggles went to his office and called Doc Neal. He told him about the uniforms and explained his hesitation over the cost.

"If those are the ones they want, then it's fine," Doc Neal said. "We've agreed that we'll buy them whichever ones they want."

We're going to need a good tailor next year, Ruggles thought as he hung up the phone, imagining all the hemming and altering that would be required to make the large uniforms fit the smaller players.

He returned to the locker room. "We'll need a set of white home uniforms and a set of maroon ones for road games," he told Newlin. "I'll call you tomorrow with the sizes and numbers."

"Sounds good," Newlin said, scarcely believing his good fortune. "You've made an excellent choice, and you won't be sorry. These uniforms are first-rate."

Before practice began the next day, Coach Ruggles and Coach Patterson measured all the players so they could buy the correct sizes. The boys were excited about the new uniforms, and knew they were getting something really special. While taking their measurements, Ruggles asked each boy what numbers he wanted for his new jerseys. They each needed an even number for home games and an odd number for away games. Most of the players opted for the numbers they had worn before. Kenny Flick selected different ones. Previously, he had worn 22 and 23, but now he asked for 4 and 5. No one knew why he made the switch. It was something he wanted to do for a personal reason. Tom had always worn 34 and 35 so Kenny now chose to wear Tom's numbers – without the 3 – as a tribute to his friend.

"Okay, we've goofed around long enough for one day," Coach Ruggles said after all the measurements had been re-corded. "Let's get out on the court and start warming up."

Ruggles asked Coach Patterson to get the boys started working on free throws while he went to call Amos Newlin with the order for the uniforms. He wanted to place the order right away so they would arrive before the season started.

If we're not the best team in the area this year, we're certainly going to be the best dressed, Ruggles thought.

The 1963-64 Appleknockers' team photo. Pictured from left: Student manager Roger Peterman, Bob Smith, Dan Marsh, Ralph Rich, Roy Witthoft, Jim Neal, Chuck Neal, Kenny Flick, Kenny Smith, Darrell Crimmins, Jim Smith, Rodney Clutts, Roger Garner, Coach Dick Ruggles.

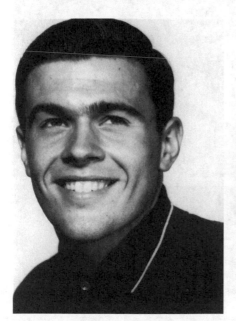

Coach Dick Ruggles in his office at Cobden High School in 1964.

Tom Crowell, a standout student-athlete at Cobden High School, in his 1962-63 yearbook photo.

Some of the Apple-knockers watch the final moments of Cobden's sectional game against Carmi from the bench. Pictured from left are Bob Smith, Kenny Flick, Jim Neal, Kenny Smith, Chuck Neal, and Coach Dick Ruggles.

Chuck Neal (54) and Kenny Smith (50) go after a rebound during Cobden's super-sectional game against Pinckneyville.

Players and fans carry Coach Dick Ruggles around the gym after the team's thrilling victory over Pinckneyville in the super-sectional.

(Photos courtesy of the Southern Illinoisan.)

Mary Ruggles holds her son Randy's hand as they alight from the train in Cobden when the team returns from the state tournament. (Photo courtesy of Dick and Mary Ruggles.)

Forward Kenny Flick takes a shot in Cobden's semifinal game against Stephen Decatur at the 1964 IHSA state basketball tournament. Also pictured from Cobden are Kenny Smith (51) and Bob Smith (21).

(Photos courtesy of the Southern Illinoisan.)

Coach Dick Ruggles and his son, Randy, at the state tournament in Champaign in 1964. Randy is pointing to an injury he sustained playing with a friend prior to the trip.

160

Chapter 11

1963-1964 Basketball Season Tips Off

Cobden opened its much-awaited basketball season in front of a capacity crowd in Shawnee High School's small gym on Tuesday, November 19. The Appleknockers were short-handed with Chuck sidelined with a knee injury, but expectations for the year were still high. Coach Ruggles had Jim Neal jump center while Chuck was out, and Jim won the tip to start the game and then knocked down a short jump shot to put Cobden up, 2-0. Shawnee took possession of the ball and slowed down the game. They held the ball for three minutes, passing it around to each other before finally drawing a foul against Cobden. Larry Lovell made the free throw for the Redskins, making the score, 2-1. Shawnee used ball-control tactics and stalled throughout the period, and the first quarter ended with the Redskins leading, 8-7.

The game was close throughout. Despite Cobden's significant size advantage, the Appleknockers could not get in a rhythm offensively, missing several free throws, and Shawnee continued to hold the ball on each possession, working for a good shot or trying to draw a foul. Both teams showed signs of nerves in their first outing of the season as they committed several miscues. Cobden began the fourth quarter with a one-point lead and extended it to five after Kenny Flick hit a 20-foot jumper and Jim Neal made a layup. It looked like the Appleknockers would put the game out of reach, but Shawnee scored the next four points to close the gap to 49-48 with 30 seconds remaining in the game. Jim Smith was fouled with less than 10 seconds left, but he missed the free throw, and the Redskins grabbed the rebound. They brought the ball down the court, but their last-second field goal attempt fell short, and Cobden hung on for the one-point win.

It was far from the auspicious beginning that everyone

expected of the Appleknockers, and the fans in attendance were surprised to see the smaller Shawnee squad battle Cobden to the wire. The Redskins had done a good job with their ball-control strategy, and Coach Ruggles knew that was something his team would have to work on. He realized that this strategy might be employed by opponents to try to offset the Apple-knockers' height advantage.

At practice the next day, Coach Ruggles divided the players into two teams, with the starters on one side and the reserves on the other.

"Gentlemen, it looks like teams are going to try to stall and hold the ball on us, and we need to be prepared," he said.

He had the reserves play a slow-down offense, hold-ing the ball and trying to keep it away from the starters who were on defense. The starters worked on their trapping defense and continually harassed their teammates in an effort to steal the ball and force turnovers. The hard work and emphasis on defense would become a theme of Cobden's practices. Coach Ruggles was confident in his team's ability to score points, and he believed if the boys improved defensively, they would be hard to stop. Each day, the Appleknockers approached practice with a defense-first mindset, working on their zone and trap for nearly an hour.

While the boys were mainly focused on basketball, a national tragedy would soon rock the country and touch the lives all Americans.

On Friday afternoon, Coach Ruggles was in his class-room, teaching a junior-senior class on current events and world problems when Charlesetta Braden, the school secretary, knocked on the door and stepped inside.

"Excuse me. I have an announcement," she said in a low voice and then paused, obviously shaken. "It's terrible news. We've just received word that President Kennedy has been shot."

Coach Ruggles and the students stared at her in stunned

silence. Whatever news they were expecting to hear, it certainly wasn't this.

"How bad is it?" Coach Ruggles managed to ask.

"He was shot. That's all we know," she said and left to continue the unenviable task of sharing the information with the rest of the teachers and students.

A feeling of shock gripped the room, and no one spoke for several moments. All of the juniors and seniors on the basketball team were in the class, and they looked at each other and Coach Ruggles, trying to make sense of the news they had just heard. Finally, a student spoke up, "Who could've done it?"

It was the question on everyone's mind. Who would want to harm the president? A popular, charismatic leader, President John F. Kennedy was beloved and respected. His wife, Jackie, and young children, Caroline and John Jr., were adored by the public, and as a family, they captured the hearts of a nation on the verge of change.

Ruggles was unable to provide the answers his students wanted and needed. Questions raced through his mind: Who would shoot the president and why? Was it a plot by the Soviet Union or some other foreign country? Was it an act of war? Was it someone deranged or mentally ill?

The students began murmuring about the possibilities as they wondered how such a terrible thing could happen in the United States. The bell rang, interrupting their thoughts and signaling the end of class. The students gathered up their books and headed to their next classes. No one had school on their minds. They wandered through the halls almost on autopilot as an eerie sensation settled over the school. If the president could get shot, it suddenly seemed as if anything was possible. They wondered what might happen next.

Word circulated throughout the school later that afternoon that the gunshot wounds had proved fatal. President Kennedy had died. The horror of that tragic event in Dallas began to register as the initial shock wore off. The students had faced a more personal tragedy with Tom's death, but the sense of heartbreak they felt for the president's family, the country, and themselves was profound. They were small-town kids, and in many ways they were naive to the ways of the world. Some of them may not have realized it at the time, but the assassin's bullets that had felled their president that day had also claimed a measure of their innocence.

Coach Ruggles called off practice that afternoon. He wondered if he should cancel the game that was scheduled for the next evening at Attucks High School in Carbondale. Ruggles called Walt Moore, the Attucks coach, and while both men expressed their disbelief and deep regret over the president's death, they decided to play the game.

The next evening on the bus ride to Attucks, all the players could talk about was the president's assassination. Television coverage had been nonstop, and the nation was consumed by the tragedy. Texas Governor John Connally had also been wounded in the assault but was expected to survive. A man named Lee Harvey Oswald had been arrested and charged with murder. Police had apprehended him in a movie theater a few hours after the assassination. Apparently, after shooting President Kennedy, Oswald had shot and killed a police officer named J.D. Tippit, and Oswald was also charged with his murder.

Coach Ruggles was engrossed in the drama as well. Like everyone else, he never could have imagined that someone would actually kill the president. He knew it was a loss that would resonate with Americans for years to come. In the locker room before the game, he tried to get the boys and himself focused on the task at hand.

"I know this game may not seem that important, but it's what we need to concentrate on right now," Ruggles said. "We have no control over what happened to the president. All we can control is what we do on the court. So let's go out there and play our best."

The teams played on even terms early in the game with Cobden taking a 15-13 lead after one period. Attucks went ahead briefly in the second quarter, but the Appleknockers regained the lead and were up, 31-27, at the half. The Blue Birds managed to keep the game close in the third quarter, but they struggled against Cobden's pressure defense and the hot shooting of Jim Neal in the final period. The Appleknockers pulled away for a 15-point win, 65-50.

This was the kind of performance people had expected from Cobden this season, and its fans cheered enthusiastically for the victory. In the locker room after the game, Coach Ruggles and the players were equally happy with the win. Ruggles was proud that the boys hadn't let outside distractions interfere with their play. Attucks was a good team, and while it stayed within striking distance for the first three periods, the Appleknockers had shredded the Blue Birds' press defense in the fourth quarter, seemingly able to score at will. In just its second game of the season, Cobden appeared to have hit its stride offensively.

Every day for the next few weeks, Coach Ruggles and the players, along with the other students, talked about President Kennedy's assassination and the aftermath surrounding it in their current events class. It provided a good outlet where the boys could share their thoughts and feelings about the terrible incident. When it came time for practice and games, they could focus totally on basketball.

The Appleknockers flourished on the court, winning handily at Hurst-Bush, 87-55, and then dismantling Gorham, 81-48, in their home opener. Coach Ruggles tempered the fast-break offense that the team had used so successfully the year before. The loss of three guards, Dale Crimmins, George Boyd, and John Marsh, to graduation last spring, and Tom's unexpected drowning, had changed the makeup of the team. It wasn't as deep and experienced at the guard spot as last year. Ruggles implemented a slower-paced motion offense that he felt was better suited to the personnel on this year's team and took maximum advantage of the players' height.

The boys embraced the change. Most of them had played for Jack Lamer and were already familiar with the slower, more deliberate offense. He had taught them that style of play as youngsters, and they had used it with great results in junior high.

An exceptional all-around player, Kenny Flick picked up right where he had left off. His teammates loved having him back. The fans who had given him a hard time for getting married last year and leaving the school now welcomed him back like a prodigal son. While Kenny remembered the way he had been treated by some of the team's supporters, he let go of any grudges. Now that he was playing ball again, he figured it was best to forget the past and move on. He and Evalena were happy and had a healthy baby boy, and that was what was most important to him.

With Kenny Flick playing forward again, Ruggles moved Kenny Smith back to the guard position and put a lot of the playmaking responsibilities in his hands. Ruggles knew this was a critical move. Last year, Tom had been the team's primary playmaker. He had been an intense competitor, but he was also steady, level-headed, and most importantly, Ruggles and his teammates trusted him to run the show. This was a new role for Kenny Smith, but Ruggles had seen some maturity in Kenny since last season, and he thought he could handle it. Ruggles spent a lot of time with Kenny at practice, teaching him the offense and running through plays with him.

"When you bring the ball up, you have to know where everyone is," Ruggles told him. "If you ever get in a bind, just hold the ball high over your head and survey the court. That's your thinking position. Your teammates know their positions. You'll be able to find 'em and get 'em the ball."

Coach Ruggles knew that with 6-foot-5 Kenny holding the ball over his head, no competitor would be able to steal it. Ruggles told all the players about the "thinking position." He didn't want them holding the ball down low where it could get stripped out of their hands by an opponent. This move proved very effective, especially with the tallest boys on the squad.

Coach Ruggles and Kenny Smith had gotten off to a rocky start, but they began forming a bond of trust that both knew was necessary if the team was going to thrive. Ruggles and the players were also looking forward to having Chuck back so their team would be at full strength.

The local press had taken note of Cobden's early-season success, and a sportswriter for the Cairo *Evening Citizen* billed its next game at Egyptian High School as one that could decide which team would be considered tops in the area. Egyptian, recently formed through the consolidation of schools in Tamms, Thebes, and Olive Branch, was 4-0 on the season. Like the Appleknockers, it had scored decisive wins over its competition. The game would pit the size and skill of Cobden against the speed of Egyptian's Pharaohs.

Cobden's fans traveled to the team's away games in huge numbers, and they packed the gym in Tamms on December 3 to witness the showdown. The Appleknockers got off to a quick start, jumping out to a 17-8 lead after the first quarter and maintaining an eight-point cushion at the intermission, 29-21. Egyptian tried to carve into Cobden's lead in the third period but was never able to mount a real threat. The Appleknockers dominated the fourth quarter to post a 67-53 victory.

Four boys – Jim Neal, Kenny Flick, Kenny Smith, and Darrell – scored in double figures in Cobden's balanced offensive attack, clearly showing the spectators who the better team was on that night.

The Appleknockers won a high-scoring affair in their next contest, beating Century High School at home, 87-52, to improve to 6-0. Coach Ruggles used his reserves for a good portion of the game, and nine different players scored for Cobden. Ruggles was glad to be able to play the subs a lot. This was the first year that Dan, Ralph, Rodney, and Roger played on the varsity squad, and they were gaining valuable experience.

The following Tuesday, Cobden hosted Trico, and it was the first time this season that Chuck dressed for a game. He had gotten the cast removed from his knee a week earlier and finally received permission from the doctor to play ball. For the past several days, Coach Ruggles had opened the gym early, and Chuck came in and ran for 45 minutes to an hour before school. He had missed the conditioning drills prior to the season, and he needed to get in shape. After school, when the other boys practiced on the main court, Chuck had run sprints on the sidelines and worked on free throws and layups.

Although the doctor said it was okay for Chuck to play again, Coach Ruggles kept him on the bench for the start of the game. He wanted to work Chuck in slowly and let him get readjusted to playing at full speed. Chuck had been off his knee for several weeks, and Ruggles wanted to avoid re-aggravating the injury.

The Appleknockers jumped all over Trico to start the game and with sharp shooting and aggressive defense, they built a 38-13, halftime lead. Coach Ruggles again used every player on the roster as Cobden eased to an 80-44 win. Kenny Smith led the Appleknockers in scoring with 22 points and looked increasingly comfortable setting up the offense and distributing the ball. Ruggles played Chuck briefly and liked what he saw. Chuck moved and rebounded well, showing no signs of favoring his injured knee and scoring four points in limited action.

Cobden's boosters were glad to see Chuck back in a uniform, and they gave him a big hand as he entered the game. He had been named the Player of the Year in the conference last year by the Evansville *Courier & Press* and was obviously one of the team's best players. It was difficult for the fans to watch him sitting on the bench in street clothes and a cast on his leg when they wanted him on the court.

Chuck practiced with the team the rest of the week,

and his knee gave him no problems. Coach Ruggles decided he was ready to go and put him in the starting lineup for the Appleknockers' game at Mounds Douglass on Friday night. Chuck rewarded his coach's faith in him by having a superb game. Playing like he was making up for lost time, he poured in 18 points and pulled down several rebounds. His teammates also played well. The Tornados were no match for Cobden's big front line as Jim Neal and Kenny Flick scored 20 and 17 points, respectively. After the Appleknockers soared to a 45-13 advantage at halftime, Ruggles again cleared the bench, letting all the players get into the act as they sewed up an 82-53 win.

On December 17, the Cairo *Evening Citizen* released its first basketball poll of the year. Cobden's record of 8-0 was good enough to get it ranked in the top spot. Anna-Jonesboro was ranked No. 2, and Egyptian followed at third.

Coach Ruggles was pleased with the high ranking, but he paid little attention to the polls. He thought they were probably more important to the fans than to the coaches or players, and he had no intention of letting the Appleknockers rest on their laurels. Now that Chuck was healthy, the team had four players standing 6-foot-5 and above, and Ruggles came up with a new way to utilize their height. He switched to a 1-2-2 zone defense and put Jim Neal out front as the point man in the one spot. Jim was tall and wide-bodied, and Ruggles liked the idea of having a big man guarding the opposing team's point guard who was usually much smaller. Ruggles believed that if the opponent's point guard was defended by Jim, he would have a hard time getting an open shot. Then if the guard tried to drive to the basket around Jim, he would be met by other defenders equally tall.

The players had become accustomed to working hard on defense, and they learned the new zone quickly. Jim Neal relished his role out front and took it seriously. He was honored that Coach Ruggles had entrusted that position to him, and he was determined not to let him down. He was also an extremely active player and liked hounding his teammates when they tried to bring the ball past the half-court line.

Coach Ruggles had the boys practice the new zone every day, and he was satisfied with their execution of it. On Wednesday, the team was scrimmaging when Darrell went up for a layup. He landed awkwardly, twisting his right ankle. Darrell rarely complained, and the players knew something was wrong when he grabbed his leg, wincing in pain. Chuck and Roy each got under one of his arms and helped him stand up and get to the sideline. Ruggles came over to take a look and saw that Darrell's ankle was already swelling.

"That doesn't look good," Ruggles observed. "Let's get some ice on it right now, and I think you better go see Dr. Hartmann right away."

The pain in Darrell's ankle kept him from protesting. Coach Patterson took over the practice while Coach Ruggles went to his office to call Dr. Hartmann about Darrell. When Ruggles told him what happened, Dr. Hartmann said to send Darrell right over, and he would work him in that afternoon. That was one of the advantages of living in a small town; people were always looking out for each other and willing to help.

Coach Ruggles asked Roger Peterman, the team's manager, to take Darrell to the clinic. Dr. Hartmann was expecting them when they arrived, and he took Darrell to a small room where he examined his ankle. Initially, the doctor thought it was sprained, but he decided to x-ray it to be sure. The x-ray revealed a break in one of the small bones in the ankle. There was no ligament damage, which was good news, but Dr. Hartmann put a soft cast on Darrell's ankle and told him to stay off of it for two weeks.

Like any competitive athlete, Darrell was disappointed to hear that he might miss some games. He was strong and in good shape, and he believed his ankle would heal faster than predicted; he hoped that was the case, anyway.

The next day, Darrell hobbled into Coach Ruggles' office before school to tell him the bad news.

"Hey, Coach. The doctor says I could be out two weeks," Darrell said. "But I think it might be less," he added hopefully.

"Two weeks?" Ruggles sighed, not hiding his disappointment. "I hope you're right and it's less, but I don't want you to push it."

Coach Ruggles was disappointed by the timing of Darrell's injury. The Appleknockers were scheduled to play in the McLeansboro Holiday Tournament in a week and a half, and Ruggles wanted all hands on deck and every player healthy for that event. Darrell was averaging nearly 10 points a game and was a good defender. Ruggles felt that he was one of the most improved players on the team this season and would miss having him on the court.

Last year, Cobden had been criticized by members of the press for playing a weak schedule so Ruggles tried to improve this season's slate. He had contacted several bigger schools during the offseason, trying to schedule games with them, but most turned him down. Although the coaches didn't give him a reason, Ruggles figured it was because they feared getting beat by a smaller school.

McLeansboro, however, agreed to let the Appleknockers participate in its tournament, and Ruggles was hoping for a good showing against the larger schools in the event. He was also glad the boys would get a chance to play against tougher competition so they could gauge where they stood as a team.

Cobden hosted Zeigler-Royalton on Friday, December 20, and with Darrell watching from the bench, the Appleknockers downed their guests, 72-40. Bob Smith was inserted into the starting lineup and had a solid game, handling the ball well and scoring 11 points. Kenny Flick tossed in 21 points to lead Cobden as it kept its record unblemished through nine games.

At practice on Monday, Coach Ruggles instructed the boys to turn their full attention to the tournament in McLeansboro.

"I know it's almost Christmas, but I don't want your heads filled with visions of sugar plums or anything like that yet," he said, circling his arm around his head. "I need you here in the gym with me today so we can get ready for Albion."

Cobden's first game in the tournament was on Thursday night against Albion, a school located in Edwards County in the southeastern part of the state. The Appleknockers had never played Albion before so the players knew nothing about the team. Coach Ruggles had never seen Albion play either, but he had obtained some information about their players and learned they were very tall. The Appleknockers had never met a team with players who matched their size, and Ruggles knew the game would be a good test for their rebounding.

The boys were excited about Christmas, but they listened to Coach Ruggles because they were taking the tournament seriously, too. McLeansboro was the team that ended their season at the sectional tournament last year, and they were looking forward to playing the Foxes again. It had been a difficult loss for the players to accept, and they were hoping for a payback opportunity.

Cobden closed school for the holiday break, and the boys enjoyed the time off, celebrating with their families. It was a really special time for Kenny Flick who was sharing his first Christmas with Evalena and their baby son, Kevin. Coach Ruggles and Mary also had a wonderful Christmas with their children, Randy and Kathy. This was the first year that Randy, now two and a half years old, seemed to understand the concept of Santa Claus, and he had a ball opening his presents. There was no shortage of packages for him to open as Mary's family showered him with gifts, and Coach Ruggles' family sent presents by mail from Massachusetts. Kathy was enthralled with the presents as well, but at nine months old, she seemed to like the colorful wrapping paper and bows as much, if not more than, the treats inside.

While it was a joyful time for most, for the Crowell family the holidays were a difficult period. They still missed Tom very much. Christmas was a time to be with family, and the festivities that came with it managed to only magnify the pain of their loss. Tom's parents and his sister, Mary, never missed a game when he played, but they found it too difficult to go to the Appleknockers' games now. Tom, Sr. went to a couple of games because he wanted to show his support for his daughter, Mildred, who was a cheerleader, and Tom's friends who were still playing, but he found it hard to enjoy the games. The loss was too fresh, and it was painful to watch the team play without Tom.

The day after Christmas, the Appleknockers boarded a bus to make the nearly 75-mile drive to McLeansboro. Cobden's fans gladly interrupted their holiday celebrations, and they were undeterred by the long distance and frigid temperatures. Many boosters showed up to ride the fan bus, and many more drove. The Appleknockers were having a terrific season, and the fans wanted to be there for every game. The players appreciated all the support they received from their classmates and people in the community. No matter where they played, their fans were there to make it feel like a home game.

Norris City beat Carrier Mills, 78-66, in the opening game of the tournament on Thursday afternoon, and then Cobden took the floor to face Albion. The Appleknockers showed no ill effects of the two-day break for Christmas as they picked apart Albion with relative ease. The Lions' players were just as big and strong as Cobden's, but the Appleknockers exhibited greater agility and skill. Cobden had a 15-point cushion at halftime, and the game turned into a rout after the intermission as the Appleknockers pulled away for a 30-point win, 73-43. Led offensively by the Neal brothers, four Appleknockers scored in double figures.

Although Cobden was much farther from McLeansboro than the other schools competing in the tournament, it had one of the biggest rooting sections, and the supporters from Cobden were glad they had made the long trip. It was exciting to watch their team put on such an impressive display over a foe from a bigger school. They always believed the Appleknockers could compete with the "big boys," and this convincing win over Albion proved it.

The only negative aspect to the game was that Bob twisted his ankle in the second half and had to go to the bench. Roger Peterman put ice on it immediately, and the injury didn't appear to be as serious as Darrell's but was still cause for concern. Coach Ruggles had Roger wrap Bob's ankle and told him to keep the leg elevated.

The Appleknockers stayed at the gym to watch the games in the evening session. McLeansboro and Ridgway hooked up in the first game, and the Foxes won an overtime thriller, 73-69. Fairfield beat Eldorado, 94-71, in the final contest of the night.

When the evening session ended, the Appleknockers loaded onto the bus for the ride home. Their opponent the next day would be Norris City, another unfamiliar adversary, but most of the talk was about McLeansboro. The Foxes had gotten a real scare from Ridgway and nearly lost their first-round game. The players had nothing against Ridgway, but they were glad McLeansboro had won. If both Cobden and McLeansboro won again the next day, they would play each other for the championship on Saturday, and that was the game the Appleknockers wanted.

The next afternoon, Cobden and its followers traveled back to McLeansboro for day two of the tournament. The hour and a half drive gave Coach Ruggles plenty of time to go over specific plays and game scenarios and make sure the players were focused on the game with Norris City. Ruggles was a great believer in preparation, but in the tournament setting, there was very little time. The Appleknockers would just have to try to dictate the style of play and make Norris City play their game. The Cardinals had looked good in their victory over Carrier Mills, but Ruggles thought the Appleknockers could beat them if the boys played up to their capabilities. Still, he was always a little uneasy when the team had to play a new opponent with no practice beforehand.

Coach Ruggles quickly saw that his apprehension was unwarranted when the game got underway. Kenny Flick and Chuck set the tone offensively, and Cobden's 1-2-2 zone proved very effective as it rolled to a 73-42 win. Bob's ankle was gimpy so Ruggles only played him briefly, not wanting to compromise the injury. Jim Smith saw increased playing time and dropped in 10 points. Darrell's ankle injury had improved dramatically, and he saw his first action since the Mounds Douglass game on December 13. He was glad to be back on the floor and played well, contributing eight points.

Now that the Appleknockers had earned a spot in the title game, the players turned their attention to McLeansboro's game against Fairfield. They watched with interest from the bleachers, waiting to see who their opponent would be. The Foxes led 40-33 at the break, but Fairfield came back strong in the second half, and the score was tied at 63 with 20 seconds left to play. McLeansboro's Junior Upton was fouled on a last-second shot attempt. He made one free throw to give his team a one-point victory, 64-63.

Now the stage for the final was set, and Cobden was getting the match up it had hoped for. The 20-point loss the Appleknockers had suffered at the hands of McLeansboro last spring had not set well, and the boys hoped to redeem themselves in the next night's game.

On Saturday, the Appleknockers, along with a host of their fans, once again journeyed to McLeansboro. This was the main event, the game they had all been waiting for. The consolation bracket game and the third-place game were contested first, and then it was time for Cobden and McLeansbore to face off.

There was a nervous energy in the Appleknockers' dressing room before the game. The feeling was distinctly different – more intense – than it had been the prior two days. Coach Ruggles went over the team's tactical game plan, making sure all the boys knew their assignments. As with the game against Norris City, there had been almost no time to prepare, but Ruggles and the players had seen the Foxes play twice so they were somewhat familiar with the team's style of play. Ruggles hoped his game strategy would bring Cobden a victory.

One thing that even the best game plan couldn't do, however, was fix Bob's ankle. It had swollen again overnight, and Ruggles decided to keep him on the bench. Bob was disappointed, and Ruggles hated to keep him off the floor, but he knew Bob's ankle wasn't 100 percent; he needed to stay off his ankle so it could heal properly.

The game tipped off and the massive crowd was loud from the start. Cobden's supporters were numerous, but they paled in comparison to the fans on hand to cheer on the home team. Both teams played cautiously but steadily in the first half, with the players making few mistakes. Close throughout, the lead changed sides multiple times. The score was tied on eight occasions before the Foxes gained a two-point edge at halftime, 32-30.

The Appleknockers had played well, but Coach Ruggles thought the players seemed apprehensive.

"You looked nervous and tight out there," he told them in the locker room. "We're doing well. You're handling everything they're throwing at you. Just try to relax a little."

The game remained close after the break, but the Appleknockers managed to take the lead from McLeansboro and move in front, 44-42, at the end the of the third quarter. Cobden extended its lead to five points early in the fourth period. It was the largest lead by either team in the game, and the Appleknockers' cheerleaders and fans rose to their feet, shouting praise and encouragement. Not to be outdone, the McLeansboro boosters cheered for the Foxes with equal vigor.

The Appleknockers were used to playing in front of big

crowds, and the noise didn't bother them, but McLeansboro seemed buoyed by the fan support, and Cobden was unable to pull away. The Foxes erased the small deficit, and the final buzzer sounded with the score knotted at 53-all. Overtime!

Chuck won the tip to start the extra session, and the Appleknockers took control of the ball. Chuck was fouled and made both free throws to put Cobden up by two. The margin became three when Kenny Smith converted another free toss, bringing the score to, 56-53, in Cobden's favor. Junior Upton tipped in a rebound for McLeansboro. Moments later, Alan Downen hit a 15-foot jumper to give the Foxes a 57-56 lead with under a minute to play. Chuck was fouled as he went in for a layup on the Appleknockers' next possession and went to the line for two shots. He missed both, but Cobden snatched the rebound and retained the ball. Jim Smith drew a foul from a McLeansboro defender and was granted a one-and-one opportunity. He made the first foul shot, but his second attempt fell short. The score was tied at 57.

The Foxes controlled the rebound and held the ball, looking for a game-winning basket. With just 10 seconds left, Jim Neal fouled Tom Strum, sending Strum to the charity stripe for a one-and-one. Strum missed the shot, but he got his own rebound, and as he tried to lay it back in the hoop, he was fouled by Darrell. Strum went back to the foul line and again missed his first attempt. But his second shot was true, giving McLeansboro a crucial one-point lead. The Foxes stole the inbound pass as Cobden tried to place the ball in play, preserving a 58-57 win.

Near pandemonium broke out when the final horn sounded as the McLeansboro fans flooded the court to congratulate the Foxes. The fans for both teams had been standing for much of the fourth quarter and the overtime period, and they couldn't contain their emotions. It was pure joy for McLeansboro but bitter disappointment for Cobden.

School officials from McLeansboro calmed the crowd so the awards could be presented. The Appleknockers were good sports as they accepted their second-place trophy. In the privacy of their locker room, they said little to each other. This was a win they had wanted desperately, and they had come up short. This was their chance to even the score, and they had blown it. Coach Ruggles was disappointed, too. He knew how important this game was to the boys, but he didn't want them to get too down about the loss. They still had a long season ahead.

"Why all the long faces?" he asked. "This was no 20-point loss. You played well, and you battled a good team to the wire on their home court and almost won it. You have no reason to hang your heads."

The players showered and changed then trudged out to the bus for the ride back to Cobden. This time there was no chatter about their next game. Instead, they rode in silence, thinking about the loss, and the cold vinyl seats did nothing to console them. Chuck and Jim Smith felt bad about their missed free throws. Jim Neal and Darrell regretted the fouls they had committed late in the game that put the Foxes at the free-throw line, giving them the chance to win. Rehashing their mistakes wasn't going to change anything, but they found it hard to push the thoughts out of their minds. It was late, and they were tired and soon many of them drifted off to sleep.

As the bus jostled and bumped its way along the southern Illinois hills in the darkness, Coach Ruggles stared out the window at a moonless sky and reflected on the game. He knew the boys were in good shape, but they had seemed to run out of gas at the end. Chuck and Jim Smith were normally good free-throw shooters, and their missed foul shots in overtime may have been a sign of fatigue. He thought playing three games in three days, coupled with all the travel and the late nights, had finally caught up with them. If the school could have afforded it, Ruggles would have put the team in a nearby hotel so the boys could have gotten more rest. If the players had been fresher for the championship game, he thought the outcome may have been different. Ruggles sighed as he remembered that the last time Cobden had played McLeansboro he had come away with the same "what-if" feeling.

After the Appleknockers' fall from the ranks of the unbeaten, Cobden took a hit in the next Cairo *Evening Citizen* basketball poll. The team remained No. 1 but only by one point over Anna-Jonesboro, and the Wildcats actually received more first-place votes than the Appleknockers, 13 to eight. It was a greater number of second-place votes for Cobden that allowed it to keep the top spot. It seemed that, despite the Appleknockers' strong showing against Albion and Norris City, the one-point loss to McLeansboro had shaken the pollsters' faith in Cobden's ability to beat top-tier teams from bigger schools. A-J's record was just 5-4 and included losses to Sparta and Carbondale, yet the Wildcats were rewarded for their body of work, with the reasoning most likely being that they played against larger schools. The pundits believed that the Appleknockers played against weaker competition, and that their record may not be an accurate indicator of their ability.

The poll results also added fuel to the long-standing rivalry between Cobden and A-J. The Appleknockers had bragging rights for the time being because of their victory over the Wildcats in last year's regional. This was a new season. With the two teams being ranked so closely, fans wanted the issue of which team was better to be decided on the court. They were hoping to get their wish at the upcoming Anna-Jonesboro Tournament.

The Appleknockers had been idle for 11 days when they went to Vienna for their next game on January 9. Coach Ruggles thought the break was good for the boys. The team had productive practices, continually working on the 1-2-2 zone defense, and Darrell and Bob had time to rehabilitate their ankles.

It appeared that Ruggles was right about the break because Cobden stormed out of the gate when the game began and never looked back. The Eagles had difficulty shooting over the Appleknockers' towering zone, but Cobden had no such troubles on offense, going up, 17-6, after one period and holding a 36-21 edge at the half. The lead swelled to 25 points for the Appleknockers by the end of the third stanza, and Ruggles inserted his reserves into the game in the fourth quarter to put the finishing touches on a 68-51 win.

The boys were all smiles in Cobden's locker room after the game. To the players, the 11-day layoff between games had felt like an eternity, with their nagging regrets about the McLeansboro game simmering just below the surface. They were happy to put that loss behind them and ready to face their next challenge.

The Anna-Jonesboro Tournament was next on Cobden's agenda. The pairings for the event had Cobden and A-J in opposite brackets, so a meeting between the schools would occur if both made it to the championship game. Since they were ranked first and second in the polls, many observers felt that scenario was likely to happen.

Coach Ruggles took nothing for granted. Mounds Douglass was the Appleknockers' first-round opponent, and that was the team they prepared for. Ruggles wanted the boys thinking about the Tornados, not about a possible game with Anna. He never wanted them to place more importance on one game over another. Every game was a learning experience, a chance to improve and get a step closer to their ultimate goal in postseason play.

On Wednesday, January 15, play opened in the Anna-Jonesboro Tournament, and Cobden got off to a slow start in its bout with Mounds Douglass. The Tornados held the ball and slowed the game to a snail's pace. When the two teams had met earlier in the season, Cobden had run away with the game, and Mounds Douglass seemed determined to keep that from happening again. After the teams ground to a 4-all tie at the end of the initial quarter, the Appleknockers tried to force the action in the second period and committed several fouls. Mounds Douglass made nine free throws and went ahead, 17-13, at the break.

"We've been working on this in practice all season," Coach Ruggles told the players in the locker room. "We've got to cut down on all these silly fouls. You know what to do out there. Trust your teammates on defense and look for good shots."

Cobden broke things loose in the second half, and this time its defense produced steals and turnovers instead of fouls. The Appleknockers capitalized on the errors made by Mounds Douglass and moved in front, 34-24, at the end of the third. The Tornados faded under Cobden's pressure in the fourth quarter, and the Appleknockers won, 52-30.

Cobden's fans cheered enthusiastically for their team's victory. They had received a scare in the first half, but they never doubted that the Appleknockers would prevail. Now they were a step closer to a much-anticipated showdown with Anna. Coach Ruggles may have been taking the tournament one game at a time, but that didn't mean the fans were. Supporters on both sides savored the opportunity to see the two rivals battle for area supremacy.

On Thursday night, A-J took care of business against a strong Metropolis club, 79-63, to earn a spot in the finals the following night. Now Cobden had to get past Cairo to set up the contest that local fans had been clamoring for.

The Appleknockers were up to the challenge. Jim Neal's hot shooting helped Cobden secure a 20-12 lead at the end of the opening frame. The Appleknockers put the clamps on Cairo defensively in the second quarter, holding the Pilots to one field goal. With time running out, Kenny Smith launched a shot from three-quarters the length of the court. The ball hit the rim of the basket and rattled out just as a Cairo defender reached high and grabbed the net. Goal tending was called against the Pilots, and Kenny was credited with the two points. Cobden went into halftime leading, 39-14.

Working their slow-paced motion offense to perfection, the Appleknockers maintained a commanding lead throughout the second half. They shot free throws well, and their tough defense forced Cairo into shooting off-balance outside shots as they stopped every attempt the Pilots made at a rally. Cobden won, 65-41, and was set to take on A-J in the final the next night.

Coach Ruggles thought this was one of the boys' finest efforts all season. The Pilots were a fine ball club, and his team had taken them seriously. He was glad the players had ignored the hype of the potential Cobden v. Anna game. It would have been easy for the boys to overlook Cairo, but they hadn't done that. Now was the time to think about Anna. Ruggles could finally admit that he was looking forward to the game himself.

Anna-Jonesboro's gym was sold out for the Friday night games, and spectators arrived more than an hour before tipoff to ensure a seat. The A-J fans believed Cobden had feasted on weak opponents all season, and they were ready to prove that the Wildcats were the best team in the area. The Cobden boosters believed that the Appleknockers were the better team and would beat A-J again like they had last year in the region tournament. The rivalry had gotten more intense as the tournament progressed. Chuck, Darrell, and Jim Neal all dated girls who attended school at A-J, and the girls had been warned by A-J supporters not to sit in the Cobden rooting section or to even cheer for the Appleknockers.

Metropolis and Cairo played in the evening's first game, with Cairo coming out on top, 51-47. By the time Cobden's game with A-J began, it was standing room only as fans continued to wedge themselves into the packed gym.

The first half of the game was close. Anna had good size in its frontcourt and solid guard play, and the Appleknockers had to work hard and play well to muster a five-point halftime lead, 22-17.

In the locker room at the break, Coach Ruggles told the boys they were playing well, and he was proud of how they were handling the pressure of the fans' expectations about this game. The team reviewed the game plan to make sure everyone knew his assignment then the players took the floor for the second half.

The words of encouragement Coach Ruggles gave the players in the dressing room paid immediate dividends. Jim Neal hit three jump shots in a row as the third quarter started, pushing Cobden ahead, 28-17. The Wildcats appeared rattled as the Appleknockers' defense allowed few clear shots at the basket, and Cobden grabbed nearly every rebound. The Appleknockers used a fierce half-court double-team trap to force A-J's guards into several turnovers, and Cobden's advantage was 20 points, 45-25, at the end of the third.

The Appleknockers increased their lead in the fourth quarter and were ahead by more than 30 points when Chuck was fouled and stepped to the free-throw line. Although Cobden won many of its games by a wide margin, Coach Ruggles never tried to purposely run the score up. As a rule, he would pull the starters once the Appleknockers had a comfortable lead.

Chuck checked the score and then looked over at Kenny Flick and said, "Kenny, can you believe we're still in?"

"You better hurry up and shoot before he realizes and takes us out," Kenny replied.

Coach Ruggles was so engrossed in the game that he was oblivious to the large lead. He glanced at the scoreboard after Chuck sank his free throw and saw that Cobden's lead had ballooned to 38 points. He called a timeout and made wholesale personnel changes, inserting the reserves into the game. The starters got a raucous ovation from the Appleknockers' supporters as they took their seats on the bench.

Cobden's subs played ably in the final minutes and kept up the scoring pace. Roger Garner closed the game in dramatic fashion. With just a second left on the clock, he heaved a shot from mid-court which fell through the hoop as the buzzer sounded, giving the Appleknockers a 42-point win, 78-36!

Cobden's fans cheered heartily. While they had expected the Appleknockers to win, no one had expected such a resounding defeat. Any doubt that Cobden deserved its ranking as the No. 1 basketball team in the area had been dispelled with an exclamation point.

The awards ceremony followed the game, and Cobden's players found this one much more palatable than the one at McLeansboro. It's amazing how much more fun it is to win, they mused. Even though the outcome of the game hadn't been in doubt since the third quarter, none of the Appleknocker boosters left early, and the ovation they gave the players when they were handed the first-place trophy shook the gym's rafters.

The players were as excited as their fans. Although Coach Ruggles wanted them to treat every game the same, there was just something special about beating Anna. It was more than just beating a rival team. Tonight they had crushed A-J on its home court in front of a packed house. This was a statement game, showing that Cobden was a team to be reckoned with no matter who or where it played. The boys had set the goal of going to the state tournament before the season started. It was a gutsy dream for such a small school, but their belief in themselves and their ability to achieve it began to solidify on that night.

Cobden was flying high after its win over A-J. It made quick work of its next opponent, defeating Trico, 96-37, on January 24. In a remarkable display of balance and depth, the Appleknockers had 11 players score in the game, with six of them reaching double figures as they bettered their record to 16-1.

Coach Ruggles' once rocky relationship with Kenny Smith continued to improve as Kenny settled into his role as the team's playmaker. They both knew how important it was for them to communicate and understand each other when it came to basketball and executing plays. Kenny took the responsibility seriously. But off the court, he still enjoyed giving

Ruggles a little grief.

Coach Ruggles required the varsity players to attend the junior varsity games. This was no big deal for the away games because they all rode together on the bus. But for home games, the players arrived at the gym separately. Kenny Smith would often sneak in the back door and sit where Ruggles was unable to see him. Then Kenny would watch Ruggles sitting on the bench, looking around and taking a mental inventory of the players to make sure everyone was there. Kenny would often remain out of sight until the third quarter of the JV game ended and all of the varsity players got up to go to the locker room to put on their uniforms. He knew this would drive Ruggles crazy, which, of course, was the reason he did it. As Kenny passed by the bench, he would give Ruggles a little wave or a knowing smile as if to say, "No worries, Coach. I've been here the whole time."

Cobden's next game was at home against Joppa, and Kenny Smith didn't try to hide from Coach Ruggles before that one. During the week, the players had gotten together and decided that they were going to wear mismatched clothes to the game as a joke and see what kind of reaction they would get out of their coach. Ruggles encouraged the boys to dress well for the games. Suits were not required, but he asked them to wear dress shirts and a nice pair of clean trousers. They were representing the school, and he wanted them to look respectable. With so many tall players on the team, they stood out wherever they went. As they continued to win, they became more recognizable so Ruggles wanted them to make a good impression.

As the JV players warmed up, Coach Ruggles saw the members of the varsity squad entering the gym, and he noticed their clothing right away. *What are these boys up to now?* he wondered. Their clothes were clean, but none of them matched, and it looked as if they had gotten dressed in the dark. Ruggles saw Kenny Smith and could hardly contain a smile. Kenny had on a kelly green and camel checked blazer and black pinstriped pants. He looked ridiculous. Ruggles realized the boys had planned this as a prank, and he decided not to take the bait.

"Hi, Coach," Kenny said cheerfully when he reached the end of the floor where Ruggles was standing.

Ruggles looked his outfit up and down. "Did you lose a bet?" he asked.

"Huh?" Kenny said.

"I didn't think you'd dress that silly unless someone made you so I figured you'd lost a bet."

Before Kenny could think of a reply, Coach Ruggles turned on his heels and sauntered into the locker room. Ruggles was smiling broadly now, but he didn't let Kenny see it.

Cobden's JV team won its game, 37-32, and then the varsity Appleknockers, who were now appropriately clad in their top-of-the-line uniforms, started their game. The boys may have been clowning around before the game, but they were completely serious when the ball was tossed up. Cobden outscored Joppa, 19-9, in the first quarter and doubled its margin to 18 points, 41-23, at the break.

The Appleknockers were cruising along in the third quarter until Jim Neal went up for a rebound. When he came down, he landed on an opponent's foot and rolled his ankle. The pain was immediate, and he was unable get up. The referees stopped the game, and the crowded gym fell silent. Chuck and Kenny Flick helped Jim to the bench so his ankle could be examined. It was getting bigger by the minute and appeared to be sprained.

"We better get some ice on that right away," Coach Ruggles said.

Cobden's fans watched in dismay as manager Roger Peterman helped Jim to the dressing room. They hoped Jim wasn't badly hurt. Injuries were a fact of life when it came to sports, but it seemed that the Appleknockers had dealt with more than their fair share this season.

In the locker room, Roger wrapped Jim's ankle with an elastic bandage and placed an ice pack on it to reduce the swelling. Jim had never sprained his ankle before, and the pain was excrutiating. He had a low tolerance for pain anyway, and this was quite a severe injury. The ice helped some but not as much as he would have liked.

Jim had been having a great game – already having scored 12 points – but the Appleknockers continued without him and had little trouble finishing off Joppa, 81-64. The cheers from Cobden's boosters were happy but subdued as they worried about the condition of Jim's ankle.

After the game, Jim went home and spent the rest of the evening in his father's recliner with his leg propped up and his injured ankle on ice. His mom was a nurse, and she was afraid he might not be able to play ball for a few weeks.

"A few weeks?" Jim asked alarmed. "I have a game tomorrow night."

"I doubt it," his mother said. "We'll go see Dr. Hartmann first thing tomorrow morning and see what he has to say."

Hearing that made Jim feel worse. He had been to see Dr. Hartmann for other injuries, and the doctor's advice was always to wait three or four weeks before playing ball again. That was something Jim dreaded hearing. Tomorrow night the Appleknockers were hosting Shawnee, and he really wanted to play in that game. Cobden and Shawnee had played each other the first game of the season, and the Appleknockers had eeked out a one-point win after the Redskins had elected to hold the ball throughout. Cobden had worked hard on defending that stalling tactic all season, and the players wanted to show Shawnee how much they had improved.

After his family went to bed, Jim stayed awake thinking about the game with Shawnee. *I can't miss it*, he thought. *I want to play*. He sat in the silence of his darkened room and tried to will his ankle to heal.

The next morning, Jim's ankle was still swollen, and

his mother took him to the clinic so Dr. Hartmann could check it out. The doctor x-rayed and examined Jim's ankle and then announced, "You should try to stay off of it for a few days and no basketball for two to three weeks."

Those were the words Jim had feared hearing, and he felt like crying. To a driven competitor like him, two or three weeks seemed an eternity. He didn't even want to miss that evening's game with Shawnee. Dr. Hartmann gave him some tablets and told him to dissolve them in hot water and then soak a towel in the water and wrap the wet towel around his ankle.

"That should help relieve the swelling," Dr. Hartmann explained.

Jim went home and went right to work on his ankle. He used the tablets like he had been told and kept his foot elevated. He followed Dr. Hartmann's instructions to the letter and by early afternoon, the swelling was down. He soon found that he was able to put weight on his injured ankle and could actually walk without too much pain.

"Hey, Chuck," Jim said to his brother. "I need a favor. Can you take me over to see Coach Ruggles?"

"Why?" Chuck asked.

"My ankle's a lot better. I want to show him I can play tonight."

"You really think you can play on that ankle?" Chuck said.

"Yeah, I've wrapped it in these wet towels all day, and it's feeling a lot better."

Chuck could see his younger brother was serious so he drove him over to Coach Ruggles' house. When they got there, Jim got out of the car and knocked on Ruggles' door. Ruggles answered and was surprised to see Jim standing there.

"Hey, Coach," Jim said. "I hope I'm not bothering you, but I wanted to show you that my ankle's all right. I've been using these tablets Dr. Hartmann gave me, and now I can walk. I think if I tape my ankle, I'll be able to play tonight."

Coach Ruggles and Mary had moved to a little white

house right by the school so he told Jim that he would meet him at the gym in a few minutes, and he would see if Jim was able to run. Ruggles grabbed his keys and headed for the school. He was skeptical about Jim's recovery, but he knew Jim had a zealous love for basketball so he thought he should give him a chance.

Coach Ruggles unlocked the gym and let Jim and Chuck in. The place was empty and quiet, and their footsteps click-clacked on the hard floor. Jim put on his high-top tennis shoes, and Ruggles taped his ankle heavily and told him to run from one end of the gym to the other. It took all the will power Jim could muster, but he ran the length of the floor and back without too much of a limp. Ruggles then had him do a few warm-up drills and asked him to shoot and jump. Jim put on a courageous show for his coach, doing his best to hide the pain that throbbed in his ankle.

"Okay," Coach Ruggles finally said after putting Jim through the short workout. "If your parents give you permission to play, you can dress for the game, but I'm not gonna play you unless we really need you for some reason."

Jim was happy to hear that, and he thanked Coach Ruggles. Now he had another obstacle. He had to convince his mom and dad to let him play. He knew his mom would want him to follow the doctor's orders and stay off his ankle so he realized his best option was to talk to his dad first. His dad had been a good athlete in high school and college and had played back in a time when players just "walked off" their injuries and stayed in the game. Jim hoped his father would be sympathetic so he asked Chuck to take him to the clinic where their dad was working.

Doc Neal didn't have a patient in his dental chair when Jim and Chuck arrived. Jim still had his ankle taped, and the support allowed him to walk without a limp.

"Dad, can I talk to you for a minute?" Jim asked.

"Sure," he said. "What's going on?"

"I saw Dr. Hartmann this morning, and he said I

shouldn't play ball for two weeks," Jim said. "But I used these tablets he gave me, and my ankle is better. We have a big game tonight with Shawnee, and I really want to play."

Jim told his dad about going to the gym with Coach Ruggles, and that Ruggles said he would let him dress out for the game if it was okay with his parents. It took some convincing, but Doc Neal finally agreed and said, "I'll talk to your mother."

"Thanks, Dad," Jim said. "I really appreciate this."

Jim knew there was no guarantee, but he now felt pretty good about his chances of dressing for that night's game. When his dad got home from work that afternoon, he discussed Jim's situation with his mother. While his parents conferred, Jim waited anxiously for their decision. After several minutes, the verdict was rendered. He was told he could play in the game. He thanked his parents over and over.

Cobden's game that night with Shawnee began with Jim Neal sitting on the bench beside Coach Ruggles. Jim knew he wasn't going to play unless the team needed him, but at least that gave him a chance. Darrell started the game in Jim's spot and played well. Both teams played physical defense, and the contest became heated. A slight scuffle broke out between the players while battling for a rebound.

Jim Neal saw the confrontation and sprang from the bench and headed across the court. Always a boisterous young man, Jim was ready to aid his teammates if needed. Coach Ruggles reached out to grab Jim's warm-up jacket and stop him, but he was too late. The referees separated the players, cooler heads prevailed, and nothing came of the incident. Jim walked back to the bench, and Ruggles told him, "If you can move that well, you might as well be playing. Go warm up and stretch your ankle. I'll put you in after halftime."

Cobden's boosters had been worried about Jim's injury, and they were glad to see that he was able to play. When he entered the game in the second half, they gave him a loud round of applause. The players on both teams behaved themselves the rest of the game, but this game had little resemblance to the one the two teams played earlier in the season. The Redskins were unable to keep up with the Appleknockers as Cobden executed its offense flawlessly and won by a comfortable margin, 80-53.

The Appleknockers' confidence and level of play continued to rise as they knocked out their next two opponents, beating Gorham, 79-58, and soundly defeating Hurst-Bush, 82-29. Cobden's record now stood at an impressive 20-1.

On Monday, February 11, the Associated Press released its ninth weekly poll of Illinois prep basketball teams, and Cobden checked in at No. 16. The Appleknockers replaced the Pinckneyville Panthers who had lost their fifth game of the season over the weekend. Cobden had garnered votes in the poll before, but this was the highest ranking it had received.

Other media outlets were also taking note of the Appleknockers' outstanding season. A sportswriter from Evansville, Indiana, came to Cobden High School that week and interviewed Coach Ruggles. After the team finished practice that afternoon, the reporter asked the players to put on their uniforms so he could take their pictures. The man was a real professional. He shot pictures from several different angles and in many formations. Some photos were simple head shots, and others were action shots with the players dribbling or shooting basketballs. The photo shoot lasted quite awhile, but the players didn't mind. They were enjoying the attention, feeling like mini-celebrities.

Cobden hosted Egyptian on Friday night. The gym was packed like it had been all year when the Appleknockers played. Sprinkled throughout the crowd were college coaches and scouts, there to evaluate the players. Interest in Cobden's games had grown so much that the gym had routinely become standing room only. Merna O'Brien, the typing teacher, was also the sponsor of the yearbook staff, and she and the students on that staff ran the concession stand at the ball games. As the season progressed, she found it increasingly difficult to get students to work in the concession stand. They all wanted to watch the games. She understood their dilemma. She loved watching the games, too. She would often help the students get the popcorn started, and then go stand at the door of the gym and watch the game through the diamond-shaped cutout window.

That night she was watching at the door as the Appleknockers took the court. Cobden's junior varsity squad won the first game, and the varsity squad got off to a strong start in the nightcap. They led 20-6 after the first period and maintained that advantage in the second. With just seconds left before halftime, Kenny Flick snagged a rebound from Egyptian's basket. He turned and launched a long shot toward Cobden's goal that appeared to be just inches short of its target. Jim Neal jumped high in the air and snared the ball, slapping it through the goal as the buzzer sounded, giving the Appleknockers a 42-24 halftime lead.

The spectators erupted with applause at the thrilling play. As Mrs. O'Brien cheered along with everyone else, she smelled something burning. She turned around and found the students who were supposed to be working in the concession stand were standing behind her, watching the game, too. Smoke poured out of the large popcorn machine. The popcorn was burning.

They all scurried back to the concession stand, fearing the popcorn machine was on fire. The students worried Mrs. O'Brien might be angry, but she wasn't. She was as guilty as they were for neglecting the concession stand. So what could she say? Except for the popcorn being ruined and the coming onslaught of disappointed customers who were expecting to eat hot popcorn at halftime, there was no harm done. And they all got to witness the phenomenal shot.

When the second half started, the Appleknockers picked up right where they had left off. Despite the efforts of Egyptian's Teddy Gleghorn, a sharp-shooter who scored 27 points, Cobden remained comfortably in front and won, 77-53.

The following evening, the Appleknockers welcomed Attucks for their last regular-season home game. It was a poignant night as the seniors were honored before the game. Kenny Flick, Chuck Neal, Kenny Smith, Jim Smith, Darrell Crimmins, Roy Witthoft, and Dan Marsh were introduced to the crowd and received a loud, heartfelt ovation. These boys had been instrumental in producing two of the most successful basketball seasons in school history, and the fans wanted them to know how much they appreciated their efforts. While it was a night of celebration, the air was tinged with sadness. Tom Crowell was on the minds of the players and the fans, and his spirit could be felt in the gym. He should have been there with them on that night, just as he should have been with them all season. He had been a good friend and a big part of the team before his tragic death, and they still missed him terribly.

There may have been an emotional hangover from the senior night ceremony because Cobden got off to a slow start and trailed the Blue Birds most of the first quarter. A last-minute scoring surge enabled the Appleknockers to go ahead, 17-16. Cobden again fell behind in the second period, but the team got hot in the final minute and took a 38-35 halftime lead.

In the third frame, the Appleknockers opened up a 13-point margin and remained in front even though they lost several players on fouls. The referees called the game extremely tight, and Chuck, Jim Neal, Kenny Flick, Jim Smith, and Bob Smith all fouled out in the second half. Four Attucks players also fouled out. Cobden's reserves got a good test as they played extended minutes in the second half, and Coach Ruggles was pleased with their effort and execution. The Appleknockers won, 81-67.

The regular season was quickly winding down. The

Appleknockers had repeated as Southern Six Conference champions and had one more game to play before the postseason tournament began. The game was on Saturday at Albion, a town in Edwards County about 125 miles northeast of Cobden. It was supposed to have been played on January 10 but was postponed due to the death of an Albion school official. The Appleknockers had already played Albion in the McLeansboro Holiday Tournament earlier in the season and won, 73-43.

On Friday night, Coach Ruggles went to a basketball game to watch Harrisburg play. He wanted to scout the Bulldogs in case Cobden met them down the road in the tournament. He was driving through Anna on his way home from the game, when he saw Kenny Smith's car go down the hill toward Jonesboro. *Was that Kenny?* he thought. Ruggles looked at his watch. It was after 11:30 p.m. *Where is he going at this hour?* he wondered. *He knows we have a game tomorrow.* Ruggles had no curfew for his players, but he thought they all understood that he expected them to be home at a reasonable hour the night before a ball game.

Kenny had spotted Coach Ruggles, too.

"Oh no," Kenny said to Chuck who was in the backseat of the car with his girlfriend, Judy. They had been on a double date and were taking Judy home. "Did you see who we just passed?"

"Was that Coach Ruggles?" Chuck asked. Ruggles was the last person in the world he had expected to see out that night.

"Yeah, it was. Do you think he recognized us?"

"Probably," Chuck said.

"Then after we drop Judy off, we're taking the back roads home," Kenny said. "In case he didn't see us, I don't want to give him another chance."

Coach Ruggles turned his car around to see if he could find Kenny. He drove around the square in Jonesboro, looking for Kenny's car, but he saw no sign of it. He finally gave up the search. When he got to the four-way stop in the middle of Anna, he saw Jim Neal filling his car with gas at a service station. Ruggles did a double take. *What are these boys doing out so late?*

Jim had been on a date with his girlfriend, Patti. He had just dropped her off and was heading home to Cobden. Unlike Kenny and Chuck, who knew Coach Ruggles disliked them being out so late the night before a game, the thought hadn't occurred to Jim. When he saw Coach Ruggles, he waved. He thought it was strange that Ruggles didn't wave back. *Maybe he didn't see me*, Jim thought as he twisted the gas cap back in place.

The next day the players met at the school to catch the bus to Albion. It was a long trip so they had to leave at 3 p.m. Coach Ruggles was already on the bus when Jim Neal climbed aboard.

"Hey, Coach," Jim said.

"What time did you get home last night?" Ruggles said, more as a statement than a question.

By his stern tone of voice, Jim could tell that he was upset, and that he really didn't want an answer. Jim moved sheepishly down the isle and slumped into a seat. Now he understood why Coach Ruggles hadn't waved at him at the gas station last night. Ruggles was angry that he was out so late. Instantly Jim felt bad. He truly respected Coach Ruggles, and he regretted that he had disappointed him.

The bus took off and after driving for over an hour, it stopped in Harrisburg so the team could eat an early supper.

"Don't go in there and eat yourselves out of the game," Coach Ruggles cautioned the boys before they got off the bus. "Take it easy on the biscuits and gravy and be respectful and act like gentlemen."

Coach Ruggles' orders to eat light were forgotten as soon as the players entered the restaurant and saw the buffet. They were big boys with big appetites, and they piled their plates high. When they went back and loaded their plates a second time, it seemed as if they were taking the all-you-can-eat sign literally. Ruggles saw how much they were eating but kept his mouth shut. He just shook his head and hoped they could still play.

Everyone finished their meals, and the team climbed back on the bus and continued the journey to Albion. The drive took another hour and twenty minutes. It was the farthest distance the players had traveled to play a game, and they were tired and restless from sitting for so long. They needed to stretch their legs.

When they finally reached their destination, they were surprised to find that Albion's gym was smaller than theirs. They also noticed that few of their fans were there. The long distance had reduced the normally large number of people who drove to the away games.

Because the trip had taken so long, the junior varsity squad had only a few minutes to warm up before its game started. The contest was close throughout, and in the final seconds, the Appleknockers had the ball and were trailing by one point. Rodney Clutts took a shot with about three seconds remaining. He missed the basket but was fouled on the play and went to the line to shoot two free throws. He failed to connect on the first one so now the best he could do was tie the game and send it to overtime. He took a moment longer to concentrate on his second shot, but he missed it, too, and Albion got the rebound. The buzzer sounded, announcing Cobden's one-point loss.

Rodney looked over at Coach Ruggles sitting on the bench. Ruggles shrugged his shoulders. Rodney figured he would be doing some extra free-throw drills at the next practice.

The varsity game got underway, and it was a physical affair from the start. As the Appleknockers had found out when they played Albion in the McLeansboro Holiday Tournament, it was one of the few teams who could match their height and size. The Lions pushed and shoved, and the officials let the boys play and called the game very loosely. Cobden wasn't playing well when Coach Ruggles called a timeout.

"What's going on out there?" Ruggles asked. "Are you still on the bus or back at the restaurant? Get your heads in the game."

Some of the players started to complain about the rough play, but Ruggles wouldn't hear any excuses.

"Just go out there and play your game," he said. "Play like you have all season."

The game was a battle the whole way, and the score was close, but the Appleknockers' execution was poor. The forceful play continued with the referees seemingly unwilling to call any fouls. Albion never backed down and won, 52-48. Cobden's 11-game winning streak was snapped.

In the locker room after the game, Ruggles was ready to explode.

"This is it guys," he said. His face red, and his tone all business. "You want to blow it right here? I saw a couple of you out last night, and I hope you've gotten that out of your systems. I don't want you being selfish and ruining it for the rest of us."

The boys were used to hearing their coach holler, but they had never seen him so steamed. Chuck and Kenny Smith stole a glance at each other, knowing Ruggles was referring to them. Chuck shifted uneasily on the hard wooden bench. Kenny Smith bent his head and trained his eyes on his shoelaces. Neither of them thought that being out late the previous night had any effect on the game, but they remained silent. They knew nothing they said would convince Coach Ruggles of that.

"We have a goal, right?" Ruggles continued, his voice rising. "We want to keep playing and winning. How did we beat this team by 30 points in the tournament, and they beat us the last game of the year? Have they improved that much? Are we going backwards, or are you starting to believe your press clippings? No one is going to give us a game. We have to earn them."

Finished speaking, Ruggles turned and walked out of the dressing room. He had said enough for now.

If the bus ride to Albion had seemed long, the ride home was even worse. The players sat quietly, staring out the windows at the dark countryside. They were accustomed to winning, and they hated the way it felt to lose. They thought they had taken the Lions seriously, but since they had already beaten Albion by 30 points, they were probably too confident going into the game. The rough play had also rattled them. Some of the boys had to admit, at least to themselves, that they were less prepared than they should have been.

Coach Ruggles was still fuming over what he thought was a lackadaisical effort by his team. *When we get back to Cobden tonight, we're going straight to the gym and practice*, he thought. As the miles wore on, his temper abated. By the time the bus pulled into the school's parking lot, it was well past midnight. *I'm not going to make them practice right now*, he thought. *Losing the game was a lesson in itself, and one they learned the hard way.*

Chapter 12

1964 Postseason Play Begins

District Tournament

The Appleknockers regrouped after the debacle at Albion. The team had some of its best practices in anticipation of the upcoming district tournament, the first step in the quest for the Illinois state high school basketball championship. The players hated having their winning streak stopped, and now they were focused and ready to get back on the winning track.

Cobden was once again the site of a district tournament. It was one of 45 schools throughout the state hosting such an event. Along with the Appleknockers, Alto Pass, Dongola, and Mounds Douglass were participating in the district at Cobden. The winner would advance to the Anna-Jonesboro Regional Tournament.

The Appleknockers opened district play on Thursday night against Alto Pass in the first game. Two-time and defending champion Cobden showed why it was the overwhelming favorite to win the title again this year. It jumped all over Alto Pass in the first quarter and put the game away early. Cobden's defense allowed just one field goal by the Apaches in the opening eight minutes of play. Jim Neal had the hot hand on offense, netting 15 points as the Appleknockers piled up a 35-4 lead after one period.

Coach Ruggles took most of his starting quintet out for the second quarter, allowing his reserves to get in on the action. Cobden continued to dominate the contest and had a 37-point cushion at halftime, leading 55-18.

"We've got control of the game," Ruggles said to his players during the break. "But I don't want you to let down. This is the tournament now. Every game counts. We have to play every game like it's our last because if we lose our focus, it will be our last game."

The Appleknockers' supremacy continued in the second half. They played at an exceptionally high level on both offense and defense as if trying to exorcize the demons of their Albion loss, proving to themselves and everyone watching that it had been an aberration. Coach Ruggles exchanged his starters and substitutes freely throughout the third and fourth quarters, maintaining a sizable lead. Nine members of Cobden's team scored at least four points in the game. With two seconds left to play, Darrell Crimmins hit a basket that put the Appleknockers over the century mark for the first time all season. Cobden won, 101-34.

The second game of the evening pitted Dongola against Mounds Douglass. A one-point game after one period, it was much closer than Cobden's game had been. Mounds Douglass eventually pulled away and defeated the Demons, 59-42, to earn a spot in the final with the Appleknockers the following night.

Cobden and Mounds Douglass were familiar foes, having played each other twice during the season. The Appleknockers had emerged victorious from both prior meetings, but in the second game, they had trailed at the intermission and had come from behind to win. In that second game, the Tornados had been successful holding the ball against Cobden and slowing the tempo in the first half. Coach Ruggles expected them to use the same tactic in the final, and he wanted his boys to be ready for it.

"We need to be aggressive and make them play our game," Ruggles told the players in the locker room before they took the floor.

"Last time they held the ball on us, and they controlled the first half of the game. I don't want to give them the chance to do that tonight. We need to be strong defensively and really battle for the rebounds."

When the final game tipped off, Coach Ruggles' suspicion was confirmed. The Tornados attempted to hold the ball, but the Appleknockers double teamed the ball handler, denying passes and breaking up plays. Mounds Douglass found it difficult to shoot over Cobden's towering zone and didn't score a bucket until under two minutes remained in the first quarter. The Tornados also committed numerous turnovers, and the Appleknockers capitalized, racking up a 24-9 margin at the end of the first period.

Cobden continued to impose its will in the second quarter, hounding Mounds Douglass at every turn. Chuck was a force on offense, stuffing in 14 points during the period as the Appleknockers cruised into halftime, leading 47-17.

Jim Neal, who had been ball hawking on defense in the first half, fouled out early in the third quarter. Even without his services, Cobden remained firmly in command. The Appleknockers put any thoughts of a Mounds Douglass comeback to rest as they outscored the Tornados 25-7 during the period. As he had done the night before, Coach Ruggles used his reserves a good portion of the game, and with victory well in hand, he let them play the final frame. The Appleknockers won, 85-44, claiming their third straight district title.

The large crowd gave Cobden a standing ovation. Coach Ruggles and the players were presented with a large plaque, designating them district champs. A sports reporter for the local *Gazette-Democrat* was there, and he took a picture of the boys and their coach posing happily with their award.

There was a feeling of satisfaction in Cobden's locker room but no excessive celebration. The Appleknockers' ability was so superior to that of the other district teams that their victory had been expected. The boys knew better than to take the title for granted, and they had prepared diligently for the games. To most of them, winning the district championship was a mere formality, a necessary stepping stone to get to the regional.

Anna-Jonesboro Regional Tournament

After winning the district title, Cobden was set to face Mound City in the opening round of the Anna-Jonesboro Regional Tournament on Tuesday night. The Appleknockers had yet to play Mound City this season, but Coach Ruggles knew the team would be a formidable opponent. The Tigers had an outstanding season, posting a record of 21-3 and were the No. 1 seed in the regional tournament. Some experts were calling Cobden's first-round game with Mound City the "championship" game of the tournament, with the winner becoming the favorite to take the title.

Other basketball pundits rated Cobden and A-J as favorites to win the tournament. The Appleknockers' supporters found that odd since Cobden had played A-J earlier in the year and scored an easy and decisive win over the Wildcats, 78-36. But Ralph Davison, Anna's coach, told a reporter that he thought his team had improved since that game, and he was quoted in a local newspaper as saying, "We only shot 29 percent in the game against Cobden and really went to pieces in the third quarter. I don't think the final score was representative of the strengths of the two teams."

Cobden and A-J were on opposite sides of the tournament bracket. If both teams won their quarter-final and semifinal games, they would meet each other in the finals. That was a rematch many area basketball fans were hoping to see.

Coach Ruggles didn't want the players to get caught up in the Cobden-Anna rivalry. The Appleknockers had to concentrate on their game with Mound City because if they lost, there would be no rematch with Anna.

Spectators packed the Anna-Jonesboro gym on Tuesday evening for the opening games of the regional tournament. Egyptian defeated Mounds Township, 73-50, in the first game, and then Cobden and Mound City took the floor for game two.

Chuck won the tipoff to start the game and swatted the

ball to Kenny Flick. Mound City immediately fouled Kenny, and he sank the free throw to move Cobden ahead, 1-0. The Tigers took possession of the ball and used quick bounce passes to keep the ball away from the Appleknockers. This ball-control tactic was effective in slowing the game, but it proved to be ineffective to Mound City on offense. Cobden's 1-2-2 zone pushed the Tigers out away from the basket, and the Appleknockers contested every shot, holding Mound City without a field goal for the entire first quarter. The Tigers' only points came on free throws, and Cobden established an 11-3 lead at the end of the period.

The Appleknockers' aggressive defense continued in the second quarter. Cobden made good use of its height as the players blocked and hindered many shots while controlling the rebounding at both ends of the floor. Mound City cracked the Appleknockers' zone occasionally, but Cobden still increased its advantage to 14 points and was up, 27-13, at halftime.

When the third quarter began, the Tigers abandoned their delay game and ball-control approach in favor of a running game. As the pace quickened, Cobden's lead grew larger. The showdown that so many spectators had expected to see between the two skilled basketball teams never materialized. On that night, the Appleknockers were superior in every facet of the game. Coach Ruggles used his reserves liberally in the fourth quarter, and Cobden rolled to a 32-point victory, 67-35.

With the win over Mound City under their belts, the Appleknockers began thinking about a possible rematch with A-J, but Coach Ruggles warned them about looking ahead.

"Egyptian looked very good in their game tonight over Mounds," Ruggles said. "They are playing good ball, and we can't overlook them."

The next day at practice, the Appleknockers prepared for their game with the Pharaohs. Coach Ruggles wanted them to take the tournament one game at a time, and Egyptian was next on the schedule. Cobden had played Egyptian twice during the season, including one game just over two weeks ago, and come away with two double-digit victories. But Coach Ruggles and the players knew the regional game would be a challenge. Egyptian was a quick team with good shooters, and the Appleknockers would have to play well to win.

On Thursday night, Cobden and Egyptian tipped off their semifinal game in front of a full house at A-J. When the game began, the normally high-scoring, speedy Egyptian ball club employed a deliberate, ball-control strategy. Not expecting this scheme, Cobden had to adjust quickly. The Pharaohs tried to hold the ball in an effort to negate Cobden's height advantage. The Appleknockers' defense made it difficult for Egyptian to get many good looks at the basket, and they managed just two field goals in the first quarter. With its aggressive play, Cobden was called for several fouls, but Egyptian hit just two-of-six free throws. Kenny Flick, Kenny Smith, and Jim Neal all supplied a pair of baskets, and the Appleknockers took a 12-6 lead after one period.

In the second quarter, sharp-shooter Teddy Gleghorn hit a couple of long-range shots for Egyptian. His offense seemed to loosen up the Pharaohs, and the game took on a faster pace. Kenny Smith matched Gleghorn's perimeter shots while he also fed the ball to Chuck and Kenny Flick for inside buckets. But the Appleknockers again committed several fouls, and Egyptian did a better job at the line as George Lawrence and Bob Houston each converted two-of-three tries. Cobden's margin at the intermission was only five points, 29-24.

Chuck and Jim Neal each picked up their fourth fouls during the third quarter. Coach Ruggles wanted to make sure he had both of them available if needed for the stretch run so he took them out and put in Jim Smith and Darrell Crimmins. Jim and Darrell played well, contributing at both ends of the floor, but the Pharaohs refused to go away. Teddy Gleghorn and George Lawrence sank three field goals apiece during the period, matching the Appleknockers' balanced offensive output and keeping Egyptian within striking distance as Cobden led,

43-38, at the end of the third period.

The Appleknockers got the tip from the jump ball in the fourth quarter, and Chuck worked inside for a layup. Kenny Smith added another bucket, giving Cobden a nine-point lead, 47-38, midway through the period. Cobden's foul issues continued to haunt them, however, and the Pharaohs made four straight free throws to get back within five points. Kenny Flick was fouled on the Appleknockers' next possession. He went to the line for his first free-throw attempt of the night. His shot wouldn't fall, and Egyptian pulled down the rebound. Teddy Gleghorn drilled a bucket from the outside, reducing Cobden's lead to three.

Coach Ruggles called a timeout. He thought the boys look rattled as they gathered around him.

"We're okay," he assured them. "Let's run our offense and look for good shots. On defense, you've got to stay in front of 'em. You can't keep fouling and putting 'em on the line, and you've gotta rebound."

The boys took deep breaths to calm themselves and play resumed. Cobden threw the ball in and dribbled up the court. Before the Appleknockers could get into their offense, Darrell was fouled and went to the line for a one-and-one opportunity. He had already made one charity toss in the game, but this shot was off the mark. Egyptian grabbed the rebound and worked the ball down the floor. Jerry Shaw tipped in a rebound for the Pharaohs, and suddenly they trailed by only one point with under two minutes left to play.

The spectators could hardly believe what they were seeing. The Pharaohs had scored eight unanswered points, and now it was anybody's game. The Appleknockers' fans rose to their feet and clapped their hands, trying to spur on their team. Egyptian's fans stood and cheered the Pharaoh's stunning rally.

Kenny Smith dribbled the ball up the court and across the center stripe. He wanted to get the ball inside for an easy basket, but before he could set up a play, he was fouled. He stepped to the free-throw line. He was having a great game offensively, leading his team with 17 points so far, and he had made the only other free throw he had attempted. Now he had a chance to give his team a little breathing room if he could knock down these shots. It was still a one-and-one situation so the first attempt was crucial. Kenny dribbled a couple of times and eyed the basket. He launched his shot. It bounced long off the iron and was no good. Egyptian recovered the rebound, giving them a chance to take the lead with less than a minute to play.

Cobden's fans let out a collective gasp of disbelief. Coach Ruggles was worried, but he stayed calm, not letting the tension show. He didn't want his players to panic. Normally his boys were good free-throw shooters, and he was afraid their nerves had affected them when they were at the foul line. From the sideline, he implored the boys not to foul.

"Be aggressive but watch your hands," he yelled. "We don't want to put 'em at the free-throw line."

The Pharaohs brought the ball slowly down the floor and passed it around to each other. No one made an attempt toward the basket. They were apparently going to hold the ball for one final shot to win the game.

Clinging to a one-point lead, the Appleknockers settled into their 1-2-2 zone defense, but they tempered their aggressiveness to avoid being called for a foul. Time drained off the clock. Egyptian continued to hold the ball. With six seconds remaining, Teddy Gleghorn launched a jumper from about 19 feet. He had been hitting consistently from the outside since the second quarter, and this shot appeared to be on the mark. The ball seemed to hang in the air forever. To Coach Ruggles and Cobden's players, who were sitting on the bench under the basket, it looked like the ball was moving in slow motion. Having fouled out of the game, Jim Neal watched helplessly as the ball traveled toward its target. He had a sick feeling in his stomach as he feared it would fall through the hoop. The ball hit the iron and rolled all around the rim. Then it fell off.

Bob Houston grabbed the rebound for the Pharaohs

and was immediately surrounded by Cobden's players as he desperately tried to take another shot. The final horn sounded and then a referee's whistle blew. Everything stopped. *Was the game over? Had a foul been called? If so, who was it on?* The noisy crowd grew quiet. People were murmuring to themselves and asking each other, "What's going on?" and "Is it over?" Neither coach knew what was happening, and they called the players to come to their respective benches while the officials sorted things out.

The referees conferred for a few moments and made the decision: the last whistle was blown after the final buzzer had already gone off. No foul was assessed, and the game was officially over. Cobden had won, 47-46. The Appleknockers had survived a great scare from the Pharaohs and had now advanced to the regional final.

The crowd applauded for both teams. Cobden's fans cheered with a sense of relief, knowing their team had dodged a bullet. Egyptian made the Appleknockers earn the win, right down to the last second.

Although they were happy, Cobden's players also felt a bit uneasy in the locker room. The victory had been a little too close for comfort. The close call reinforced the fact that this was the tournament now. Every team was going to bring its "A-game" because no team wanted its season to end.

"They aren't always going to be easy," Coach Ruggles said to the boys. "That was a close one, but we did it. We're in the finals now, and we've got to come ready to play tomorrow night."

The Appleknockers never got the chance to play the much-anticipated rematch with Anna-Jonesboro in the regional final. The Wildcats were upset in the second semifinal game by Cairo Sumner. A-J had maintained a slight lead through most of the contest, but the Red Devils came from behind in the fourth quarter to gain a dramatic one-point win, 61-60.

The finals were set: The Appleknockers and Cairo Sumner would battle for the title.

After watching two exciting semifinal games the previous night, fans filled A-J's gym on Friday for the regional final hoping to see another thriller, and that's just the way the game began. Cairo Sumner struck first to go up, 2-0, but Cobden came right back to tie the score. The Red Devils matched the Appleknockers bucket for bucket in the first quarter thanks mostly to Joe Williams' excellent outside shooting. Cobden was more efficient at the free-throw line, though, hitting six-of-eight attempts compared to Cairo Sumner's one-for-four performance, and the Appleknockers led, 20-15, at the end of the period.

A close game continued in the second quarter. The Red Devils moved the ball much better, especially after Kenny Smith picked up his third foul, and Coach Ruggles was forced to put him on the bench. Joe Moore scored eight points, and Jerome Johnson went seven-for-seven from the foul line as Cairo Sumner cut into Cobden's lead. But Jim Neal netted seven points, and Kenny Flick and Jim Smith each added four, and the Appleknockers retained a one-point margin, 35-34, at the half.

Cobden came out of the locker room with renewed energy following the break. The Appleknockers went on an 8-0 run to start the third quarter. Jerome Johnson made a free throw for Cairo Sumner, and then Cobden scored five more points to open up a comfortable 13-point advantage, 48-35. The Appleknockers' tough zone stifled the Red Devils' offense, allowing just a single basket, and Cobden took a 51-37 lead after three quarters.

A minute into the fourth period, Jerome Johnson, Cairo Sumner's center, was called for his fifth and final foul. He had done a good job defensively on Chuck, holding him to just five points in the first three periods. Now with Johnson on the bench, Chuck had more room to work inside. He tossed in three field goals. Joe Williams got hot from the outside and helped bring the Red Devils within seven points at 59-52 midway through the frame. Then Cobden scored nine straight points to take a 68-52 lead. The Appleknockers lost Kenny Smith and Jim Neal on fouls late in the fourth, but the victory was already wrapped up. Cobden won, 69-54, and claimed its second straight regional championship.

After shaking hands with the players from Cairo Sumner, the Appleknockers began whooping and hollering. They hugged Coach Ruggles and each other. The cheerleaders clapped and cheered loudly, and Cobden's fans joined them, showering the team with appreciation for their achievement.

The players wanted to cut the nets down from the goals to keep as victory mementos. They asked for a ladder, but an official from A-J refused.

It was common practice for the winning team to take the nets after it won a big tournament, and Coach Ruggles was confused by the man's hesitation.

"We'd like to cut down the nets for our trophy case," Ruggles told the official. "We need a ladder."

"I'm not sure you're going to get the nets," the man replied.

"Why not?" Ruggles asked.

Before the man could answer, John Lipe intervened. As the assistant principal at A-J, he had been asked to present the regional championship plaque to the winning team.

"What's the problem with the nets?" Lipe asked.

"Ask him," Ruggles said, motioning to the official.

"These boys want to get on a ladder and cut the nets down, and I don't think that's necessary or safe. This is our gym, and one of 'em could get hurt," the official said.

The crowd started to get restless, wondering what was holding up the awards ceremony.

"If safety is all you're concerned about, I'll get a custodian, and he'll get the nets down," Lipe said. Turning to Ruggles he added, "Hang on. It won't take long."

The man continued to protest, but Lipe paid him no attention. A custodian was found, and he removed the nets from both goals and gave them to Lipe.

"Congratulations," Lipe said, shaking Coach Ruggles' hand and giving him the nets and regional plaque.

The large crowd again erupted in applause. As the cheers died down, a photographer from the local paper approached the team.

"Coach Ruggles can I get a quick photo of you and the boys?" he said.

The players lined up. Ruggles stood on one side of the group, and Lipe stood on the other. It was a nice moment for the team. Not long ago, Lipe had been their basketball coach and teacher. All the boys liked him, and he was fond of them. It seemed fitting that he was there to share their victory. Even though his feelings were hurt when the Cobden School Board removed him as their coach, he was excited they were doing so well and wished them continued success.

The boys celebrated in the locker room, smiling ear-to-ear as they recounted key plays. The mood was more festive than it had been after they won the district tournament. Although they had won the regional title last year, it was still a feat that was seldom accomplished by Cobden. The boys weren't taking the win for granted.

Coach Ruggles stopped to talk to the sports reporters. Although the regional had just concluded, most of their questions were about the upcoming sectional tournament. Ruggles tried to keep focused on one game at time, but he knew there was no time for the team to rest on its laurels. On the tournament trail, games came fast and furious. Thinking ahead to the next opponent, he was distracted as he entered the locker room and found himself surrounded by his exuberant players.

One of them hollered, "Shower!"

All of a sudden, the boys grabbed him and carried him to the shower room. It took a split second for Coach Ruggles to register what was happening, but by then he knew there was no use fighting. He was outnumbered, and the boys were determined. The whole group was howling with laughter when they dropped him in a shower stall and soaked him with water.

"You're a bunch of wise guys now, huh?" Ruggles said after he gathered himself and tried to shake the water off his clothes.

The players were still grinning, pleased with their ambush and waiting for further reaction from their coach.

Taking it in stride, Ruggles simply smiled at them and said, "You boys better get in here for your showers before I use all the hot water."

Coach Ruggles and Mary invited the players over for supper on Sunday evening. It was, in part, a gesture of congratulations for winning the regional tournament while also giving the team a chance to get together away from the basketball court. They had played three games that week, and Coach Ruggles wanted the players to know how much he appreciated their effort and commitment.

Chapter 13

1964 Sectional Tournament

Cobden once again found itself being called a "Little David" by the press after winning the regional title. It was the smallest school still in the tournament, and newspapers throughout the region began to show a greater interest in the Appleknockers. The Cairo *Evening-Citizen* and the *Gazette-Democrat* in Anna had covered the Appleknockers all season, but now Coach Ruggles was receiving phone calls from his old pal in Evansville, Indiana, as well as papers in St. Louis, Missouri. Other newspapers from towns in lower southern Illinois, whose teams were no longer in the tournament, also called to get interviews.

The Associated Press poll was released, and Cobden was picked as the favorite to win the Eldorado Sectional Tournament. The Appleknockers received 11 votes in the poll. Its opponent in the opening round of the sectional, Carmi, got two votes. The other entries in the tournament, Harrisburg and Cave-In-Rock, received two and zero votes, respectively.

Although Cobden was the decisive choice in the state-wide poll, many local papers were hesitant to cast the Appleknockers in the role of favorite. Perhaps they were swayed by memories of Cobden's performance in last year's sectional tournament. For whatever reason, the local reporters seemed to be rooting for Cobden, but hedging their bets and favoring Harrisburg and its top player, Guy Lee Turner.

While it was fun to see their names and pictures in the papers, Coach Ruggles and the players never lost sight of the reason why they were receiving the press coverage. The games were the important things, and Ruggles made sure he had the players' full attention when they were in the gym. Last year when the Appleknockers played in the sectional, Ruggles felt they could have been better prepared. He was determined to have them ready this time.

Having not scouted Carmi, Coach Ruggles had to rely on reports from some of his former classmates at SIU who had seen the Bulldogs play. He was told the Bulldogs were a well-balanced team that often used a ball-control strategy in games. They had a starting quintet that boasted plenty of height with their tallest player, Darrell Hankins, standing just over 6-foot-4. Another player, Jim Anderson, was 6-foot-4, while Wayne Ackerman stood over 6-foot-3. Even with Carmi's considerable size, Cobden had a decided height advantage. Ruggles knew that rebounding would be key. He was also worried about turnovers and felt it would be important to limit ball-handling mistakes.

Every day at practice, the Appleknockers went over the game plan that Coach Ruggles developed for Carmi. The players listened carefully to what he said. They were a competitive group, and they were taking this game as seriously as he was. They didn't want a repeat of what happened last year when they had lost to McLeansboro. No team from Cobden had ever won a sectional game. They were determined to be the first.

On Thursday, the Appleknockers took the bus to Eldorado for the game. It was a long ride, and Coach Ruggles thought some of the players looked uptight. He felt some of the boys had gotten the jitters last year at the sectional, and the tension had affected their play.

"Relax," he said to the boys as they pulled into the gym's parking lot. "Focus on Carmi. You're ready."

As he got off the bus, Jim Neal felt more confident. Having played in the sectional tournament last year, he had a better idea of what to expect, and he thought that experience would help him and his teammates. He watched Kenny Flick striding across darkened asphalt ahead of him. Kenny was the only starter who had never competed in the sectional tournament, but that didn't concern Jim. Kenny was a fierce competitor and could handle any challenge on a basketball court. Jim, like all the other boys, was thankful to have him back on the team. Going into battle, Kenny was someone Jim wanted on his side.

Four thousand fans filled the bleachers to watch Cobden and Carmi, but the loudest, and perhaps most excited fan, was on the sideline. He was Roger Burnett, the Appleknockers' new mascot. The cheerleaders had asked Roger to wear baggy denim overalls and a checkered shirt and cheer with them at the games. Cobden had received plenty of attention, and sometimes grief, for its unusual nickname. Now when someone asked, "What's an Appleknocker?" they could point to Roger.

Roger was happy to be the team's mascot. Tonight was his first time playing the role of the Appleknocker, and he was a natural. He shouted cheers with the cheerleaders and strutted up and down the sideline, encouraging the large group of Cobden's fans to clap and cheer. His energy was contagious. When the Appleknockers ran out on the floor, they were met by one of the loudest ovations they had received all year.

Cobden controlled the tipoff to start the game, and Chuck nailed a 15-foot jump shot from the circle to give the Appleknockers a quick 2-0 lead. Carmi threw up a 30-foot jumper on its first possession that missed its target. Cobden got the rebound, and Kenny Smith hit a shot from the corner. Chuck added a free throw, and the Appleknockers moved ahead, 5-0. On defense, Cobden used its tough 1-2-2 zone to harass the Bulldogs and disrupt their plays.

The Appleknockers' demeanor made it clear from the beginning that this year they were ready for sectional play. They had come prepared and were determined to take control of the game. Cobden's aggressive play garnered foul calls from the referees, but Carmi failed to take advantage, making only three free throws in seven tries during the quarter. Chuck and Kenny Smith contributed two more field goals apiece before Chuck was called for his third foul with 30 seconds left in the quarter. Coach Ruggles removed Chuck from the game and put Darrell Crimmins in. Kenny Flick scored a layup to bring the period to a close with the Appleknockers leading, 15-9.

Because of Chuck's foul situation, Coach Ruggles kept him on the bench to start the second quarter. Jim Neal jumped center, giving Cobden the tip. Kenny Smith tossed in a 20-footer to extend the Appleknockers' advantage. Kenny Flick drilled a shot from the corner, and Jim Neal made a pair of free throws while Darrell hit one to push Cobden in front, 22-12, with four minutes remaining before the half.

The Bulldogs weren't used to being at a height dis-advantage and had trouble penetrating Cobden's towering defense. Kenny Smith was hot from the outside and drilled another 20-foot jumper. Jim Smith sank a free throw, and Jim Neal contributed a basket to increase the Appleknockers' lead to 27-14 with a minute and a half to play. But the Bulldogs rallied. Darrell Hankins was fouled and dropped in two free throws. Jim Anderson hit a field goal as Carmi closed the quarter with four straight points to trail, 27-18, at halftime.

Although not pleased with the Bulldogs' flourish at the end of the half, Coach Ruggles felt good about his team's effort. The boys had played with confidence, not showing the nerves he was afraid they might. In the locker room, they reviewed their game plan, and then the players returned to the court to warm up for the second half.

Kenny Flick scored two fast field goals to open the third quarter, igniting a 10-2 Appleknocker run. Jim Neal pumped in a 15-foot jumper. Tom Mears then scored for the Bulldogs, but Chuck came back with a bucket and two free throws, and Cobden led, 37-20, halfway through the third quarter.

Carmi began using a press defense that flustered Cobden briefly and slowed its scoring pace, but Jim Smith handled the ball skillfully, and the Appleknockers adjusted to the new tactic. The Bulldogs committed several fouls while trying to press. Jim Neal made good on four-of-five free-throw attempts while Chuck converted two foul shots. The brothers each pro-vided another bucket, putting Cobden up, 47-34, at the end of the third.

The Appleknockers began the fourth stanza right where they left off in the third. After winning the tip, Chuck scored a layup off a nice feed from Kenny Smith. J.O. Walling hit a jumper for Carmi. Then Kenny Flick drained four straight free throws, and Kenny Smith added two more and a field goal as Cobden opened up a 21-point lead, 57-36, with four minutes and 15 seconds remaining. The Bulldogs ran into foul trouble. They lost starters Jim Anderson and Wayne Ackerman on fouls during that stretch, and the Appleknockers continued to pull away as they had Carmi easily outmanned.

Jim Neal was called for his fifth foul and went to the bench, but Cobden maintained a significant lead during the last four minutes of the game. Coach Ruggles began pulling his remaining starters from the lineup. Each received an enthusiastic ovation as he went to the bench. Although Carmi was a much bigger school than Cobden, a clear majority of the crowd was rooting for the Appleknockers. Basketball enthusiasts from communities throughout lower southern Illinois had joined Cobden's fans in support of the team.

Carmi began to foul frantically in the final stages of the game in an effort to gain possession of the ball and cut into Cobden's lead. Bob Smith made three-of-four free throws, and Rodney Clutts went two-for-two from the foul line, keeping Cobden well in front as it breezed to the first sectional win in school history, 71-53.

The Appleknockers' fans cheered wildly for their team's impressive win, but the spectators who had just watched Cobden play for the first time this season were almost too stunned to clap. They had heard about the Appleknockers and expected them to be good, but the dominating display they had just witnessed surprised them. Cobden thoroughly dismantled Carmi, convincing many of those in attendance that the Appleknockers could win the sectional title.

The players were ecstatic in their dressing room. Winning this sectional game felt great and was a big boost to their confidence. A year ago, this was where their season had ended with a loss to McLeansboro. But not tonight. This time they had come out on top. They had now gone further than any other Cobden team, and they weren't finished yet.

Coach Ruggles gathered the boys around him to try to focus their energy on the next game. The Harrisburg Bulldogs had beaten Cave-In-Rock on Wednesday and would meet Cobden in the finals the next evening.

"This win was great, but we have another bunch of Bulldogs waiting for us tomorrow night," Coach Ruggles told the players. "If we're going to be ready, we have to start thinking about Harrisburg now."

On the bus ride back to Cobden, Coach Ruggles and the boys had a strategy session on Harrisburg. Ruggles had scouted the Bulldogs in case Cobden would have to play them. Guy Lee Turner was Harrisburg's unquestioned star. A highly skilled All-State performer, he was a formidable 6-foot-4 and 240 pounds and played with a grace that earned him the nickname the "Elegant Elephant." Stopping him would be an important factor, but Ruggles wanted to avoid targeting the defense only on him. The Appleknockers planned to use their patented zone defense with some minor adjustments for Turner. Ruggles felt that his players were big and strong enough to keep up with Turner. He and the boys discussed a game plan that they believed would be successful against the Bulldogs.

The boys found it difficult to concentrate on their studies the next day. They, along with most everyone else at school, were thinking about the big game that night. During the lunch hour, Coach Ruggles called the players into the gym so they could run through plays they were going to use in the game. Harrisburg was an unfamiliar opponent, and there was no time to have a regular practice after school. Ruggles wanted to use this free period to make sure everyone knew their assignments when a particular play was called.

After putting on their gym shoes, the boys spent the

next half hour running through different game scenarios. The impromptu practice quickly drew a crowd, and students gathered on the bleachers to watch. Everyone was so engrossed in the makeshift session that they were startled when the bell rang, beckoning them back to class.

The rest of the day the boys simply went through the motions in their classes and were relieved when the dismissal bell sounded. They went home and got their gear together, ate, and rushed back to school to catch the bus. During the 90 minute ride to Eldorado, Coach Ruggles went over the game plan again and told the boys to stay calm and concentrate on Harrisburg. It was the same thing he had told them the night before about Carmi, and it had paid off.

When the Appleknockers arrived at the Eldorado gym, it was already beginning to fill with people. There had been talk that the game might be a sellout. Many of Cobden's supporters had come early to make sure they could get seats. By the time the teams took the floor to warm up, about 4,500 fans packed the bleachers. It was estimated to be the largest crowd at the gym since Marion and McLeansboro played in a supersectional there two years earlier. Many of the spectators were rooting for Cobden, and they yelled loudly when its starting lineup was introduced.

Coach Ruggles gave the boys a little pep talk in the huddle.

"You know what to do now," he said. "You've worked hard to get here so keep it going. Just play your game."

With those words in mind, the Appleknockers took the floor.

Cobden won the opening tip and took a 1-0 lead over the Bulldogs when Jim Neal was fouled and made a free throw. Kurt Feazel hit a basket from the baseline for Harrisburg, but Kenny Flick came right back with a layup, giving Cobden a 3-2 advantage. The Appleknockers profited from turnovers by the Bulldogs and dashed out to a 14-6 lead as Kenny Smith and Jim Smith each hit a pair of jump shots, and Kenny Flick, Jim

Neal, and Jim Smith all contributed a free throw. Cobden's scoring drive was stalled when Jim Neal and Kenny Flick were both whistled for offensive fouls, and Chuck was assessed his third foul while grabbing a rebound. The Bulldogs scored the last five points of the first quarter to trail Cobden, 14-11.

The Appleknockers did a good job defensively on Harrisburg's star Guy Lee Turner in the initial period, limiting him to four points, all on free throws. He came alive in the second quarter, however, dumping in three field goals and two more free throws. Chuck picked up his fourth foul just two minutes into the period so Coach Ruggles replaced him in the lineup with Bob Smith. The Bulldogs pulled even at 17-all, and then took the lead at 21-19 when Kurt Feazel buried a jump shot.

The Appleknockers' fans were tense in the stands. They dreaded seeing their team fall behind, and they were worried about all the fouls on Chuck and the other starters.

Bob was fouled on Cobden's next possession and made both free throws to tie the game again, and the score remained close throughout the period. With 45 seconds left and the score tied at 28, Harrisburg gained possession and tried to hold the ball for the last shot. The Appleknockers broke up the stall pattern and stole the ball. Then Kenny Flick drove in for a layup, and Cobden owned a two-point halftime edge, 30-28.

After a fast start, the Appleknockers' starters were hit hard by fouls in the first half, but Bob and Darrell Crimmins came off the bench and played well, and Cobden was able to maintain a slim lead.

The referees were Ford Peebles of Murphysboro and Fred Gibson from Centralia. Similar to many officials in southern Illinois, they were known for calling games extremely close, where the slightest contact between players resulted in a foul. Both teams played aggressively in the first half, but Cobden bore the brunt of the foul calls as its starters were tagged for multiple infractions. This upset the Cobden faithful, especially in light of a rumor that had been circulating around town. Word had spread that Peebles had said district teams like Cobden had no business in sectional play and didn't belong with the "big boys." Whether the story was true or not, many of the Appleknockers' fans and players believed the rumor, and they were afraid his officiating might adversely affect the game's outcome. Many of Peebles' calls were met with suspicion and disdain by Cobden's supporters.

Coach Ruggles and the players weren't overly concerned about the foul situation. Throughout the season, Ruggles always felt he had a starting lineup of seven instead of a starting five. The four big guys – Chuck Neal, Kenny Flick, Kenny Smith, and Jim Neal – were the regular starters. Jim Smith, Bob Smith, and Darrell Crimmins also started at different times during the season. When not in the starting lineup, they would come off the bench when needed and do a good job. Being big, physical players, the four regulars often got in foul trouble so the reserves had seen a lot of action and contributed valuable minutes all year. This allowed the bench players to gain confidence and important game experience, and the boys had grown accustomed to playing with different combinations of players on offense and defense.

Since Chuck had four fouls, Coach Ruggles kept him on the bench at the start of the second half. Jim Neal moved to the center spot and performed admirably, pacing Cobden with eight points in the third quarter. Kenny Flick and Kenny Smith each added a bucket for the Appleknockers as they gained a seven-point lead at 41-34. But the Bulldogs were still fighting. Guy Lee Turner and Kurt Feazel furnished all of the offense for Harrisburg, and they closed the gap to five points, 44-39, at the end of the period.

Coach Ruggles put his regular starting lineup back into the game to begin the fourth quarter. Using deliberate ball control and consistent free-throw shooting, Cobden extended its lead to 10 points midway through the period. Chuck was called for his fifth foul with three minutes and 45 seconds remaining. Saddled with foul trouble the entire game, he had played cautiously and went to the bench scoreless for the first time all season.

Guy Lee Turner made one of his free-throw attempts to bring Harrisburg within nine, but Bob, who had come in to replace Chuck, was fouled and made both free throws, giving Cobden its largest lead, 59-48, with just over three minutes to play.

The Bulldogs needed to make something happen, and they had to do it quickly. They turned to their ace, Guy Lee Turner, who had carried them all season. Turner drove the baseline and scored a layup, drawing a foul on Kenny Flick. Turner made the bonus shot to trim Cobden's lead to eight. Jim Neal found an answer for the Appleknockers on their next possession and knocked down a jump shot, restoring their 10-point lead, 61-51.

The Bulldogs got the ball to Turner again, and he drove down the middle of the lane, again knocking into Kenny Flick. Cobden's players and fans thought Kenny had established position in the lane. They wanted a charging foul called on Turner. The crowd expressed its displeasure with a chorus of boos when the referee signaled a blocking foul against Kenny. It probably hadn't helped Kenny's case that after he was assessed a foul on the previous defensive play, he told the referee, Ford Peebles, exactly what he thought of his officiating. It wasn't complimentary. The normally soft-spoken senior had never mouthed off to an official before, but this was an important game – this was for the sectional title – so emotions were running high, and Kenny had made his feelings known. It was his fifth foul, and he exited the game with just over two minutes left. Turner made both foul shots as Harrisburg crept within eight points.

Coach Ruggles put Darrell back in the game to replace Kenny. The Appleknockers passed the ball around. They had the lead and were in no hurry to take a shot. Harrisburg couldn't afford to let Cobden stall. The Bulldogs had to get the ball back if they were going to cut into the lead. They tried to steal the ball but got whistled for a foul instead. Darrell went to the line and sank both free throws to put Cobden back up, 63-53. But Harrisburg and Turner weren't finished. He worked the ball inside time and again, drawing fouls on Cobden's defenders and going to the free-throw line. His tenacious play was taking a toll on Cobden. Kenny Smith fouled out with a minute and 15 seconds on the clock, making him the third Appleknocker starter to be sent to the bench. Coach Ruggles inserted Roy Witthoft into the game to take Kenny's place. A few moments later, Turner bullied his way into the lane again, and Jim Neal was charged with his fifth foul. He was forced to join the other three starters on the sideline.

Coach Ruggles looked down his bench for a replacement and this time he called Rodney Clutts' number. The sophomore was nervous about going into the game at such a critical juncture. He had played in a lot of games throughout the season, but it was usually when Cobden had a big lead and the victory was assured. Ruggles could see Rodney was tense.

"We've got the lead and there's just a minute to play," Ruggles told him as he stepped onto the court. "Relax. This is just like practice. Just hold onto the ball."

Harrisburg whittled away at Cobden's lead, but the Appleknockers played valiantly against the surging Bulldogs. Cobden still held a five-point advantage, 64-59, with 12 seconds on the clock when Turner was fouled and stepped to the free-throw line. He sank the first free throw to pull Harrisburg within four. He missed the second shot intentionally, hoping the Bulldogs would get the rebound. They did. Carl Reynolds grabbed the ball and dribbled around the key, desperately looking for an open shot. He launched a jumper from the top of the circle, and the ball dropped through the hoop with just three seconds remaining. Cobden's lead was down to two points. There was only enough time for the Appleknockers to inbound the ball. Roy Witthoft threw the ball in, and Jim Smith caught it and wrapped his arms around it, embracing it like a small child. He refused to let Harrisburg get possession of the ball, holding it until the final buzzer sounded. Cobden had won,

64-62! The Appleknockers claimed their first ever sectional championship.

The players jumped from the bench, hugging each other and Coach Ruggles.

"We won it! We won it!" Chuck yelled as his teammates tossed their warm-up jerseys high in the air.

The boys lifted Coach Ruggles onto their shoulders and took him on a victory ride. Cobden's fans were too excited to stay in their seats. They rushed onto the court to celebrate with the team. They watched the boys cut down the nets from the hoops and receive the large sectional championship trophy, brimming with pride at the accomplishment of their team.

Reporters followed the Appleknockers to their locker room. They interviewed Coach Ruggles and spoke with the players about their historic win. Photographers asked Ruggles and the boys to pose for some pictures. The boys held up the big trophy and the nets and smiled broadly for the cameras.

The press left after they got the stories and photos they wanted. When the team was alone, one of the boys shouted, "It's time!"

The players picked up Coach Ruggles and carried him to the showers. They pushed him into a stall and turned on the water, drenching him with the cold spray. The boys laughed heartily. Ruggles figured that this had become the boys' ritual after a big victory, and he didn't try to stop them. Instead, he had come prepared. Before he left for the game, he had packed a set of spare clothing to wear home.

While the Appleknockers celebrated in the dressing room, Cobden's fans still mingled on the court and throughout the gym. They basked in the atmosphere of victory and were in no hurry to leave. Fans and coaches from other schools in lower southern Illinois also lingered. There was a special feeling in the gym. Cobden's win represented more than a sectional championship. It showed that schools from the farthest end of the state were capable of playing with the best teams in the state – no matter where they hailed from. This was the second straight year that a team from lower southern Illinois advanced to the Sweet 16 of the state basketball tournament. Metropolis, a little town on the banks of the Ohio River in Massac County, had accomplished the feat last year, eventually making the Elite Eight.

In the past, teams from lower southern Illinois had been largely ignored in the state basketball polls. Even when a team compiled an impressive record, it was generally viewed as having played a weak schedule and not beaten a "proven" opponent. These victories by Cobden and Metropolis seemed to prove that teams in the far south were now a force to be reckoned with.

The following night, a pep rally was held in a field behind Cobden High School. A bonfire blazed as a large group of boosters celebrated the Appleknockers' sectional championship. The crowd not only consisted of students but also many of Cobden's adult residents. The basketball team's accomplishments had excited the whole town, and the rally gave the students and people in Cobden a chance to share in the team's success.

Several of the Ruggles' friends and neighbors were there, and Coach Ruggles could almost feel the affection oozing from the crowd as he enjoyed the rally with Mary and their children. He and his family had been welcomed so warmly when they had moved to Cobden nearly two years ago, and they really appreciated that. The school and townsfolk backed the team unconditionally. These victories probably meant as much to the town as they did to the team.

Coach Ruggles looked at the players assembled around the fire, their faces illuminated by the blue and orange flames. Some of the boys had brought their girlfriends, and others sat with their friends and classmates, chatting contentedly. They seemed relaxed and happy, not a care in the world. Ruggles was glad they were having a good time. Tonight was for fun and celebration. They still had plenty of work ahead of them, and he was quite certain they knew it. Even as he listened to the cheerleaders and Roger Burnett lead the crowd in cheers, his mind had already drifted to the super-sectional game coming up on Tuesday night.

🍎 Chapter 14

1964 Super-Sectional Game

Cobden's opponent in the super-sectional would be Pinckneyville. The Panthers had defeated Belleville Township, 69-61, in the sectional held at Pinckneyville. This was a mild upset since Belleville was ranked No. 12 in the final regular-season Associated Press poll and was picked by most to win. But the Panthers' win was certainly no big shock. Pinckneyville had been ranked in the polls during the year and was among the best teams in the state.

It had been a bad postseason for ranked teams. Of the 16 teams in the AP's final poll, only six survived regional and sectional play and made it to the Sweet 16. When the Sweet 16 was set, the AP ranked the remaining teams in the following order: 1. Collinsville (28-0), 2. Crane Tech (23-1), 3. Centralia (27-1), 4. Stephen Decatur (30-1), 5. Pekin (26-3), 6. Galesburg (23-3), 7. Pinckneyville (24-6), 8. Rockford Auburn (20-5), 9. Springfield Lanphier (22-6), 10. Rock Island Alleman (17-10), 11. Streator (24-6), 12. Evanston (17-7), 13. Cobden (29-2), 14. Glenbard East (23-6), 15. Bradley (20-7), 16. Arcola (25-5).

Coach Ruggles and the team were unconcerned with the Appleknockers' No. 13 ranking and had no problem being considered underdogs against Pinckneyville. After all, the favorites had not faired particularly well this year. The boys had no time to worry about where they were rated or what other people thought of them. They had to prepare for Pinckneyville.

The Panthers were a fast-moving team, paced by center Ben Louis who averaged more than 20 points per game. He was their tallest player, standing over 6-foot-3. Other than Louis, Pinckneyville didn't have a lot of size, but it had superb shooters, speed, and a great press defense. Coach Ruggles had seen the Panthers play during the regular season, and he knew the Appleknockers would have to slow them down to be successful.

At school on Monday, Coach Ruggles had the boys practice during lunch hour again. They ran through plays in their street clothes and sneakers for 30 minutes and then had a full practice after school. Ruggles wanted the players to be as prepared as possible. The boys had never played in a game of such significance. He wanted them to feel confident when they took the floor. The players willingly put in the extra time. They wanted to be ready.

That afternoon, the school received a telegram from Leon Sitter, a former Cobden coach from 1950 to 1956. He was now working at Arcola High School, a town in central Illinois established by the Illinois Central Railroad. The message read:

"Congratulations, Appleknockers, Cobden,
Illinoisans everywhere are proud of you.
I hope Cobden and Arcola can play in Champaign."

Arcola had beaten Champaign High School, 46-41, in the Champaign Sectional to reach the Sweet 16. Some of the players remembered Coach Sitter and thought it might be fun to play against his new school.

"We're not to Champaign yet," Coach Ruggles reminded them. "Let's get past Pinckneyville first. One game at a time."

A restlessness permeated Cobden High School on Tuesday. Tonight was the big game, and it was all anyone could think or talk about. If it had been difficult for the boys to focus on school on Friday, today it was impossible. At 2 p.m. the teachers finally gave up. The players were dismissed from classes and sent to the gym. They were standing around waiting for Coach Ruggles when Merle Jones, a sportswriter from the *Southern Illinoisan*, showed up. The boys recognized him from seeing his picture by his newspaper column. He was there to talk to Coach Ruggles, but when he saw the players, he stopped to chat.

Jones was a well-known sports writer. His column and articles were widely read in southern Illinois. Although the *Southern Illinoisan* was based in Carbondale, a town about 15 miles north of Cobden, he had covered the Appleknockers very little during the season. When he did write about Cobden, his comments were seldom flattering. He thought the Appleknockers were a nice bunch of boys, and Coach Ruggles had done a fine job as their coach, but in his judgment, Cobden had played a poor schedule and would be unable to compete against the larger schools. Even when Cobden beat Harrisburg to win the sectional championship, Jones considered the Appleknockers to be more lucky than good as he wrote in his column:

"The big Appleknockers performed as one might expect to see the state's only surviving district tournament winner perform. They would move to a good lead, then fall into a series of errors, which would allow Harrisburg to get close.

"Excessive and often needless fouls kept Ruggles from having his regular lineup on the court for much more than 10 minutes. The thing that saved the Appleknockers in the long run is that they made 11 straight free throws in the early part of the fourth quarter when they began to hold the ball against the pressing Bulldogs.

"The Appleknockers quit going to the basket in the hope that time would run out while they were still ahead. They just barely were saved by the bell."

In his most recent column that morning, Jones picked Pinckneyville to beat Cobden in the super-sectional. Some of the players had read the article, and they didn't appreciate his prediction.

"So you don't think we have a chance tonight, huh?" Jim Neal asked him.

All the players gathered around to hear his response.

"Well, I didn't say you don't have a chance," Jones said. "I just said Pinckneyville was favored to win."

"Tell you what," Jim Neal said with a mischievous grin.

"When we beat Pinckneyville tonight, don't come to our locker room unless you want your butt in the shower."

When the super-sectional tipped off on Tuesday night, the West Frankfort gym was overflowing. Supporters for Cobden and Pinckneyville had turned out in force to cheer on their teams in the important battle. More than 4,500 boisterous fans were there to watch the action, and in this gym the action was up close and personal. Bleachers surrounded the court, stopping just inches from the inbound line. Many people who were unable to attend the game sat at home near their radios to listen to the broadcast as it was beamed to the local stations.

At the start, both teams played cautiously. The players knew what was on the line, and the stress seemed to affect their rhythm. Two minutes elapsed before Jim Neal scored the first basket, a short jump shot, to get the Appleknockers on the scoreboard. Chuck followed that shot with a layup, giving Cobden a 4-0 lead. Pinckneyville scored the next five points, however, to go ahead by one. Jim Smith hit a 10-foot jump shot to get the lead back for Cobden, but Jon Bruns put the Panthers back on top with a jumper of his own. In the final minute and a half of the first quarter, Kenny Flick made layups on two straight possessions to push the Appleknockers' lead to 10-7. Ben Louis then dropped in a layup for Pinckneyville to bring the quarter to a close with Cobden leading, 10-9.

There was no scoring drought to start the second period. Cobden won the tip and 10 seconds into the action, Ben Louis fouled Chuck. Chuck made the free throw, giving Cobden an 11-9 lead. The lead did not last long as Pinckneyville got its up-tempo game going. The Panthers shot well from the outside, and with Kent Ragland doing most of the scoring, they grabbed an eight-point lead. With 11 seconds left, Bob Smith was fouled and sank two free throws, cutting Cobden's deficit to six points and making the halftime score, 26-20, in favor of Pinckneyville.

In the locker room, Coach Ruggles faced his team. The

boys had made a few mistakes, but Ruggles thought that was mostly due to nerves. They had shot poorly, hitting just 36 percent of their shots compared to Pinckneyville's 42 percent. His players were unaccustomed to being behind at halftime. But Ruggles thought they would be fine if they could control their emotions.

"We're all right," he told them. "We're down six, but we're okay. You're doing a good job on Louis, especially in the second quarter, but Ragland is hurting us. They're good shooters. We've got to go out quicker to contest their shots and make them drive. If they try to go inside, that's where we have the advantage."

With their coach's words in mind, the Appleknockers headed into the second half. The Panthers won the tip to begin the third quarter, and Kent Ragland knocked down a 20-foot jump shot to give them an eight-point lead. It was not the start Coach Ruggles was hoping for. He had just warned them about Ragland. Because of Cobden's size advantage, he always got aggravated when the Appleknockers lost the jump ball. Besides, he had just told the boys to close out faster and do a better job guarding Pinckneyville's shooters.

"Get to him quicker," he shouted from the bench.

Cobden's fans began to get anxious, but the players showed no outward signs of nerves. Jim Neal and Kenny Flick hit back-to-back jump shots to trim the lead to four points. The Appleknockers used their tough zone defense to force Pinckneyville to shoot from the outside while Cobden was able to work inside and score on high-percentage shots. Kenny Flick nailed a 15-foot jumper with 15 seconds remaining in the third period to give Cobden a 38-36 lead. Kent Ragland responded with a 20-footer 10 seconds later, and the score was tied at 38 at the end of the quarter.

Cobden controlled the tip to start the fourth quarter, and Kenny Smith hit a 10-foot jump shot to put the Appleknockers up, 40-38. Kenny Flick added a pair of free throws on the next possession to make the margin four, but Cobden was unable to hold the lead. The Panthers scored the next six points to go ahead by two, and the game was a seesaw battle throughout. Fans for both teams would cheer wildly when their team made a basket and then groan when the opposing team scored. As usual, Roger Peterman sat on Cobden's bench with his fingers crossed for good luck. They were really getting a workout tonight.

The players felt the tension, too. Tired and short of breath, Chuck called timeout and headed to the bench.

"Are you all right?" Coach Ruggles asked.

"I'm winded," Chuck replied. "I'll be okay. I just need a minute."

Chuck had missed a lot of conditioning prior to the season because of his injured knee, and he never felt his stamina was at the level it should be.

Roger handed Chuck a cup of water and draped a wet towel around his neck. Cobden's cheerleaders and fans looked on with concern, hoping nothing was seriously wrong.

"Maybe you should ask for another timeout," Coach Patterson said to Ruggles. "Give him a little more time to rest."

Ruggles agreed and took a second timeout.

When play resumed, Ruggles put Jim Neal in. He had been on the bench when the fourth quarter started due to his three fouls. Once back in the game, Jim got right to work. He scored two field goals and made a pair of free throws that gave Cobden a 54-52 lead with one minute and 20 seconds left to play. His defense out front was first-rate as he helped stop Pinckneyville's fast break. Cobden's zone defense pushed the Panthers out away from the basket, but Gary Decker had his outside stroke working, and he canned a 25-footer that tied the score at 54-all with one minute remaining. The Appleknockers threw the ball away on their next possession. It was one of the few turnovers they had committed. Cobden had been holding its own against Pinckneyville's famed press. The Panthers missed a shot, and Cobden regained control with just a few seconds left on the clock.

Coach Ruggles called a timeout to set up a last-second play. There was no time to break through Pinckneyville's press and dribble down the court for a good shot so he turned to Darrell Crimmins, one of his strongest players. Being a quality baseball pitcher, Darrell had a solid throwing arm and good aim. One day when the boys were shooting baskets before practice, he stood behind the baseline and threw the ball into the hoop at the opposite end of the floor. Ruggles knew Darrell could get the ball to the goal.

"When you throw the ball in, throw it high and long. Throw it to the basket," Ruggles told him. "We don't have much time, and the pass is quicker than the dribble."

Ruggles instructed Chuck, who was fully recovered by now, to stand at the foul line and told Kenny Flick to stand at the end line under Cobden's basket.

"When play starts, Flick, you break hard toward Chuck and set a screen to free him up. Chuck, I want you to roll toward the basket and look for the pass. Then when you catch the ball, lay it in. If you can't catch it, make sure you at least get a hand or finger on it. We have to touch it before it goes out of bounds."

If the ball went out of bounds without a Cobden player touching it, the clock wouldn't start. It would be a violation, and the Panthers would get the ball back under their own basket. With so little time left, that would give them a big advantage, and they would have a chance to score.

Coach Ruggles told Jim Neal and Kenny Smith to stay in the back court to try to draw a couple of Pinckneyville's defenders away from the basket.

"You guys are decoys back here," he explained. "Kenny, you can break toward Darrell like you're expecting him to throw you the ball but stay on this side of the court."

The referee handed Darrell the ball out in front of Cobden's bench. He blew the whistle, and Darrell saw his teammates waiting in their positions under the goal. He hoisted a high-arcing pass over the heads of the defenders. It was plenty long enough and was headed straight toward the basket. Unfortunately, the Panthers broke up the play. They blocked Chuck from getting positioned in the lane where he could catch the ball. Kenny Flick reached high in the air, and the ball went off the top of his outstretched fingertips and out of bounds. Pinckneyville inbounded the ball and threw up a long shot that missed its target. Time ran out with the score tied at 54. Overtime!

Pinckneyville wasted no time getting on the scoreboard as John Margenthaler buried a 20-foot jump shot just 10 seconds into the extra frame, but Chuck pulled the Appleknockers even at 56-all when he drained a pair of free throws. Ben Louis then struck for the Panthers, putting them up two points on a 10-foot jumper. Chuck again answered for Cobden. He worked inside the lane and put home a layup to tie the contest at 58-all with a minute and a half left to play. Both teams had scoring opportunities in the final minute but neither could connect, sending the game into double overtime.

The Panthers suffered a blow early in the second extra session. Gary Decker was chasing Bob as he dribbled down the court. Kenny Flick set a screen, and Decker ran into Kenny, picking up his fifth foul. The Appleknockers were relieved to see Decker go to the bench. His outside shooting had been killing them, especially in the second half. Kenny Flick missed his free throw, but Kenny Smith got the rebound and scored on 10-foot jump shot to put Cobden ahead by two. Kent Ragland still had the touch and drilled two long-range bombs, putting Pinckneyville back up, 62-60, with 50 seconds left.

The Pinckneyville fans erupted in joy, but Cobden's players seemed oblivious to the crowd's reaction. They calmly worked the ball around, searching for a good shot. With less than 20 seconds on the clock, Jim Neal caught a pass on the right baseline. He lofted the ball from about 12 feet, and it fell through the net, tying the game at 62. Chuck blocked a shot attempt by Gary Svanda, and the Panthers were unable to score. Triple overtime!

The game had turned into a battle of wills. Coach Ruggles and his players huddled together before the third overtime period began. He praised the defensive effort they had been giving throughout the game and encouraged them to keep it up. As he looked at the faces of the boys gathered around him, he knew his words were not necessary. He saw no fear or fatigue, only determination. He knew these young men were going to give it everything they had. They would leave it all on the court. Win or lose, he was proud of them.

There was a discussion going on at the scorer's table where an official was suggesting that the game be decided in sudden death with the first team to score being declared the winner. Coach Ruggles overheard part of the conversation and broke away from the huddle.

"We won't play sudden death," he informed the referees and scorekeeper. Ruggles was adamant. He had a bad memory about a sudden death overtime game that he had played in as a senior in high school. He wasn't going to let that happen again.

"We want to play the full overtime. We won't play sudden death," he told them again.

"Okay. That's fine, Coach," one of the referees said. "We were just discussing it, and we're going to play the full three minutes."

Satisfied, Coach Ruggles sent his players out on the floor.

The Appleknockers won the tip to start the third overtime. Jim Neal was fouled on a shot attempt and stepped to the free-throw line. *I don't care if we have to play 100 overtimes,* he thought, *we're not going to lose this game.* He sank both foul shots to give Cobden a two-point edge, but just seconds later Gary Svanda tossed in a shot to tie the game again. Bob was fouled on the Appleknockers' next possession and calmly made both free tosses, putting Cobden in front with one minute and 50 seconds left. Before Pinckneyville could take a shot, Chuck stepped in and intercepted the pass. Cobden regained the ball.

Coach Ruggles signaled for a timeout. In the huddle, he told the boys that they were now in the driver's seat.

"We've got the lead and the ball," he told them. "We have to play this smart. Take your time and make good passes. Look for a good shot. If they want the ball back, they'll have to come after us, and then we have to make free throws."

Kenny Smith threw the ball in, and Cobden worked down the court through Pinckneyville's defense. The Apple-knockers passed the ball around, draining time off the clock and looking for an open shot. Chuck caught a pass out near the half-court circle. Suddenly, the left side of the floor opened up. He spotted a clear path to the basket and drove in for a layup. The ball rolled into the basket, giving Cobden a 68-64 lead with a minute and 10 seconds to play.

Cobden's fans roared their approval. The cheerleaders and Roger Burnett cheered wildly. They hoped the Apple-knockers could hold this lead, but they knew the game was far from over.

The Panthers raced up the court. Time was their enemy now. John Margenthaler missed a shot from the right baseline, but Pinckneyville got the rebound and retained possession. The players worked the ball around, trying to penetrate Cobden's smothering defense. Margenthaler put up another shot. He missed, and Kenny Flick grabbed the rebound. Jon Bruns fouled him immediately, and Kenny walked to the free-throw line. There were 35 seconds on the clock, and he could put the game out of reach. He shot the free throw but the ball didn't drop, and the Panthers grabbed the rebound. They were still alive but just barely.

Once again, they hurried up the floor. Kent Ragland, who had already scored 24 points, took a long shot that missed its mark. Pinckneyville grabbed the rebound, but the Apple-knockers' defense wouldn't allow another clear shot. The

Panthers probed Cobden's scrappy zone unsuccessfully as the seconds ticked away. Finally, Ben Louis worked inside, and the Appleknockers allowed him to score unguarded right before the buzzer sounded. It was over! Finally! Cobden had won, 68-66! The Appleknockers were headed to Champaign and the Illinois High School Association State Basketball Tournament.

Cobden's fans streamed from the bleachers and onto the floor. Men and women, adults and students, celebrated the milestone victory. It seemed as if all of Cobden was there to share in the celebration, and the excitement multiplied with every win. Players, cheerleaders, and fans hugged one another and clapped their hands, reveling in the joy of the moment. Albert Flamm was among the Cobden fans who got swept up in the frenzy and scrambled down the bleachers. His foot got tangled in someone's coat lying in the stands, and he heard the material rip. He was too excited to stop and survey the damage. He kept right on going. Rushing onto the floor, he hugged every Cobden player he could find. He didn't even care that they were sweaty. Coach Ruggles found Mary, and they shared a quick embrace before they were jostled apart by the mob.

The players and fans corralled Coach Ruggles and raised him up on their shoulders. They carried him on a victory lap around the gymnasium, and he was happy to go along for the ride.

It took several minutes for the noise and excitement to ebb. The game had been incredibly close and intense. Both teams had played their hearts out, and the spectators respected the effort and execution displayed by the players. Fans were still buzzing around the court when the Appleknockers cut the nets down from the goals.

Still high on adrenaline, the players finally broke away from the crowd and headed to their locker room. As soon as Coach Ruggles walked in the door, the boys took a hold of him and pushed him into the shower room, dousing him with water. Although they had done it after the regional and sectional victories, they still found it hilarious and couldn't contain their laughter. Several reporters had followed the team, and one of them snapped a picture of Coach Ruggles as he emerged from the shower dripping wet.

Jim Neal noticed that Merle Jones from the *Southern Illinoisan* was among the group of reporters wanting to speak with Coach Ruggles. Jim thought about what he had said to Jones at school earlier in the day. Jim looked at the other boys and knew they remembered, too.

"Are you ready for a shower?" Jim Neal said to the reporter.

He grabbed a hold of one of Merle Jones's arms, and Kenny Smith grabbed the other. Jim Smith and Bob helped them half drag and half pull Jones toward the shower room. The other boys laughed and cheered on their teammates, ready to help. The players had Jones almost in shower when Coach Ruggles stepped in.

"Let him go, guys," Ruggles said. "Come on now. Let him go. He has a job to do, and he doesn't have a change of clothes."

The boys looked at each other, torn as to what to do. They really wanted to put Jones under the shower, but instead they listened to their coach and reluctantly released him.

"Sorry about that," Ruggles said to Jones. "They just got a little carried away."

Even though Ruggles apologized to the journalist, his main concern was not for Jones but for his players. The way the boys were horsing around, he was afraid one of them would turn an ankle or injure something, and they had more basketball to play. Truth be told, he would have liked seeing Jones soaked in the shower.

To Jones's credit, he was a good sport. "It's just kids being kids," he said, brushing off the incident. "No harm done."

The players showered and changed while Coach Ruggles talked to the reporters and answered their questions about Cobden's historic win and the Appleknockers' upcoming trip to the state tournament.

The ride home on the fan bus was raucous. The cheer-leaders and Roger Burnett led cheers all the way back to Cob-den. The long trip and the late hour did nothing to dampen the enthusiasm of the passengers who were still pumped up from the exciting game. Everyone sang and chanted Appleknocker cheers, yelling until their throats were hoarse.

The atmosphere on the players' bus was more sub-dued, but the boys were just as happy. As they rode back to the school, they thought about the game and what they had achieved. *We're going to the state tournament*, Kenny Smith thought. *We're really going to state.* It was something he had thought about since he had started playing basketball in junior high. He always believed that his team was good enough to play in the state tournament. He had even told people they were going to make it to state. Now it was truly happening, and he was even more excited than he had ever imagined.

The other boys were having similar thoughts. Jim Neal recalled what Coach Ruggles had told them at the first practice of the season back on October 1. He had said, "Gentleman, with a lot of hard work and a little luck, you have the talent to be playing basketball on the last day of basketball season next spring." Ruggles had believed they had the talent to go to state, and they believed it, too. Now here they were, headed to Champaign.

It was around midnight when the busses filled with players and fans got back to Cobden High School. Doris Gar-ner, the school's superintendent, told the players that they could report to school at 9 a.m. the next morning, an hour later than usual, to allow them to get a little extra sleep.

The players and other students headed home to get some much-needed rest, but the Appleknockers' adult fans were too keyed up to sleep. They were feeling good and many decided to go to Fuzzy's tavern to continue the celebration. When they entered the bar, they found a party already in full swing. Several fans who were unable to go to West Frankfort to attend the game had listened to it on the radio at Fuzzy's, and they had been celebrating ever since. After Cobden won, more fans crammed into the tavern and crowded on both sides of the bar that stretched nearly the full length of the building. Gray cigarette smoke hung thickly in the air, dimming the bar's neon lights.

It seemed as if the whole town was there, except for Coach Ruggles and Mary. The party seemed incomplete without the Ruggles there to share in the festivities so the fans decided to call them. Albert Flamm, the Ruggles' friend and former neighbor, got the coach on the phone.

"Hey, Coach," Albert said. "You and Mary are missing the party. Come on up to Fuzzy's and join us."

Mary had already put Randy and Kathy to bed so she couldn't go.

"Go on up," she said, encouraging her husband. "It's a special night, and you probably won't be able to sleep right now anyway."

Ruggles decided to go, and when he walked into Fuzzy's, everyone cheered, welcoming him like a conquering hero. They offered him free beers and treated him like a celebrity. People talked about how great the basketball team was and how proud they were of the boys. The fans started chanting, "Speech! Speech! Speech!"

Ruggles wasn't sure what everyone wanted to hear, but there were too many people there to refuse. At their insistence, he finally climbed up on a table, and the place grew quiet, waiting to hear what he had to say.

"So did any of you happen to catch the game tonight?" he asked with mock innocence.

The place howled with laughter at his little joke.

"No, seriously," he said. "I guess all it takes to get a free beer around here is to win a super-sectional."

There was more laughter, and then Coach Ruggles got serious.

"I want to thank all of you for supporting the team all year. I don't have to tell you what a fine group of young men are on this team. They're good students and hard workers, and we're going to go to Champaign to show everyone what it means to be an Appleknocker."

Everyone applauded and whistled as Ruggles got down from the table, and the party continued. The fans seemed reluctant to go home. The night had a magical feel to it, and no one wanted to break the spell.

People went to Fuzzy's that night who had never been there before. The Appleknockers had brought the townspeople together like nothing else in recent memory. Whether they were sports fans or not, the folks in Cobden were behind their basketball team 100 percent. For much of the season, there had been two factions in town. One believed that the team had the ability to win the state championship if they played their best. The other thought the team was great, but they probably couldn't compete with teams from larger schools. While there may have been some people who still subscribed to the latter school of thought, it would have been very difficult to find anyone in Cobden who doubted the Appleknockers on that night.

At school the next day, the students talked about nothing but the dramatic win. They found it difficult to settle down. No one felt like studying, including the teachers. When the players arrived at school at 9 a.m., the entire student body congregated in the assembly room on the second floor. The players entered and received a loud round of applause from their classmates. Coach Ruggles spoke on behalf of the team.

"We want to thank you for all the support you've shown us all season," Ruggles said to the students and teachers. "We really appreciate it. Your support has been a big help to us. We're going to do the best we can in Champaign to represent Cobden in a positive manner and win as many games as possible."

Mr. Garner announced that some telegrams had been

sent to the school, congratulating the players on their victory and wishing them good luck. In a fine display of sportsmanship, Harry F. Quillman, the principal at Pinckneyville High School, sent a message that read:

"Coach Ruggles and Team
Bring the big trophy to southern Illinois.
We are with you all the way."

Another telegram came from Hebron High School in northern Illinois. In 1952, Hebron had an enrollment of less than 100 students when its basketball team won the state title by defeating Quincy, 64-59, in overtime. It was the only district school to claim a state basketball championship. As Cobden moved along the tournament trail, people had started comparing the two schools because of their size.

When the assembly was over, the students drifted back to their classrooms, but everyone knew there wouldn't be much studying going on. The basketball players were excused from classes. The local radio station in Anna invited them down for an interview. Coach Ruggles had several things to take care of so he stayed at school, and Coach Patterson went with the team to the station.

After seeing the players off and reminding them to behave like gentlemen, Ruggles went back to his little office by the gym to get to work. Unlike the boys, he had arrived at school early that morning to make plans for the state tournament. He found out that Galesburg had defeated Springfield Lanphier, 79-66, in the super-sectional at Springfield. The Galesburg Silver Streaks would be the Appleknockers' opponent in the quarter-finals on Friday in Champaign. He had never seen Galesburg play so he had no idea what to expect.

He called some friends and coaches who were familiar with Galesburg to gather information on the team. The Pinckneyville coaches had scouted Galesburg, and they were kind enough to give him their scouting report. He also spoke with his former teammate at SIU, Don Hepler, who had agreed to scout the Silver Streaks for him. Ruggles had prepared his players for every game they had played this season, and he believed Cobden could compete with any team as long as the boys were prepared.

As the day wore on, Ruggles switched from scouting to other tasks. He had to make travel arrangements and also line up a place for the team to practice in Champaign. Then there was the media; reporters from local newspapers showed up at school to talk to him. He also received phone calls from sportswriters with papers as far north as Chicago and Rockford, and all points in between. The Appleknockers qualifying for the state tournament was an unprecedented event, and the press was eager to cover the story. Ruggles told the reporters that he anticipated a good showing by his team in Champaign.

"We have gained more confidence with each game," he told one of the reporters. "We don't know much about Galesburg, but we'll give them a battle."

Ruggles' next statement indicated his concern about the challenge of the upcoming tournament.

"The only thing that worries me is that the boys seem a little tired today," he said. "I know the boys are in shape, but they are all big boys and just youngsters. If we should play two games on Saturday, I won't know what to expect."

Once he had dealt with the reporters, Coach Ruggles went back to his preparations for the tournament. The Illinois High School Association arranged the lodging and assigned the Appleknockers to the Paradise Inn, a hotel a few miles south of the tournament site. Champaign was 220 miles north of Cobden, and transporting the team that distance would be no easy task. Ruggles and Mr. Garner discussed the travel options and both thought that taking the train was the best choice. Passenger trains no longer stopped in Cobden, but after several phone calls, officials with the Illinois Central Railroad agreed to make a special stop. The company's No. 8 "Creole" passenger train would stop in Cobden and pick up the team before 11 a.m. the next day and take the players to Champaign. The company even said it would bring the Appleknockers back to Cobden on Sunday morning when the tournament was over.

Coach Ruggles and Mr. Garner were still working out the details when Ruggles got another phone call. This one was from Mary.

"Honey, are you busy?" Mary asked.

Although he had been going nonstop since early that morning, he was never too busy for his wife, and he knew she wouldn't be calling if it wasn't important. "No, what's going on?"

"It's Randy," she said. "He was playing out in the yard with Rusty Flamm, and I went inside to answer the phone. I was only gone a moment, but Randy came in with a pretty bad cut under his eye. I'm afraid it may need stitches. Can you come and take a look at it?"

"Sure. I'll be right there," he said, putting down the phone.

Ruggles repeated to Mr. Garner what Mary had told him and said he would be back as soon as possible. The superintendent told him that he hoped Randy was all right and to take as much time as he needed. Mr. Garner said he would work out the remaining logistics.

When Coach Ruggles got home, he checked out Randy's cut. It was still bleeding quite a bit, and he thought they better take him to the doctor. Rusty's mom, Carolyn, their good friend, was already there. She apologized for Rusty's involvement in the incident, but both Coach Ruggles and Mary said the apology was unnecessary. When kids play together, accidents happen and there was no need to place blame. Carolyn babysat Kathy while Coach Ruggles and Mary took Randy to the doctor in Carbondale.

Young Randy was a real trooper while his doctor cleaned the wound and closed the gash with a row of stitches. The doctor covered the stitches with a bandage and said Randy was fortunate that the cut wasn't a little higher; otherwise it might have damaged his eye. As it was, he was going to be just fine and the stitches would come out in a week.

Coach Ruggles and Mary thanked the doctor for seeing them on such short notice. He told them it was no problem.

"One more thing," he said as they left the office. "Good luck at the state tournament."

When Coach Ruggles got back to school, the players had returned from the radio station and were in the gym lobby, huddled around a radio listening to a delayed recording of their victory over Pinckneyville.

"Hey, movie stars," Ruggles called out to the boys. "Let's not get too full of ourselves. We still have work to do."

The boys laughed and went to the locker room to change into their practice clothes, and then Ruggles led them through a light workout. He thought some of them had seemed tired that morning so he wanted to take it easy.

After practice, Ruggles told them about the arrangements that had been made for the state tournament. He said the train was going to stop in Cobden tomorrow and take them to Champaign. He asked the boys to pack practice attire and enough street clothes to last through the weekend and to be at the downtown depot by 10 a.m.

"Do we have to take our own basketball?" Roger Peterman asked.

Some of the boys laughed at his question, but then realized none of them really knew the answer.

"I'm sure the balls will be provided for the games," Ruggles said. "But it might not be a bad idea to bring one to use when we practice."

He put Roger in charge of bringing the basketball and then dismissed the boys with orders to rest and get a good night's sleep.

While Ruggles was making plans for his team, the school board was dealing with the all-important issue of tickets for the tournament. People kept calling the school to find out how to obtain tickets for the big event. H.R. Clutts and Doc Neal had driven to Champaign early that morning to pick up the tickets allotted to Cobden. Garner told the ticket seekers that when Doc and H.R. returned, the tickets would be available at the bank. He said the school had requested 1,000 tickets, but it was unclear how many they would get.

Doc Neal and H.R. got back to Cobden late Wednesday evening with only about a third of the tickets they had hoped to receive. Assembly Hall holds more than 16,000 people, but only 4,500 seats were saved by the IHSA for the four schools playing in each session. Each school received a minimum of 300 tickets regardless of size. The remaining 3,300 tickets were allocated based on enrollment. The Appleknockers were in the afternoon session with Galesburg, Evanston, and Stephen Decatur. Those schools had enrollments of 1,750, 4,100, and 1,600 students, respectively. With a student body of just 147, Cobden was a mere fraction of their size and received only 370 tickets.

The men knew this wouldn't be enough to meet the needs of everyone who was requesting tickets. The school had gotten 825 tickets for the super-sectional, and fans had purchased every one of them. Although Cobden's population was only around 900, many people from the surrounding area were now supporting the Appleknockers. Doc and H.R. asked for additional tickets, but the IHSA had to follow its disbursement policy and couldn't give anymore.

The school board members had asked the bank to sell the tickets on Thursday. Since there was such a limited number, they decided to offer them to the students and their parents first. They thought that was the fairest way to dispense them. Then if any tickets remained, the bank could open the sale to the general public.

🍎 Chapter 15

On to State

Light spilled through the window of Chuck's room on Thursday morning and woke him from a fitful sleep. He had tried to sleep like it was any other night but his subconscious betrayed him, and he kept waking up. *We're going to state today*, he thought, feeling a mixture of excitement and apprehension. He had gone to the state tournament as an observer a year ago, but this time was going to be very different. He was going to do more than watch this year. He and his teammates were going to actually play.

A similar scene played out in the bedrooms of the other players as they woke up, anticipating what awaited them in Champaign. And it wasn't only the players. Practically everyone in Cobden found it hard to get a good night's sleep. They were all involved in the trip to state in some way. No one wanted to miss seeing the Appleknockers compete in the state tournament, and the fans were busy scheduling their own trips to Champaign.

People rushed to the bank early on Thursday morning to get tickets, and by the time the bank opened, a long line had formed. With so few tickets available, fans snapped them up in a matter of minutes. As feared, there weren't enough to satisfy everyone who wanted to attend. Many people left the bank disappointed but vowed to go to Champaign anyway and try to get tickets at the box office at Assembly Hall.

Hotel rooms in Champaign proved almost as hard to get as tickets. The tournament drew spectators from throughout Illinois and the surrounding states, and most hotels were booked solid. But Cobden's fans were undeterred. Nothing was going to stop them from following their team. A large contingent of supporters contacted a former Cobden resident named Melvin Lockard. He was now a banker in Mattoon, a town about 50 miles south of Champaign. They told him they were looking for rooms to rent for the weekend, and he arranged accommodations at a Mattoon hotel for several people from Cobden.

Jim Smith's dad, Clyde, didn't have to worry about finding a place to stay in Champaign. He worked for Otteson Mobile Homes in Carbondale, and when his boss, Gene Otteson, found out that the Appleknockers were going to state, he was thrilled. Jim worked part-time for Gene on the weekends, and Gene was fond of him. Gene knew Clyde would be attending the tournament, and he offered him the use of one of the company's campers. Clyde and his wife, Geneva, gladly accepted. The camper was nice. It could carry six to eight people comfortably so they invited Cecil and Lucille Smith, Kenny Smith's parents, to go with them. Lucille went to all of her son's games, but Cecil had little interest in sports and never went to the games. The Appleknockers were causing such a sensation now, however, that even Cecil had gotten caught up in the excitement, and he and Lucille decided to join them.

The residents of Cobden had heard that the train was going to make a special stop in town to pick up the players and take them to Champaign. Many of them gathered at the depot, along with the grade school and high school students, to give the players a big sendoff. The Cobden High School band was on hand in full uniform, providing musical accompaniment for the rally.

When Coach Ruggles and the boys arrived at 10 a.m., a large crowd met them. Many of the students wore white t-shirts, and they asked the players to autograph them. The boys were flattered by the outpouring of support from the townspeople and their classmates, but they thought it was kind of funny that the other kids wanted their autographs. *This is unbelievable*, they thought as they made their way through the crowd to the station platform. All the people made the boys increasingly aware of what a big deal going to state was, not only to the school, but the entire community.

Store owners prepared to close their businesses the next day. Mayor Frank Petty proclaimed Friday to be "Appleknocker Day" in Cobden. A sign in a window at the bank warned, "The bank will close all day Friday to let employees follow the team. Also Saturday if necessary. We will be open until 4:30 p.m. Thursday to accommodate your needs."

Coach Ruggles and the players weren't thinking that far ahead. They knew they had to take the tournament one game at a time, and their first challenge was Galesburg. Several reporters showed up at the train station, and they asked Coach Ruggles about the matchup with the Silver Streaks.

"I am confident that we can compete with Galesburg from what I have heard about them if we battle them on the boards and stop their fast break," Ruggles told the press. "We did a good job against Pinckneyville, and they play the same way."

The Illinois Central Railroad's "Creole" train came to a halt at the station, and the team began boarding. Coach Ruggles was taking Mary and Randy with him to Champaign. They went to all the games and were his biggest supporters. His family meant more to him than anything else in the world, and he was glad they would be at the tournament to share in the experience. Unfortunately, Kathy wasn't going to make the trip. She was turning a year old the following day, and he and Mary thought she was just too young to go. They decided to leave her with Mary's parents.

Roger Peterman, the manager, Roger Burnett, the mascot, Coach Jack Lamer, and Donald Ballance, the gentleman who had been keeping the scorebook for the Appleknockers during postseason play, were all riding up on the train with the players. Coach Patterson planned to travel with the cheerleaders to the tournament the next day and join Ruggles and the team on Friday.

Once all the riders and their luggage were aboard, the train pulled out of the small depot shortly after 10:30 a.m. amid exuberant cheers and with the band playing. More than a dozen people climbed onto the roof of the station for a better vantage point. A few even crawled to the roof's pitch to watch the train cut a path through the thick forest that blanketed the northern edge of Cobden and begin its 220-mile journey to Champaign.

As the boys settled into their seats, they had a hard time hiding their apprehension. Coach Lamer was as nervous as the players and didn't even bother to find a seat. He was restless and walked to the back of the train to look out at the countryside. Like the train he was riding on, spring was moving through the area, pushing out the drab grays and browns of winter and bringing warmth and color to the land. He watched as Cobden became smaller and more distant until the town finally disappeared from view when the train rounded a bend in the tracks.

Coach Lamer had been to every state basketball tournament since 1951 but had never looked so forward to one like this before. When he coached these boys in junior high, he knew they were going to be good in high school, but he had no inkling they would make it to state. It was so rare for a team from such a little school in a little town to make it. But here they were, on their way to the tournament. *It couldn't have happened to a finer group*, he thought. They were good boys from good families, and he was proud to be associated with them. The "Creole" glided past Carbondale before he was finally able to sit down.

The train rolled along on its trip northward through the Illinois prairie, and the passengers soon realized that this would be no ordinary ride. Mary looked out the window and saw a farmer, standing in the middle of a field and holding up a sign that read, "Go Appleknockers."

Coach Ruggles sat beside her, looking at the scouting reports he had gotten on Galesburg and working on a game plan. Mary nudged him.

"Honey, look at that," she said, pointing out the window.

He saw the sign and then looked at his wife with a bewildered smile. "How'd he know we were going to be coming by?" he asked.

The farmer wasn't the only one who knew the Appleknockers' schedule. The boys saw several more people holding similar signs of encouragement as the train passed by other fields and through small towns. The folks in southern Illinois had gotten behind Cobden during its postseason run, and they were really pulling for the Appleknockers. Their visible show of support added to the players' enthusiasm, and some of the players waved out the windows as a way to thank their unknown supporters.

The boys thoroughly enjoyed the train ride. For some of them, the trip marked their first time on a train. The passenger car was spacious and comfortable and gave them plenty of room to spread out. This was particularly important for Cobden's tall players who required a lot of leg room. One aspect of train travel didn't impress Kenny Flick, however. He went to the snack car to buy a soda and found that they cost twice as much on the train as they did in the grocery store. As a young man with a family, he knew the value of a dollar. He was never loose with his money and returned to his seat without a drink.

The players talked anxiously among themselves, musing about what the state tournament would be like and the fact that they were going to be playing basketball on TV.

"Remember last year when we told Coach Ruggles we'd be going to state?" Chuck asked as he sat down by Kenny Smith. "Can you believe we made it?"

"Yeah, I can believe it," Kenny said. "That was our goal...but I wish Tom was here with us."

"I know," Chuck said. "I think about him all the time, not just during basketball season either."

"Me, too, but it really hurts sometimes," Kenny admitted.

Chuck stared out the window a few moments before responding.

"I know," he said.

Kenny knew that Chuck was one of the few people who understood. The two of them were linked forever by that terrible event that had claimed their friend's life. They rarely talked about that horrific day. It was just too painful, but it was never far from their thoughts. They both wished desperately that there was a way to go back and change what happened.

"You know, I think Tom is happy we're going to state," Chuck said after the two of them had ridden in silence for awhile. "I think he helped us get this far."

"I want to win this tournament for him," Kenny said.

"I do, too," Chuck said, and they shook on it.

When the train made a stop in Arcola, a town about 38 miles south of Champaign, the Appleknockers received a warm and noisy welcome. More than 100 screaming fans and two fire engines with their sirens wailing greeted the team. A large banner declared: "Arcola Backs Cobden All The Way."

After Arcola High School's run at the state title ended at the hands of Stephen Decatur in a super-sectional game on Tuesday night, the 280-student school had "adopted" Cobden as its choice to win the tournament. Arcola felt a connection to Cobden since its superintendent, Leon Sitter, had gone to school in Cobden, and he and his wife, Patricia, had both worked at the school. Mrs. Sitter had even taught some of the boys when they were in junior high. In a show of support, the Arcola basketball coach, Bob Avery, and several of the Purple Riders basketball players boarded the train and rode with the Appleknockers for a few miles.

Cobden's and Arcola's players were strangers, but they had basketball in common so they found plenty to talk about as they discussed their respective seasons. Arcola had a great year, going 25-6 and winning regional and sectional championships. The team had hoped to make it to state and have a chance to play in Assembly Hall, but had fallen just short. Coach Avery and his players hopped off the train when it stopped in the town of Tuscola. They said goodbye and wished the Appleknockers the best of luck.

With their visitors gone, the boys became more contemplative as the train rumbled out of the station toward their final destination. Their conversations with the players from Arcola reminded them of how fragile success in tournament play could be, and they recognized how truly fortunate they were to be one of only eight teams in all of Illinois to be playing in the state tournament. Their game with Pinckneyville had taken three overtimes to be decided. It could have gone either way, and they knew they were fortunate to have come out on top. Bob Smith felt his heartbeat quicken as the train approached Champaign. He had no idea what to expect at the tournament, and he began to feel nervous. *Can we really compete with all the big schools?* he wondered.

Thirty minutes after leaving Tuscola, the "Creole" pulled to a stop at the station in Champaign. When the Appleknockers emerged from the train, they were met by a legion of reporters, cameramen, and curious basketball fans. Newspapers all over the state had reported on Cobden's victory over Pinckneyville, and their readers were fascinated by stories about the big team from the small southern Illinois town. Many people had turned out to get a look at the boys for themselves. If they had been skeptical about the heights reported for the players, they soon saw that the Appleknockers were as tall as advertised.

The group from Cobden carried their luggage out to the platform at the depot. None of them had known what to expect when they reached their destination, and they were surprised that there were so many people there to see them. They were also surprised by the weather. It had been short-sleeve weather down in Cobden when they had boarded the train, but now a gunmetal gray sky in Champaign was spitting snow. The players pulled their letter jackets tightly around them to ward off the chill.

The sports reporters approached Coach Ruggles and began asking questions about the team. The photographers snapped some candid pictures of the boys and then asked if they could set up some shots.

"Hey, Coach," one of the photographers said. "Can I get a picture of you and few of your boys here on the platform?"

The man pointed to some crates, indicating that he wanted Ruggles and the boys to sit on them. He noticed one of the players had a chessboard.

"Let's have a few of you here playing chess," the man said.

The photographer must have seen the hesitation in Coach Ruggles' eyes.

"Come on. Our readers love these kinds of pictures," the man explained. "They show how you passed the time on the train, and they show people that you're just a bunch of regular guys with interests outside of basketball."

"Okay," Coach Ruggles said. He had never brought a team to state before, and he was willing to go along with the photographer's suggestions.

Darrell Crimmins had brought the chessboard because he and Chuck played together quite a bit. He, Chuck, and Roy Witthoft were recruited to join Coach Ruggles in the picture. The photographer moved the boys around and finally settled on a shot where Chuck and Roy were playing a simulated, good-natured game of chess while Darrell and Ruggles looked on with simulated interest.

Mike Basler, who operated the feed store in Cobden, and school board member H.R. Clutts had agreed to drive to Champaign and meet the boys at the station. They were going to chauffeur the Appleknockers while they were at the tournament. Mike and H.R. arrived a few minutes after the boys had gotten off the train, but they had no trouble spotting them among the crowd of reporters. They made their way to the platform to let Coach Ruggles know they were there.

When Coach Ruggles saw them, he excused himself.

"I've got to get my boys to the hotel," he told the press.

"How was the trip?" H.R. asked Coach Ruggles.

"Well, we all made it in one piece," he said.

They loaded their luggage in the trunks of Mike's and H.R.'s cars, but it soon became apparent that two cars weren't going to be enough to transport the whole gang and their gear to the Paradise Inn. Lee Patterson was coming up the next day and would also drive the players around, but right now they only had the two cars. They began discussing their options and were thinking of calling for a taxi when a man, who had overheard their conversation, offered a solution.

"I've got a station wagon," the man said. "I can carry several people, and I'll be glad to take you to your hotel."

"Are you sure?" Coach Ruggles asked, a little surprised that a total stranger would be so generous.

"Yes," the man said. "It would be my pleasure to drive the Appleknockers."

Coached Ruggles gratefully accepted. He made sure Mike and H.R had directions to the hotel, and then everyone found seats in the cars. Kenny Flick, Kenny Smith, Jim Neal, and Bob Smith climbed in with Mike. Darrell Crimmins, Rodney Clutts, Roger Garner, Roger Peterman, and Roy Witthoft squeezed into H.R.'s car. The remaining players got into the station wagon with Coach Ruggles, Mary, young Randy, Roger Burnett, Jack Lamer, and Donald Ballance.

Mike pulled out of the parking lot, followed by the man in the station wagon and then H.R. As the procession of cars headed down the street, several vehicles carrying reporters fell in line behind them. The press was going to their hotel, too, because they wanted to gather more stories about the Appleknockers.

As Mike drove through downtown Champaign, he got separated from the cars behind him when he made it through a traffic light that turned red before the others went through.

"Well, we've lost your friend," the man driving the station wagon remarked to Coach Ruggles. "But I can probably catch him."

"Don't worry about it," Ruggles said. "He knows where he's going."

"It's no worry," the man replied, flipping on a siren. "I'm a funeral director."

The gentleman stepped on the gas and slapped a flashing light on the top of his station wagon. All of a sudden the little motorcade resembled a parade, barreling through the middle of the city. All Coach Ruggles could do was look at Mary and shrug as they sped down the street.

In a few minutes, the passengers in the station wagon heard another siren. A policeman had pulled alongside and was signaling for the car to pull over. *Oh no*, Coach Ruggles thought. *What have we gotten into now?* The driver did as the officer requested and maneuvered to the side of the street.

"What's going on?" the policemen asked, obviously confused as he peered into the funeral director's window and saw his passengers.

"These are the Cobden Appleknockers," the funeral director replied. "They needed a ride, and I'm taking them to their hotel."

The officer was a basketball fan so he leaned in for a closer look.

"I've heard all about you Appleknockers," he said. "You're up here for the tournament."

"That's right," the funeral director said. "They just got off the train."

"Where are you staying?" the cop asked.

"The Paradise Inn," the funeral director piped up again. He had apparently appointed himself the spokesman for the team.

"I understand you need to get them to their hotel," the policeman said. "But you can't use your light and siren just to haul a basketball team."

The funeral director apologized and removed the light

from the roof of his vehicle. The officer didn't issue any citations or warnings. He just sent them on their way with a little advice.

"Slow down a little," the policeman said. "You want to get them there safely."

Mike and his passengers got to the hotel before the others so they waited in the parking lot for the rest of their party to arrive. Coach Ruggles had the information they needed to check in, and they wondered what was taking him so long. Some of the reporters who were at the train station had followed them to the hotel, and they came over to talk to the boys.

A photographer convinced Kenny Flick, Kenny Smith, and Jim Neal to stand beside a tree at the edge of the parking lot and hold apples up to the branches as if they were picking the fruit. The tree branches were still bare of leaves, but the boys played along, laughing at the thought of picking apples in the spring, and not the fall, while the man snapped their picture.

H.R. pulled into the lot and parked beside Mike. The boys scrambled out of his car to see what their teammates were doing. No one wanted to miss a thing.

"Where's Coach Ruggles?" Mike asked H.R. "He was right behind me."

H.R. tried to stifle a grin.

"The last I saw of him, a policeman had pulled over his car. I guess if he doesn't get here soon, we'll have to find out where the police station is."

"He got pulled over?" Mike asked in disbelief.

"Yeah, that man with the station wagon put on a flashing light and a siren and took off through town. I could hardly keep up with him until that cop stopped him."

Mike and H.R. both started laughing. By the time Coach Ruggles arrived, all the players and sportswriters had heard about his car being detained by the police. Ruggles had a sheepish grin on his face as he looked out the window at the people waiting for him. He could tell the whole group had enjoyed a good laugh at his expense. He saw the reporters and thought, *I hope this doesn't make the papers.*

Ruggles got out of the station wagon and held up his arms. "Look everyone, no handcuffs," he announced with a smile. "No one got arrested. No harm done."

Now that everyone was accounted for, they checked in, and the boys paired off and took their luggage to their rooms. It was early afternoon, and the players had no problem letting Coach Ruggles know that they were hungry and ready to eat. The Paradise Inn had a restaurant so Ruggles told them to go in and get a sandwich and then he was taking the whole group to see Assembly Hall, the venue for the state tournament.

After everyone finished eating, they loaded back into the cars to go to Assembly Hall. The funeral director had stayed and volunteered to drive some of the players. He also promised he would watch his speed and not use his siren. It had been a long train ride, but the boys felt no weariness from their travels. They were all too excited about this adventure to think about rest. They stared out the car windows, taking in their surroundings as they rode back into Champaign and onto the campus of the University of Illinois.

The sky was clearing and a hint of sun shone through the clouds and glinted off the dome of Assembly Hall as the Cobden crew approached the colossal edifice. *That's the biggest darn building I ever saw*, Jim Neal thought as the building came into view and his nerves tingled.

To some of the players, the big arena resembled a futuristic spacecraft or a giant mushroom. Two concrete bowls placed face-to-face made up the mushroom's cap and a solid bank of vertical windows looked like the short, thick stem.

Open only a year, the arena had cost $8.3 million to construct and was an engineering marvel. Assembly Hall was billed as one of the world's largest edge-supported structures and had no interior supports or pillars. Instead, 614 miles of steel wire circled the dome, holding the structure together at its base.

The arena was virtually empty as a building custodian led Coach Ruggles and the boys through an entrance that opened onto the second-level concourse. Ruggles knew the huge arena could be intimidating, and he wanted to bring the players so they could see the layout before they had to play a game there the next day. He turned to look at the boys and saw them standing with their eyes open wide and their mouths agape. Only Chuck, Darrell, and Roy had been to the arena before, and he could tell the others were clearly in awe.

Oh no, Ruggles thought. *They're going to get scared.* The players were being too quiet, and Ruggles knew he had to think of something to say.

"Boys, it's the same size as our floor at home, just a little bit longer," he told them. "Don't worry about it. Just play like you have all year."

In truth, Ruggles didn't know how the boys would respond when they stepped on the court to face Galesburg. They were used to playing in small gyms, and this was a completely new environment. He wondered how they would handle the pressure that came with playing in the state tournament.

"Go ahead," Ruggles told the players. "Explore a bit."

He wanted the boys to become familiar with the vast hall so tomorrow at game time they could relax – if that was possible – and play ball.

Following their coach's suggestion, some of the boys ran all the way to the top of the arena. At its peak, Assembly Hall rose 128 feet above the center of the floor and could hold 16,128 people. Bob stood on the highest level, gazing 400 feet across to the other side.

"You could stack a lot of hay in here," he said, getting a laugh from the other boys.

"You'd need binoculars to see someone sitting on the other side," Jim Smith observed.

Chuck gazed out at the same massive expanse and then

looked down at the court far below. *Coach Ruggles is right*, he told himself, calming his nerves. *The court is basically the same size as ours.*

The boys raced back down to the ground level of the arena, growing more excited with each step. They were actually going to get to play ball in this amazing building. It still seemed unbelievable. The custodian who had let them in took them to see the locker room they would be using for their game the next day. To the boys' surprise, the locker room was as small as the arena was big. It was smaller than the dressing room at Cobden's gym. Jokingly, they wondered if tournament officials had given them such a small room to make them feel at home.

After taking time to check out Assembly Hall, the group drove over to Champaign High School. Teams were not permitted to practice in Assembly Hall so Coach Ruggles had made arrangements for his team to workout at Champaign High's gymnasium. While on the train, Ruggles had devised a game plan for Galesburg based on the scouting reports he had gotten from various sources. He walked the boys through some plays that he thought would be effective in their game with the Silver Streaks. The players ran through drills and then had a short scrimmage. Ruggles just wanted them to work up a sweat and get the kinks out from sitting on the train for so long.

Forty to 50 students from Champaign High gathered in the gym to watch the Appleknockers practice. They had read about Cobden's unlikely victory over Pinckneyville and had heard that the Appleknockers were going to be using their gym. Even though school had dismissed for the day, several kids stayed around to see the team play.

The students weren't the only ones showing an interest in the team's practice. The press, who had followed the Appleknockers to their hotel, had now come to the gym. They snapped several pictures of the players and scribbled furiously in their notebooks about the team's personnel. For many of the reporters, this was the first time they had seen Cobden on a basketball court. They were trying to figure out who was who and acquaint themselves with the players' names and the positions they played. With all the Smiths and Neals on the team, this was no easy task. The Appleknockers also had an unorthodox starting lineup with four players 6-foot-5 or above. For those unfamiliar with the team, it was difficult to tell the difference between the boy who played guard and the one who played center. Coach Ruggles was fine with having the reporters around as long as they didn't create a distraction and interfere with what he was trying to accomplish with the players.

Lee Cabutti, the basketball coach at Champaign High, had agreed to let the Appleknockers use his gym. He stood on the sidelines as Coach Ruggles put the boys through their paces.

"Just look at that. Four guys 6-foot-5 or better from a town of 900," Cabutti said to a reporter, shaking his head. "I'm going to get some of those Cobden dads to tell the fathers up here what they feed their kids. We have more than 50,000 people and can't get one guy as tall as any of theirs."

The workout helped the players loosen up like Coach Ruggles had hoped, and it got their minds focused on basketball. That was the reason they were here, and he wanted them to start thinking about Galesburg. Before going back to their hotel, they stopped at a steakhouse for supper. Ruggles wanted the boys to have plenty of protein in their diets, and the players happily obliged. The school was paying the expenses of the trip, and since the players didn't have to worry about money, they ordered and ate some of the finest steaks they had ever had. Ruggles shook his head and grinned as he watched the boys eat. Their appetites never ceased to amaze him. *If we're up here too long*, he thought, *the school might go broke on the meals alone.*

When they got back to the Paradise Inn, the basketball team from Pinckneyville was checking in. Although the Panthers had lost to Cobden in the super-sectional, the players and coaches had come to Champaign to watch the state tournament. By coincidence, they ended up staying at the same hotel as the Appleknockers. Coach Ruggles was afraid the situation might be a little awkward since Pinckneyville had lost to Cobden on Tuesday night. But the gang from Pinckneyville was very cordial, and they wished the Appleknockers good luck in the tournament. Cobden was carrying the banner for the schools from the southern end of the state, and Pinckneyville wanted them to represent the area well.

More reporters found out where the Appleknockers were staying, and they rushed to the hotel seeking interviews. Most of the sportswriters from northern Illinois had never even heard of Cobden until the team beat Pinckneyville earlier that week. Now they all wanted to talk to the "Little David" team about its chances at state. The unfamiliarity with the Appleknockers led to a humorous moment for one reporter from a Chicago newspaper. He struck up a conversation with Jack Lamer and began questioning him about the team. Lamer was obviously quite knowledgeable about the players and the interview went on for several minutes. It wasn't until the reporter heard another journalist address Coach Ruggles by name that he asked Mr. Lamer who he was and found out he had been talking to the wrong man the entire time.

While Coach Ruggles dealt with the media, some of the players decided to look around the hotel a little before going to bed. Just being up there was a big deal to them. Being away from home and staying in a hotel was a new experience for a lot of the boys, and they wanted to take full advantage of the situation. They were pleased when they discovered that the Paradise Inn had a pool table. One of the few sources of entertainment in Cobden was shooting pool at the pool hall, and many of the boys played regularly.

Chuck and Kenny Smith racked up the balls and decided to play a game. Some of the other boys watched them and then decided to get in on the action. They didn't get a chance to play too many games before Coach Ruggles showed up.

"Come on, fellas," he said. "It's been a long day, and you need to get to bed. We didn't come up here to shoot pool. We came to play basketball, and we've got a big day ahead of us tomorrow."

The boys obediently went to their rooms, but they were excited about the tournament and sleep did not come easy. Chuck tossed and turned before he finally drifted off. Then he was in the locker room, getting dressed for the game. He looked up and saw Tom Crowell walk in.

"What are you doing here?" Chuck asked. He could hardly believe his eyes. Tom was wearing his letter jacket, and he looked fine and very much alive.

"Where else would I be?" Tom said. "This is where I belong."

Chuck knew this was impossible, but he was so happy to see his friend that he didn't want to question it. He looked around the locker room to make sure his teammates could see that Tom was there, too. Suddenly, he was alone again.

Chuck's eyes popped open, and he sat up in bed. The room was dark, and he didn't know where he was. He began to get his bearings and recognized the silhouette of Jim Smith, his roommate, sleeping soundly in the other bed. Chuck realized he was in his hotel room at the Paradise Inn. It had been a dream. It had seemed so real, but it was just a dream. He lay back down and his head sank into the pillow. In the stillness of the night, he could still feel Tom's presence and was comforted.

Chapter 16

State Tournament - Cobden's First Hurdle: Galesburg

Coach Ruggles woke up early Friday morning, feeling more nervous than he anticipated. He had been so busy since Cobden won the super-sectional on Tuesday that he had hardly had time to think about where he was and to fully take in the gravity of the situation. Now it was game day, and in a few short hours the Appleknockers would take the floor to compete in the state tournament for the first time ever. It was an exhilarating thought but also an unnerving one. He and his players were about to step onto Illinois high school basketball's biggest stage. The Appleknockers had played in big games before, but they had never experienced anything like the pressure-packed environment of the state tournament. Ruggles was the youngest coach at the tournament, and even at 27 years old, he knew that these kinds of opportunities didn't come along very often. He thought about what Doc Neal had said to him when he recruited him to work at Cobden. "The Appleknockers are a special team," Doc Neal had said.

Now it was time to show the entire state just how special they were.

At 9 a.m., Coach Ruggles and the players met in the hotel lobby for a team meeting. Ruggles told the boys to gather up their gear. They were going to have breakfast and then go to Assembly Hall for the games.

"This is what we wanted, isn't it?" he asked the players, trying to sound as relaxed as possible. "This is where we wanted to be, right? Let's enjoy it."

Ruggles thought the boys showed some signs of nerves. He understood if they were nervous or apprehensive because he felt the same way. He just hoped the tension would wear off before the game started.

After the meeting, Coach Ruggles went back to his room. He and Mary called Mary's parents' house to wish their daughter, Kathy, a happy first birthday. They hated being away from her on her big day, but they planned to have a party for her when they returned from Champaign.

A half an hour later, the boys were consuming a big breakfast at a restaurant close to the Paradise Inn. A few reporters had been at the hotel that morning, and they followed the team to the restaurant. They asked Ruggles about his game strategy, and photographers took pictures of the boys while they ate. The players weren't used to this much scrutiny and attention, and they found it amusing. Roy stole a glance at Darrell.

"Can you believe they came here to watch us eat?" Roy asked.

The players found it hard to keep straight faces if they looked at each other so they kept their eyes trained on their plates to keep from laughing.

The Appleknockers were a hot story, and the press wanted to cover their every move. The unusual height of the players, the unique nickname, and the small-school Cinderella angle seemed to have mass appeal to their readers. Considered a decided underdog by most of the basketball pundits, Cobden wasn't expected to be around very long so the reporters figured that they better get their stories while there was a story to tell.

Coach Ruggles himself was also an object of fascination for many of the reporters. The handsome young coach with the Boston accent was affable and accessible to members of the media. He answered their questions freely and honestly, and his natural wit provided them with good quotes for their articles.

Coach Patterson accompanied Cobden's five cheerleaders and their honorary sponsor, Evalena Flick, to Champaign on Friday morning and took them to the Alpha Omicron Pi women's fraternity house on the campus of U of I where they would staying during the tournament. He gave them an itinerary, reminding them that their game against Galesburg started at 3 p.m. that afternoon. Once the young ladies were settled, Patterson headed to Assembly Hall where he caught up with the team.

Coach Ruggles and the players watched Stephen Decatur and Evanston play in the first quarter-final game. The game was close in the first quarter before Decatur began to take control in the second. Decatur's players were an impressive bunch: strong, seasoned, and confident. This wasn't lost on the Appleknockers.

"Decatur's got some great athletes," Jim Neal remarked to Bob. "They're a really good team."

At halftime, the Appleknockers went to their dressing room to prepare for their own quarter-final game with Galesburg. The players changed into their uniforms while Roger Peterman performed his managerial duties, gathering up towels and balls and filling water bottles. Team mascot Roger Burnett put on a pair of over-sized overalls and a big flannel shirt. He stuck a red handkerchief in his back pocket, donned his maroon Appleknocker hat, and he was primed for action.

Once everyone was ready, Coach Ruggles spoke up.

"It's pretty simple now, boys," he said. "If we win today, we move on and play again tomorrow. If we lose, we go home."

He let the words hang in the air for effect before he continued, "We've got to take this tournament one game at a time, and right now we need to focus on Galesburg. Let's push all the distractions of the tournament aside and give this game our full attention."

After Coach Ruggles briefly went over the game plan, the boys filed into the hallway outside their small locker room. They waited in the tunnel and watched Decatur put the finishing touches on its 73-59 victory over Evanston. Then they ran onto the court to warm up for the first game Cobden had ever played at state.

The crowd greeted the Appleknockers with generous applause. Cobden's cheerleaders and Roger Burnett led the Cobden rooting section in cheers, but they soon realized, to their surprise, that they weren't alone. People all over the mammoth arena joined in a loud ovation for the school from the tiny town.

As the boys went through their usual warm-up routine, they took in their surroundings. They had visited Assembly Hall yesterday when it was empty, but now the arena was filled to capacity with more than 16,000 basketball fans. The size of the building was intimidating. So was the size of the crowd. The Appleknockers had never played in front of so many people.

Kenny Smith looked into the stands at the sea of faces, and the first two people he saw were his mom and dad. His mom attended his games, but his dad never went. When Kenny saw his dad in the crowd, he understood how special this game was, and it meant a lot to him that his dad had come.

Some of the other boys spotted their family members and other familiar faces in Cobden's cheering section. These were many of the same people who had been going to their games all season, and the players were happy they were here for the biggest game of the year. Evalena Flick was on the sideline with the cheerleaders, and even though young Kevin had stayed home with his grandparents, Kenny was pleased his wife was able to make the trip.

Coach Ruggles had told the boys to concentrate on the game so they tried to ignore their nerves and the large crowd. They continued to shoot and go through their normal drills, trying to get a feel for the unfamiliar floor and goals. During the warm-up, Bob noticed that the floor had "dead spots" in certain areas that caused the ball to bounce awkwardly. He knew he would have to keep that in mind when he dribbled.

When the warm-up period was over, the boys returned to the bench. The public address announcer called out the starting lineups for both teams, and Cobden's players were introduced first. Jim Neal was the first starter announced, and when he ran onto the court, one of Cobden's cheerleaders followed and did a special cheer just for him. That was the custom for many teams during starting lineup introductions. The Appleknockers had done it all season, but they added a new twist for their first game at state. Roger Burnett brought five red apples – one for each starter – and he stuffed them into the pockets of his baggy overalls. When Jim Neal's name was called, Roger ran out on the court along with Jim and the cheerleader. He pulled out one of the apples and placed it on the floor.

Chuck's name was announced next, and he jogged out onto the court, followed by another cheerleader. Roger pulled another apple from his pocket and placed it on the floor by the first one.

The same routine was used for the other three starters: Kenny Flick, Kenny Smith, and Jim Smith. It was a little corny, but the spectators loved it. Many in attendance thought of the Appleknockers as a bunch of country bumpkins anyway, which was true to an extent, but it was also refreshing to see that the folks from Cobden had a sense of humor about their image. Encouraged by the cheers from the crowd, Roger's actions became more animated with each player. Before he put Jim Smith's apple on the court, he pretended to give it an elaborate spit shine. Everyone clapped and howled with laughter.

Coach Ruggles stood on the sideline, watching. Usually he was all business at game time, but even he was amused. While he didn't like adding unnecessary hoopla that could divert the players' attention, he realized this was a special time for all of Cobden's students, and he let Roger and the cheerleaders have their fun.

As the lineup was announced, Mary Ruggles glanced down at her husband on the sideline, knowing his concentration was solely on the game. He had always been able to tune everything out when he was coaching basketball, but like the other fans in the arena, she and young Randy were enjoying Roger's antics. She often got anxious before the games started, and Roger's show had helped her relax just a little.

The whistle blew, and the game tipped off. The nervousness that the players had been feeling quickly abated. This was what they had waited for. It was time to play basketball. Cobden got off to a fast start. Capitalizing on their height advantage, the Appleknockers worked the ball inside where Kenny Flick and Chuck netted field goals to produce a 4-0 lead. Cobden extended the margin to 7-2, but the Silver Streaks' quickness seemed to bother Cobden as they drew several fouls on the Appleknockers. Jim Neal scored only once before going to the bench with three fouls with nearly four minutes left in the quarter. Galesburg demonstrated excellent passing ability and featured a balanced offensive attack. Four different players contributed a bucket in the first period, but the Streaks didn't shoot particularly well against Cobden's tough 1-2-2 zone. The Appleknockers had shooting troubles of their own, but Chuck and Kenny Flick carried the load offensively, and Cobden held a 12-10 edge at the end of the first quarter.

Cobden opened the second frame much like the first with baskets by Kenny Flick and Chuck to move ahead by six. Galesburg scored the next six points, knotting the score at 16-all. Jim Neal was charged with his fourth personal foul so Coach Ruggles took him out and put Bob back in the game. Chuck soon joined Jim on the bench after picking up his third foul, and Ruggles sent Darrell in to replace him. The bench strength of the Appleknockers, a weapon they had used all season, was soon evident to the spectators at Assembly Hall. Bob and Darrell performed well as reserves, and even though Cobden had two of its starters sidelined with foul trouble, it continued to battle the Streaks on even terms. The score was tied on four occasions during the period. With six seconds remaining in the half, Galesburg led by two. Kenny Flick was fouled and made both free throws, sending the contest to the intermission deadlocked at 26.

Coach Ruggles was pleased with his team's effort but not the foul situation, and he talked to the boys about it in the locker room.

"The refs are calling this game close so we have to adjust and play smart," he told them. "You can't be reaching in and grabbing. Move your feet and stay in front of your man. It's a tie game so we're in good shape. Stick to the game plan, and we'll be fine. And remember, use the 'thinking position' if you get in trouble."

Galesburg scored first in the third quarter when Rick Callahan sank a free throw, putting the Silver Streaks up, 27-26, but Kenny Flick and Kenny Smith hit back-to-back shots to give the Appleknockers a three-point lead. Kenny Flick and Mike McCreight then traded baskets before Galesburg got hot from long range and rattled off nine straight points to go up, 38-32, with three minutes left in the period. With both Neal brothers on the bench, Cobden's height and heft advantage was reduced. The Streaks were finally able to work inside for close jump shots.

Coach Ruggles signaled for a timeout. Galesburg was on a hot streak, and he wanted to cool the team off. He also wanted to make sure his players weren't panicked from falling behind.

"We've got to slow them down and check their shooters," he said to the boys as they huddled around him. "They're getting inside too easily. We need to tighten up the middle and force them out.

"You're doing a good job against their press," he assured them. "We're going to be all right. Let's take care of the ball and look for good shots."

The players heeded Ruggles' orders and became more

active defensively. They tried to deny the Streaks' interior passes and cut off their driving lanes. On the offensive end, Kenny Smith and Jim Smith both provided field goals, while Kenny Flick and Bob each hit a free throw, and Cobden closed the gap to four points, 44-40, at the end of the third period.

Chuck and Jim Neal returned to action to start the final quarter. Cobden controlled the tip, and Chuck hit a short jump shot on the first possession, slicing the deficit in half. Mike Davis scored for Galesburg, and Marv Harris added a free throw, pushing the Streaks' lead to 47-42. Kenny Smith then made two free throws, bringing the Appleknockers back within three. With nearly six minutes left in the game, Jim Neal was called for a foul on Mike McCreight. McCreight missed his free-throw attempt, but the foul was Jim's fifth, sending him to the bench for the remainder of the contest. Coach Ruggles put Bob back in. Moments later Rick Callahan was fouled and connected on two charity tosses, restoring Galesburg's five-point cushion, 49-44, with five and a half minutes to play.

An uneasy feeling began to ripple through the Cobden fans, who by now accounted for nearly all of those in attendance, minus the Galesburg rooting section. The hundreds of supporters who had made the trip from southern Illinois to cheer on their team had been joined by thousands more people —strangers really— who had jumped on the Cobden bandwagon. The underdog Appleknockers had been dubbed the "People's Choice" by the press, and they were certainly the crowd favorite. But now they were down by five points with one of their best all-around players on the bench. The spectators worried that Galesburg would begin to pull away.

Cobden's players thought otherwise. Kenny Flick scored on a tip-in, and after a Galesburg turnover, Bob drained two free throws to cut the Streaks' lead to one. Marv Harris drove in for a layup and a three-point Galesburg advantage, but Chuck brought Cobden back within one when he put in a layup of his own with four minutes left to play. Thirty seconds later, Chuck was fouled and converted one-of-two foul shots, tying the game at 51-all.

The Appleknockers ratcheted up their defensive intensity, and the Streaks threw the ball away on their next possession. Kenny Flick was fouled and dropped in a pair of free tosses, making the score, 53-51, and giving Cobden its first lead since early in the third quarter. Energized with new life, the Appleknockers' defense came through again as Galesburg failed to score, and Cobden regained the ball. Kenny Smith was fouled and stepped to the charity stripe for two shots. He made the first, but his second shot bounced off the iron. Kenny Flick jumped high in the air and slapped the ball back through the goal, putting the Appleknockers up, 56-51, with less than two and a half minutes on the clock.

The throngs of people in the massive arena rose to their feet, roaring in approval for the stirring comeback. In just over two and a half minutes, Cobden had dug itself out of a five-point hole and rallied for a five-point lead. The Appleknockers showed remarkable poise for a team that was playing its first game at the state tournament. Cobden never wavered under Galesburg's attack. The players refused to buckle under the pressure and had seized command of the game.

Galesburg called a timeout.

"We're up five, but we can't get careless," Coach Ruggles cautioned the boys.

The finish line was in sight, but the game wasn't over, and he wanted them to maintain their concentration.

"Continue to play good defense but try not to foul them," he said. "We don't want to stop the clock because time is on our side. Slow down on offense. Make them come after you. And you're gonna to have to make free throws."

The Streaks inbounded the ball and dribbled quickly up the court. Cobden's zone defense met them as they crossed the center stripe. Even with Jim Neal on the bench, Cobden still had three defenders on the floor who stood 6-foot-5 or taller. Following Coach Ruggles' direction about avoiding fouls, the players were less aggressive on defense than they had been, but they did their best to make it difficult for Galesburg to get a clear shot. The Streaks passed the ball around the zone. They finally found an opening and scored. It was their first basket since before the four-minute mark of the period and got them back within three points.

Galesburg applied a furious press, trying to steal the ball or force a turnover, but Bob maneuvered skillfully through the defenders and got the ball safely across the half-court line in the allotted time. Once in their own territory, the Appleknockers slowed their offense to a stall. They were in no rush to shoot and passed the ball to each other as the seconds ticked away. Trailing by three, Galesburg had no time to waste and realized they would have to foul to get the ball back, and then hope Cobden would miss its free throws. The Streaks fouled Bob, and he walked to the foul line. As he prepared to shoot, the crowd fell silent, not wanting to disturb his focus. Bob gripped the ball and took a deep breath, relaxing his muscles. He was three-for-three from the line so far in the game. He made both free throws, remaining perfect and pushing Cobden's margin back to five points.

Galesburg hustled up the floor, racing against time and a determined opponent. There was under a minute to play, and the Appleknockers' defense was stifling. The fans cheered loudly. They could feel an upset coming. Cobden, the upstart "Little David" team from a small school at the far southern end of the state, was on the verge of eliminating a talented, veteran team and advancing to the state semifinals. The Streaks continued working against the Appleknockers' zone as precious time drained off the clock. With less than 20 seconds left, they broke through and scored to once again pull within three.

When Cobden threw the ball in, Galesburg's press again came in full force, but it was to no avail. The Appleknockers got the ball across the center line unscathed. The Streaks had no choice but to foul, and this time Jim Smith was the recipient. With only seven seconds left to play, he strolled confidently to the foul line, knowing he could ensure victory for his team if he made his free throws. Both shots found their target, and Cobden reclaimed a five-point lead. The fans erupted in applause. They clapped and cheered loudly. Cobden's cheerleaders squealed in delight and hugged each other. Some people didn't even realize that Galesburg had come back up the floor and scored a bucket just before the final horn blew, bringing the game to a close with the score, 60-57. Cobden had done it! In this single-elimination round of the tournament, the Appleknockers had survived their first test; they would play another day.

The crowd continued its loud ovation as the players celebrated on the sidelines, shouting and clapping their hands. Kenny Flick found Evalena for a victory hug and kiss before going to the locker room with his teammates.

When they reached the locker room, the players continued their celebration. They were elated over their win. Few of the so-called experts had given them much of a chance to beat Galesburg, but they had remained confident and proved the doubters wrong. They had also proven to themselves that they truly belonged there. It wasn't just a fluke. They hadn't just been lucky; they had the ability to compete with the best teams in the state, no matter how much bigger the other schools were.

"Just two more games, gang," Kenny Flick said to his teammates. He had led the team in scoring with 20 points. "Two more games and it's the state title."

Sportswriters surrounded the Appleknockers' dressing room after the game. A few of them wedged their way into the small room.

"Is this the best your team has played this year?" one of the reporters asked.

"No. We've looked better," Ruggles said. "I think we looked better against Pinckneyville than we did today. Although Galesburg may be a better team."

The reporters jotted notes as Ruggles spoke.

"You and your team looked very composed during the

game," another reporter noted. "Were you nervous?"

"We were a little wobbly at first," Ruggles admitted. "But any team going out on that floor is going to be nervous."

"Do you think all the cheering from the fans helped your team?" inquired another journalist.

"I think it was probably helpful," Ruggles said. "Being so far away from home, we really appreciate the support."

Meanwhile, over in the Galesburg locker room, Coach John Thiel told a much smaller gathering of the press that the Silver Streaks were adversely affected by the cheers for their opponents.

"Every time they scored it sounded like the Yankees had won the seventh game of the World Series," he said. "I wish my boys could have forgotten about the crowd."

In the winner's locker room, the reporters continued to pepper the Appleknockers with questions.

"You held the Streaks to 38-percent shooting from the floor," a reporter said. It was the second-worst shooting performance for Galesburg this season. "How did you prepare your defense?"

"We work very hard on defense in practice, and we have all year," Ruggles said. "We didn't know exactly what to expect from Galesburg because we weren't able to scout them due to a lack of money. It's a problem common to most small schools. We wanted to battle them on the boards and limit their fast-break opportunities, and I thought we did a pretty good job of that."

Coach Ruggles said he was a little concerned that his team had to come from behind to win.

"I guess we just had some trouble with their press," he said. "But we'll have to get that straightened out if we plan to stop Decatur. Those guys have it down pat."

"How do you plan to stop Decatur?" all the reporters wanted to know.

After all, along with Centralia, Stephen Decatur was considered by almost everyone to be a favorite to win the tournament. Called the Runnin' Reds because of their speed, Decatur's players were also known for their physical strength and rebounding prowess. They had played stiff competition and lost only one game all season.

"We'll just have to limit our turnovers and battle them on the boards like we did today," Ruggles said, knowing it was easier said than done. But he had confidence in his team. He wanted the boys to know that he honestly believed they could compete against Decatur, and he wanted them to believe it, too.

"How will you stop their running game?" asked a reporter.

"We're going to use our zone, and we'll just have to take care of the ball," Ruggles said.

"They can't run if they don't have the ball," Kenny Flick added.

The sports reporters had done their homework on Cobden, especially after the team won the super-sectional game against Pinckneyville. By now most of the reporters knew about the tragic drowning death of Tom Crowell. They were aware that the Appleknockers had dedicated their season to Tom, and they asked the team about him.

Ruggles paused a moment before answering. "Tom was the playmaker and probably my steadiest performer," he said quietly. After a slight hesitation, he added, "I know we all miss him."

A flicker of sadness showed on the faces of all the Appleknockers as the pain of losing Tom suddenly became immediate and present in their minds.

"We've been playing ball for Tom all year," Chuck said. "We don't say 'win this one for Tom' just to build up our morale. It's just the way we feel."

"Tom was a great guy and a great ball player," Darrell added. "We know he should be in the lineup, and he's not. It makes us all work harder."

A couple of the other players shared their thoughts about Tom. As the boys spoke of their friend, it became apparent that he was still very much a part of their team. Their initial sadness gave way to smiles as they recalled all the happy times they had spent with Tom.

The press conference wound down, and the journalists, satisfied that they had their stories, filed out of the locker room. As the tallest entry in the tournament, the Appleknockers' size had been the topic of many columns and conversations. On his way out, one of the reporters asked a final question. "How did your players get so tall?"

Without missing a beat, Ruggles said with a grin, "They drink apple cider between halves."

After the game, the cheerleaders and Evalena Flick returned to the Alpha Omicron Pi women's fraternity house where they were not only greeted by the fraternity sisters, but also several members of the press. It seemed as if the Appleknockers' story was going to be covered from every possible angle.

"Newspapers have called here several times today," one of the fraternity sisters informed the cheerleaders. "We didn't know the Appleknockers were so famous."

The reporters asked the girls about their thoughts on their team competing in the state tournament and playing in a huge venue like Assembly Hall. As good cheerleaders should, they told the reporters that they were very proud of Coach Ruggles and the players. They said that even though Cobden had never played in such a big facility, they were confident the boys could win it all.

Roger Burnett had been a hit with the fans at Assembly Hall when he set the apples out on the court when Cobden's starters were introduced. One of the reporters inquired about the mascot.

"We asked Roger to dress in overalls, a sloppy flannel shirt, and Appleknocker hat because if anyone would earnestly cheer, Roger would," cheerleader Marilyn Draper explained.

"Roger took on the role of the Appleknocker when the

sectional tournament began," cheerleader Kathryn Gunn said. "He's been cheering with us ever since."

When the reporters left, the girls treated their guests to a special candlelight dinner, serving among other things, applesauce.

A large group of Appleknocker supporters was staying in Mattoon, a town about 50 miles south of Champaign. After the game, they returned to the hotel and took over the bar with their revelry. Every so often someone would ask, "What's an Appleknocker?"

The rooters from Cobden were more than happy to tell them.

While the Appleknockers' game with Galesburg was in progress, the town of Cobden resembled a ghost town. The streets were deserted and nearly all of the businesses were closed with signs on their doors that read, "Gone to State." The few people left in town were either watching the game on TV at home or at Fuzzy's or the Tip Top. When the television flashed the final score, 60-57, for the victorious Appleknockers, the folks in Cobden cheered as loudly as the fans in Assembly Hall.

People who had been watching at home rushed into town and started driving around, honking their horns. A small, impromptu parade formed, and the cars circled the loop in downtown Cobden several times, blowing their horns in celebration. It was louder than any Fourth of July fireworks display. The townspeople couldn't have been happier or more proud. Shouts of "Go Appleknockers!" echoed over and over throughout the Shawnee hills hamlet.

A few reporters had come to Cobden to record the locals' reaction to their basketball team's success. After the Appleknockers beat Galesburg, most people were smiling and laughing too much to be interviewed.

A shopkeeper at one of the few stores that stayed open

told one reporter, "I'm glad we beat at least one of those big upstate schools. They're always bragging on how good they are."

Another local fan said, "We'll be giving that team the biggest reception anyone ever had in Cobden when they get back, win or lose."

The players were unaware of the festivities going on in Mattoon and in their hometown. Once they showered and changed into street clothes, the whole crew went out to eat. The team celebrated its win with a big dinner and then went straight back to the hotel. Coach Ruggles told the boys to relax and get some rest. They were in good physical condition, but they'd had a tough battle with Galesburg. Whether they felt it yet or not, he knew the game had taken its toll on their young bodies. They still had two games to play the next day.

The evening session of the state tournament tipped off at 7:30 p.m. In the first quarter-final game, Rock Island Alleman beat Centralia, 57-56, in overtime. This was a huge upset. After the Orphans defeated Collinsville in the super-sectional at Salem, many basketball experts picked Centralia to win the state championship. When another title-contender, Crane Tech, lost to Evanston in double overtime at the Evanston Super-Sectional, and Stephen Decatur scored a decisive win over Arcola at the super-sectional in Normal, many pundits labeled Centralia and Decatur as co-favorites to take the title.

Now the Orphans had been eliminated by a lightly regarded Alleman team that was ranked 10th among the Sweet 16 contenders. Centralia's 6-foot-8 All-State center Cliff Berger had a big game with 26 points and 15 rebounds, but it wasn't enough to offset the inside-outside duo of Alleman's John McGonigle and Steve Spanich. McGonigle scored 16 points and Spanich had 22, including the game-winning basket.

Pekin dismantled Glenbard East, 84-43, in the last quarter-final game. The hot-shooting Chinks led, 42-19, at the intermission and continued to dominate in the second half to post the 41-point win.

The semifinal match-ups were now set. Cobden would face Stephen Decatur the next day at 12:15 p.m., and then Pekin and Rock Island Alleman would square off immediately after.

Some of Cobden's players had watched the tournament on TV back at their hotel. They were as shocked by Centralia losing as everyone else. The Orphans were an excellent team and had received a lot of coverage in the *Southern Illinoisan* and other downstate papers throughout the season. But the games weren't played on paper; the outcomes were decided on the court. This was something the Appleknockers and the Alleman Pioneers had proven today.

"I can't believe Centralia got beat tonight," Bob Smith said to Jim Neal as they headed to their room. "I was afraid that we would be the ones to lose."

"Why did you think that?"

"Well, we always hear about how good these big teams are," Bob said. "I was scared we might come up here and make fools of ourselves."

"We can play with anybody up here," Jim said. "But don't worry. Since we won today, you'll have another chance to make a fool of yourself tomorrow."

It was late and most of the players had retired for the night. Some went right to sleep, exhausted by the events of the day. Others stayed up into the wee hours of the morning, talking with their roommates about their big win over Galesburg and what lay ahead for them tomorrow. Their dream to win the state tournament was just a day away. Could they make it come true?

The boys were in their rooms for the night, but Coach Ruggles was still on the move. He was in demand by the media and had given dozens of interviews to newspaper reporters. It seemed as if everyone wanted to talk about the Appleknockers, especially now that they had defeated Galesburg.

Ruggles was also busy tracking down information about Stephen Decatur. He contacted a couple of friends, who were familiar with the Reds, to get a scouting report on the Appleknockers' next opponent. Everyone he spoke to had high praise for Decatur. He and the boys knew they would be a formidable opponent. They had watched part of Decatur's game with Evanston in the quarter-finals, and Decatur had been impressive, winning, 73-59. Once you get to this point in the tournament, everyone is good. There are no pushovers remaining.

Ruggles was good at sizing up an opponent. He was able to spot mismatches and find ways for his players to take advantage of them. He gathered as much information on Decatur's players as he could, learning their tendencies, strengths, and weaknesses. Although his knowledge of the Reds was limited, he worked with Coach Patterson to devise a plan for the game.

"We'll run through this with the boys in the morning," Coach Ruggles said, realizing the lateness of the hour. "Let's call it a night."

When Ruggles finally made it to his room, Randy was sound asleep, but Mary was waiting up for him.

"I was starting to get worried about you," she said.

"Sorry I left you two up here alone. But there was no need to worry," he assured her. "I was just talking basketball."

"You look tired," Mary said. "You need to get some sleep. Tomorrow is a pretty big day."

Chapter 17

State Semifinal:
Cobden v. Stephen Decatur

A brilliant orange sunrise announced the arrival of
Saturday morning on the Illinois prairie, painting the landscape
in warm hues of pink and coral. The Appleknockers barely
noticed. Coach Ruggles, Coach Patterson, and the players had
risen early, but not to enjoy the scenery; they were preparing
for their game with Stephen Decatur.

Ruggles shared the information he had gathered on
the Reds with the boys. He went over a personnel report on
Decatur's players, telling his team about Charles Currie, the
All-State forward, and Jack Sunderlik, who was averaging
18 points per game in tournament play. Ruggles didn't dwell
too long on any particular player. Cobden rarely focused its
defense on an opposing team's star player. It used its zone to
thwart its opponents' offensive schemes.

"They're a very talented bunch," Ruggles said. "You
saw them play yesterday so you know how good they are.
They're a physical team, but I think we match up well with
them in terms of strength. They're a good rebounding team
and have a good press. They're also quick, and they like to
run. If we're going to beat them, we have to slow them down
and not turn the ball over."

The players listened intently as Coach Ruggles went
over the game plan he and Coach Patterson had drawn up the
night before. Every team is different and brings new challenges to the floor so Ruggles thought it was vital to prepare
for every game. At this point in the season, however, he felt
that Cobden's best chance for success was to simply play its
own game. This was no time for dramatic changes. The Appleknockers needed to rely on the play that they had used to win
31 games already; the same play that had gotten them to the

semifinals of the state tournament.

Once the players were fully debriefed on Decatur, they packed up their gear and headed to Assembly Hall. The media followed the team everywhere, but Coach Ruggles had asked the reporters to direct all their questions to him and to give the boys some space. He wanted the players to be able to concentrate on playing basketball and not get too caught up in the circus-like atmosphere. He thought the boys had done a good job of handling themselves in front of the press so far. He noticed at breakfast that morning the boys had hardly paid any attention to the reporters. They were focused on Decatur. The Reds were going to be a tough opponent, and Cobden's players knew that they were going to have to be at the top of their game to beat them.

The Appleknockers were in their dressing room, getting ready for the game when a telegram arrived. Coach Ruggles handed the bulky package to Roger Peterman and asked him to read the contents. Roger pulled the telegram from its envelope and began to unfold it. The team watched curiously as the paper continued to unfurl and extend to 20 feet in length. It was a message of good luck from people in Cobden and other southern Illinois communities and contained more than 1,000 names. The players poured over the telegram. Some of the names were familiar. The boys were all quite impressed when they found the names of Clyde Choate, a state representative; John Gilbert, a state senator; and Albert Fred "Red" Schoendienst, a former professional baseball player for the St. Louis Cardinals.

A commotion in the hallway pulled the boys' attention away from the telegram. Stephen Decatur's players walked past Cobden's locker room to go out on the floor, and they chanted, "We're gonna make applesauce. We're gonna make applesauce."

The telegram had been a great morale boost for the boys, reminding them of how many people from southern Illinois were rooting for them. Now listening to the sing-song taunt from their opponents only fueled their motivation. *You're gonna make applesauce, huh?* the players thought. *We'll see about that.*

Decatur was already warming up when the Apple-knockers dashed onto the court and were welcomed by a spirited ovation from the crowd. Fans rose to their feet, clapping and cheering enthusiastically and leaving no doubt that Cobden was the sentimental favorite.

While the crowd embraced the underdog, the sportswriters and pundits still favored Decatur to win the game. Stephen Decatur already had four state basketball titles to its credit, with the most recent being 1962. Considered one of the best teams in the state, Decatur had been ranked near the top of the Associated Press poll all season. Now that Centralia was out, the Reds were the odds on favorite to win the championship.

Cobden, on the other hand, was playing in its first state tournament. The team had won a lot games this season, but most experts thought the victories had come against relatively weak competition. Although the Appleknockers had been impressive in their come-from-behind win over Galesburg a day earlier, few experts thought that an inexperienced team from such a small town could handle Decatur's quickness, rebounding ability, and physical strength.

Coach Ruggles paid no attention to the odds or the experts. What did they know? Most of them had never seen Cobden play before the tournament started. He thought they underestimated the Appleknockers' ability and determination. He knew what his team was capable of better than anyone else. He couldn't imagine having a better group of young men to coach. His boys were talented, intelligent, and hard-working. In practice, they did everything he and Coach Patterson asked.

They loved basketball and had a great understanding of how to play the game. Ruggles could draw up a play in the huddle, and more often than not the team would execute it to perfection the first time. As he watched his players warm up, he could see they were also sizing up the Reds at the opposite end of the court. The Appleknockers showed no signs of intimidation. If anything, they seemed less nervous than when they took the floor the previous day with Galesburg. His boys had never backed down from a challenge, and he didn't expect them to start now.

On the sidelines, Roger Burnett led the energetic Appleknocker rooting section in lively cheers and chants. They were proud of their team, and they weren't bashful about letting it show. Roger shouted encouragement to the players as they warmed up, but he was starting to get a little worried. It was almost game time, and Cobden's cheerleaders were nowhere in sight.

While the boys spent the morning getting ready for their game, the cheerleaders had their own preparations to attend to. After having breakfast at the women's fraternity house, the cheerleaders decided to go into Champaign to do some shopping. They wanted to get a gift for Coach Ruggles to show him how much they appreciated everything he had done for them. They also wanted to get a souvenir for Kenny and Evalena Flick's baby son, Kevin.

The girls knew the game started at 12:15 p.m. so they split up into two groups, three girls in each, to save time shopping. One group went to find Coach Ruggles' present while the other went to get Kevin's. The idea worked great. The Ruggles' group found a maroon tie monogrammed with the initial "R." Kevin's group got a small gold trophy, like the one they hoped his dad, Kenny, would soon be winning. It wasn't until after they had made their purchases and were attempting to rendezvous that the girls discovered the flaw in their plan. Champaign was a big city compared to Cobden, and the separated cheerleaders were unable to find their designated meeting place.

They started getting nervous as they walked through the unfamiliar city. The streets and buildings of downtown Champaign seemed to blend together, furthering their confusion. It was no fun being lost, and when the girls finally found each other, they were relieved and grateful. Fearing they would be late for the game, they quickly flagged down a taxi to take them to Assembly Hall.

By the time the cheerleaders arrived, the starting line-ups for both teams had already been announced. The girls felt bad that they had missed cheering for their assigned players, but Roger had kept the crowd entertained in their absence. He had been a one-man show with his apple routine, placing one on the court for each starter, and the fans again responded with cheers and laughter.

"Where have you been?!" Roger demanded when the cheerleaders joined him on the sideline. "I was worried something happened to you."

The girls told him about their excursion into Champaign. They apologized for being late, but there was no time to dwell on the incident. They had something much bigger to focus on now. A whistle blew, signaling the start of the game.

Cobden won the tip on the opening jump ball and took a quick 4-0 lead when Kenny Smith made a 15-foot jump shot and Kenny Flick tipped in a rebound. Dave Scholz hit a jump shot for Stephen Decatur, but Jim Neal answered with a bucket, and Kenny Smith added a free throw to put the Appleknockers in front, 7-2. Jack Sunderlik then scored for the Reds, and Charles Currie sank a free throw, trimming Cobden's lead to two. Kenny Smith drilled a jumper from the corner, and the Appleknockers held a 9-5 edge at the end of the first period.

Kenny Flick made a layup to begin the second quarter, giving Cobden a six-point lead. Chuck was called for his third personal foul just a minute into the action so Coach Ruggles took him out and sent Bob Smith into the game. Decatur took advantage of Chuck's absence in the middle as Jack Sunderlik drove inside for two layups. He also hit a free throw, which cut the Appleknockers' lead to one. Jim Smith popped in a clutch jumper, and Jim Neal was fouled and drained a pair of free shots for Cobden to send the margin back to five. Then Dave Scholz and Charles Currie each contributed a free throw for

Decatur to make the score, 15-12, in favor of the Appleknockers.

With about a minute left in the quarter, Bob was fouled
and went to the line to shoot a one-and-one opportunity. He
made the first shot, but his second one bounced off the rim.
Kenny Flick grabbed the rebound and stuck it back through
the hoop. He was fouled in the process and went to the line to
shoot his bonus shot. He missed the free throw, but this time
Kenny Smith was there to gather in the rebound and toss it in.
Kenny was also fouled on the put back and made the free throw
to complete what was essentially a six-point play for Cobden.
In a span of less than five seconds, the Appleknockers saw their
lead balloon from three to nine points.

The pro-Appleknocker crowd at Assembly Hall cheered
loudly as they felt momentum swing firmly behind Cobden.
Kenny Flick fouled Dave Scholz on Decatur's next possession, and he made a pair of free throws to temporarily quiet
the crowd. But moments later Kenny Flick was fouled and
knocked down two free throws of his own to give the Appleknockers a 23-14 halftime edge.

Basketball experts and fans marveled at the way the
Appleknockers had handled the Reds' fierce press. Although
Cobden had committed several turnovers, the players never
became rattled and were able to dictate the pace of play. The
Appleknockers' defense had been superb in the first half, holding Decatur to only four baskets on a dismal 14-percent shooting from the floor. The Reds missed 13 of their first 15 shots.
Analysts were impressed with Cobden's play in the first half,
but most of them thought that Decatur would rally and win.
They believed that the talent, speed, and physical strength of
the Reds would wear Cobden down similar to what they had
done to all but one of their opponents this season.

Not everyone was ready to count the Appleknockers
out, though. Dolph Stanley, a highly successful coach, who in
1934 had brought a team from the small southern Illinois town
of Equality to a third-place finish at state and then won a state

championship at Taylorville in 1944, was impressed with the Appleknockers' talent and composure.

"I hope this little team goes on and wins the state championship because I know what it will mean," he said. "They'll be talking about this for 100 years in Cobden. In Decatur, they won't even remember it this summer."

Gene Haile, the basketball coach at McLeansboro High School, was more familiar with the Appleknockers than most of those in attendance since his team had played them earlier in the season.

"They're not doing bad now, but you give that Cobden bunch a year-long schedule in a good conference, and they just might walk over this field," Haile said.

Cobden continued its deliberate style of play in the third quarter. With a nine-point lead, the Appleknockers were in no hurry to shoot. Kenny Flick and Jack Sunderlik exchanged buckets during the first minute of action, and Cobden remained in front, 25-16. With just over two minutes gone in the period, Chuck fouled Sunderlik, and he converted one of his two free-throw attempts. The foul was Chuck's fourth so Coach Ruggles again sent Bob in to replace him. Dave Scholz furnished another free throw for Decatur and then Kenny Smith hit one for Cobden. The Appleknockers displayed exquisite ball control, executing crisp passes and draining time off the clock with every possession. The fans at Assembly Hall showed their approval as they showered Cobden with applause. Kenny Flick hit a basket, staking Cobden to a 10-point lead at 28-18. The Appleknockers continued to fluster the Reds with their 1-2-2 zone defense, holding them scoreless for over three minutes. Jack Sunderlik finally broke the drought for Decatur with a 12-foot jump shot late in the quarter. Kenny Flick gave the Appleknockers the last word in the period when he splashed home a bucket with just one second on the clock, putting Cobden up, 30-20.

The Reds got the tip to start the fourth quarter and

scored two quick field goals, cutting Cobden's lead to six. Coach Ruggles called a timeout.

"You have to hang on to the ball," he told the boys in the huddle. "They're getting too many steals. We have the lead, but there's plenty of time for them to come back if we get careless. We can't let these guys run on us."

During the timeout, Cobden's cheerleaders took the floor to perform. The crowd hopped to its feet, and when the cheerleaders shouted out the cheer, it seemed as if everyone in the hall yelled with them.

When play resumed, Kenny Smith buried two field goals and a free throw, and Bob added a pair of free tosses. The 7-0 run put the Appleknockers ahead, 37-24, with just over four minutes left in the game. Decatur chipped away at Cobden's lead, but the Appleknockers retained their poise and continued to dictate the tempo. They stalled the ball, and the Reds were forced to foul to gain possession. The strategy was unsuccessful for Decatur, however, as Cobden cashed in at the free-throw line. In the final minute and 20 seconds of play, Kenny Flick made four foul shots and Bob supplied two as the Appleknockers moved to a 44-36 advantage with 10 seconds remaining. With victory no longer in doubt, Cobden allowed Decatur to score unhindered just before the final horn sounded. The Appleknockers won, 44-38!

They had done the improbable – what some even deemed the unthinkable – defeating tournament co-favorite Decatur and earning a spot in the IHSA state final. What the basketball experts underestimated, or perhaps simply failed to understand, was the team chemistry and confidence the boys had for each other and their coach. The Appleknockers hadn't just come to the tournament to play. They had come to win.

Thunderous applause echoed throughout Assembly Hall. The capacity crowd made it clear that the efforts of the underdog Appleknockers were appreciated by all those who watched them play. Even the security officers, custodial staff, and snack vendors cheered for Cobden. The Cobden rooting section, in particular, went wild with joy. Everyone jumped up and down, giddy with excitement, and hugged each other freely. The Cobden fans and the Appleknockers' cheerleaders were more than happy to share the celebration with the thousands of new Appleknocker supporters.

Jubilation reigned in Cobden's locker room. The players whooped it up, shouting and slapping each other on the back. They were thrilled with their win over the heavily favored Reds. They had defeated an outstanding ball team, and they knew it. Reporters and photographers swarmed into the hallway leading into the locker room. Everyone wanted to document this unlikely story.

"That was quite an upset you pulled off," said one of the sportswriters. "Did you really think you had a chance against Decatur?"

"Sure we did," Coach Ruggles responded quickly. He knew there were a lot of doubters out there, but his team continued to prove them wrong. "I have a lot of confidence in these boys, and they're confident in themselves."

"Is this the best game your team has played this year?" a reporter asked Ruggles.

"It was a great effort," Ruggles answered. "But we had too many turnovers today."

"Aside from turnovers, do you think this was your team's best game?" the question came again.

"No," Ruggles said. "I think our best effort was our 101-34 win over Alto Pass in the district. We played well from start to finish in that game."

The reporters seemed a little shocked and even a bit amused by his answer. Most of them had never heard of Alto Pass, and they doubted the town had a team comparable to Decatur's.

Ruggles didn't mean to equate Decatur's and Alto Pass's teams. He was trying to make a point about his own team's performance. Seeing the curious looks on the reporters' faces, he continued.

"Today's game was tough from the start," he said. "Those couple of tip-ins we got at the end of the first half really helped. Decatur's press was very tough, and we've faced some good ones. They are a great running team and their press got the ball from us a little too often to suit me."

The reporters hung on every word Ruggles spoke. Flashbulbs popped, recording the scene.

"How did your players remain so poised against their press?" another reporter queried.

"Well, we knew what to expect, and we reacted well," Ruggles answered. "They really turned it on, but we always squeezed out of it."

"How were you able to stop their running game?"

"We used our zone defense and ball-control offense to slow things down," Ruggles explained. "We simply didn't want to play their game but wanted to force them to play ours."

Cobden had shot more than 46 percent from the floor, while holding Decatur to a paltry 26 percent. The reporters wanted to know why Cobden's defense was so effective.

"Defense is something we've concentrated on all year," Ruggles said. "The boys work hard on defense everyday in practice, and it shows in our games. We worked hard today to frustrate their fast-break and fast-ball offense."

"Look ahead to tonight," a reporter said. "What are your thoughts on the championship game?"

Ruggles scratched his head and said, "I think we can do it, but we've never had to play two games in one day before, and this game was a real battle for us. I'll be interested to see who our opponent is."

As the press conference wound down, a man poked his head into the cramped locker room and approached Coach Ruggles.

"I'm Paul Judson," he said. "I just wanted to congratulate you and your team on the win today."

Paul and his twin brother, Phil, had played for Hebron in 1952 when their team won the state basketball championship, becoming the only district school to do so.

Photographers lingered in the dressing room, taking pictures, and they couldn't pass up the opportunity to capture on film this meeting between two powerhouse district teams. They snapped a couple of shots of Judson as he spoke with Kenny Flick.

Now the question on everyone's mind was: Can Cobden go all the way and join Hebron, becoming the second district school to capture a state crown?

After Judson left, the photographers asked the Appleknockers to line up for a group shot. Ruggles knew his players needed to get some rest before that night's game so he told the reporters that they needed to wrap things up.

"Just one more picture, Coach," one of the photographers said as he lined up his shot. "Just one more."

"Just one more," the players repeated.

Quickly realizing that one was the number of games they needed to win in order to be state champions, they spontaneously adopted the line as a rallying cry. "Just one more, just one more," the boys shouted over and over in the dressing room.

Coach Ruggles laughed at his players' enthusiasm. He let them enjoy the moment and then said, "Hit the showers, gang."

Jack Kenny, Stephen Decatur's coach, was obviously disappointed when he talked to the press after the game. When asked why his team was unable to beat the Appleknockers, he shook his head and said, "The main reason we lost is because we couldn't handle their size. It was one of those games where nothing seemed to go right. We've never shot so poorly."

"Was Cobden better than you expected?" a reporter questioned.

"Cobden is a good ball club, but I don't know if they were that good or we were that bad," Kenny said, apparently not in the mood to lavish praise on his opponent. "It might have been different if we'd gone ahead at anytime. But since we fell behind, we had to go after the ball. I thought our press was okay. They came out and played 'Mickey Mouse ball' and we just had to force the play."

While the "Mickey Mouse" comment was a less-than-flattering assessment of the Appleknockers' style of play, the coach complimented Cobden's defense, saying, "They had one of the best defenses we've faced all season...big and tough. We had trouble shooting over them from the outside."

Meanwhile, down in Cobden, the fans who had stayed at home celebrated the victory over Decatur with another parade of honking cars. They drove around the village's small downtown loop while the fire station blew its piercing siren for 20 minutes.

Coach Ruggles remained at Assembly Hall to watch some of the semifinal game between Pekin and Rock Island Alleman. He wanted to see who his team would face in the finals. He had missed most of their quarter-final games, but he knew both teams would offer stiff competition. Pekin jumped on top early, leading by five points after one quarter. With a fast-paced offense and solid defense, the Chinks continued to pull away in the second frame and were up, 33-17, at halftime. Alleman's upset victory over Centralia seemed to have left it drained as the Pioneers shot only 26 percent from the floor. As many as 10 players saw action for Pekin, and eight of them scored as Coach Dawson Hawkins used his bench liberally in the second half, resting his starters. The Chinks cruised to their second straight lopsided win, 69-36.

Pekin was well coached, well balanced, and very quick. The team's center and tallest player was Jim Sommer who stood 6-foot-3. The Chinks' guards were good shooters, and they liked to push the ball up the court. Cobden had a significant height advantage, but Coach Ruggles knew his team would have its hands full.

Cobden's players had returned to the Paradise Inn after their game with Decatur. Coach Ruggles asked them to get some rest, but most of the boys were too keyed up to sleep. They tried to relax, but found they were too excited about beating the Reds and too anxious about their upcoming game to get any real rest.

After the Pekin v. Alleman game, Coach Ruggles met the players back at the hotel.

"We've got Pekin tonight," he told the boys. "They're a good team with a lot of speed. They like to run and shoot, and they shoot well."

Coach Ruggles relayed to his players everything he had learned about the Chinks from watching them play, and they discussed their strategy for the upcoming game. With such a quick turnaround between games, there was little time to prepare, but Ruggles wanted the boys to be as informed and ready to compete as possible.

After the strategy session, the whole Appleknocker entourage – Ruggles, Mary, young Randy, Lee Patterson, Donald Ballance, Jack Lamer, Mike Basler, and the boys – all went to a nearby diner for the pre-game meal. The large group took up several tables at the restaurant.

"You're the Appleknockers, aren't you?" asked the restaurant manager. "I've read all about you in the papers. You're doing quite well."

"Thank you," Coach Ruggles said.

"Just let us know what we can do for you," the manager said. "It's our pleasure to serve you."

Coach Ruggles thanked the man again, and the players looked at each other and shrugged in amazement. It was hard to believe that a stranger in Champaign would know who they were. There had been a lot of reporters hovering around and following the Appleknockers since they had arrived at the tournament, but Ruggles had done his best to keep the boys shielded from the spotlight. The state tournament was a nerve-wracking event, and since the boys had never been in a situation like that, Ruggles tried to keep the distractions to a minimum.

Although the excitement had kept the players from sleeping at the hotel, it did nothing to diminish their appetites. They all ate a hearty supper. The mood around the tables was festive. Smiles came easy and often. Even though there was more work to do, everyone was enjoying the accomplishments the Appleknockers had already achieved. They knew that life is a journey not a destination. While the ultimate goal was still out there, the path to achieving it had already been a lot of fun, and the team was soaking up the experience.

The other patrons must have overheard the manager or recognized the team from the recent newspaper coverage because when the group from Cobden finished eating and got up to leave, everyone in the restaurant clapped. Surprised by the reaction, the boys just stood there for a moment, looking around. Coach Ruggles was also a bit taken aback, but then he quickly acknowledged the unexpected applause. He smiled and nodded at the other customers and shook hands with those who were close enough to reach, thanking them for their support. The rest of the group followed his lead, and by the time they left the eatery, they had shaken hands with nearly everyone in the establishment.

Chapter 18

State Final: Cobden v. Pekin

Stephen Decatur had a narrow lead over Rock Island Alleman in the tournament's third-place game when the Apple-knockers arrived at Assembly Hall and climbed into the seats to watch. The Decatur Reds began to pull away in the second half and won, 73-54. The boys were in the stands watching when Coach Ruggles was informed by an IHSA official that Pekin was already dressed for the title game.

"When will your boys get ready?" the official wanted to know.

When the team had come back to the hall, Ruggles had inquired at the scorer's table about the starting time of the championship game. He was told it would begin at 9 p.m. He checked his watch and saw that there was still plenty of time.

"We're looking forward to this game," Ruggles assured the man. "We won't be late."

The official looked skeptical. "You know your game starts at 8:30, right?"

"Eight-thirty? No," Ruggles said, shaking his head. "I was told it started at nine."

The official sighed. "No. I'm sorry. It's scheduled to go at 8:30, right after this game ends."

There were only a few minutes left in the consolation game so Coach Ruggles and Coach Patterson hastily rounded up the players and herded them into the locker room.

"I got the time wrong, fellas," Coach Ruggles told them. "We play at 8:30."

The boys rushed to change into their uniforms. While the players dressed, Roger Peterman hurried to gather towels and balls and fill the water bottles. He was going through the same routine and preparations he had done for every game when reality hit him. This wasn't just any game. *This is the state championship*, he thought. *Cobden could win the state championship!* It was an awesome thought and set off a feeling of butterflies in his stomach.

The players were excited, too. They had been on a high since they beat Decatur earlier in the day. The Reds were the best team they had played all season, and they had emerged from the game victorious.

Ruggles could see that the players were still fired up about the Decatur game, and he wanted to make sure they were now focused on Pekin.

"Here we are guys," he said. "This one is for all the marbles. We just have to play our game. If we do that, we can win this whole thing."

After a few last-minute instructions, the boys spilled out into the corridor and came face to face with Pekin's players. Since his boys had been late getting ready, Coach Ruggles thought Pekin would have already taken the floor. That wasn't the case. The Chinks were waiting for the Appleknockers. Apparently Pekin's coach, Dawson Hawkins, had figured out that the vast majority of the crowd was rooting for Cobden. He was a veteran of tournament play, having already coached a high school team in Nebraska to a state title. He didn't want his players to be intimidated before the game started so he was determined that the two teams would enter the court together.

Ruggles knew what Hawkins was doing and thought he would have a little fun. Knowing the game couldn't start without either team, Ruggles decided to let the Chink's mentor stew awhile longer. Ruggles told the boys to relax and let the tension out, and they talked about everything but basketball. As the moments stretched out in the crowded hallway, the players felt a little awkward. They had no clue why their coach was stalling, and they wondered among themselves, *what are we waiting for?*

Ruggles could see his players were getting restless so he asked them, "Are you ready?"

"Let's go," they said.

Both teams took off and ran out of the tunnel together. The sound that greeted them when they hit the floor was like an explosion. The roar from the crowd was deafening. The noise, lights, and colors seemed even more intense than they had in previous games. Everyone stood and cheered, eager to watch the main event.

The Appleknockers went through their normal warm-up routines, trying to loosen up and work out the kinks. They felt confident they could win, but there were definitely some pre-game jitters.

Coach Ruggles called the boys to the sidelines just before the game started. He talked to them about playing their roles and tried to make them feel like this was just any other game.

"We haven't had a lot of time to think about Pekin or prepare for them," he said. "We just have to play our game and take care of the ball."

The public address announcer broke through the racket in the huge hall, informing the crowd that the game was at hand. He began to call out the starting lineups for both teams, and the Chinks were introduced first. Amel Massa, Jim Couch, Jim Sommer, Ron Rhoades, and Dave Golden were called one by one and ran out on the floor to a rousing ovation from Pekin's fans.

Then it was Cobden's turn. Jim Neal was the first player announced. When he ran onto the court, the fans leaped to their feet and cheered wildly. Roger Burnett ran out and placed an apple on the court, and the applause grew louder and more vigorous. The PA announcer called out Chuck, then Kenny Flick, then Kenny Smith, and finally Jim Smith. Their names were barely audible over the din of the crowd. The boys just looked at each other and shrugged, and then ran out when they thought it was their turn.

The five starters for Cobden stood on the court astonished by the howling, whistling, cheering support that poured down on them from every corner of the vast hall. With wide eyes, they turned and looked into the stands on all sides. *Is this really all for us?* they wondered. It wasn't just the Cobden rooting section that was making all the noise. Everyone in the place, except for the small section of Pekin fans, was on their feet, clapping and cheering for the Appleknockers. It was almost overwhelming.

Coach Ruggles and the players on the bench were overwhelmed by the crowd's reaction as well. Ruggles figured the fans would be cheering for his team like they had in the first two games, but he hadn't expected such a vocal outpouring of support for the starting lineup. *So much for this being just any other game*, he thought.

"Look around you," he said to the boys, motioning to the crowd with both arms. "This is all for you. You earned this with your play."

In the stands, Mary hugged Randy tightly. She was filled with emotion and goose bumps covered her arms. She was so proud of her husband and the boys.

Cobden's fans, those who were actually from Cobden, were also surprised when they saw that nearly everyone in the hall was standing and cheering for their team. Energized by the volume of support, the fans kept the ovation going strong and loud for several minutes. When the crowd finally quieted, a referee's whistle blew, and the game began.

The final game tipped off, and Cobden got the ball. Chuck scored on a short shot from the side just eight seconds into the contest, putting the Appleknockers up, 2-0. Dave Golden hit an 18-foot jump shot for Pekin, knotting the score. After a turnover by Cobden, Golden knocked down a 10-foot jumper, pushing the Chinks ahead by two points. Kenny Smith floated home a 15-foot jump shot to tie the score again, but Ron Rhoades responded with a field goal from the top of the key, giving Pekin a 6-4 lead. Jim Neal worked inside for a nifty reverse layup, but the referee waved off the basket and assessed Jim with a charging foul. Jim Smith was then called for a foul against Jim Sommer, and Sommer sank the free throw, increasing Pekin's lead to three. Chuck was fouled and made his free throw, bringing the Appleknockers back within two points, but Jim Couch nailed a 16-foot jumper, stretching the Chinks' lead to four. Chuck tapped in a missed shot by Kenny Flick, making the score 9-7 in favor of Pekin with two minutes and 30 seconds left to play in the period.

Although the game was close, Ruggles noticed that his players seemed more tense than usual. The Appleknockers didn't have the same zip that they had had earlier in the day against Decatur. Pekin's easy victory over Alleman had left the Chinks the fresher team. Pekin employed a full-court press that seemed to bother Cobden at times.

Dave Golden popped in another outside jump shot, and and then Jim Sommer shook loose for a layup, and the Chinks had a six-point edge, 13-7. Jim Neal was fouled and converted one free throw. A lapse in defense by Cobden allowed Golden to score a fast-break layup for Pekin with 15 seconds remaining. Golden then fouled Bob Smith, giving him a chance to slice into the lead with the clock stopped. But Bob missed the free throw, bringing the quarter to a close with the Chinks in front, 15-8.

The jump ball to start the second frame was botched so the official threw up the ball again, and Cobden won the tip. Kenny Smith missed a shot in the Appleknockers' first possession, and then Ron Rhoades nailed a 20-footer for Pekin. Bob was fouled but wasn't able to connect from the charity stripe, and the Chinks got the rebound. Dave Golden buried a 10-foot jumper, staking Pekin to an 11-point lead, 19-8. Jim Neal made a layup – the Appleknockers' first basket of the second period – and Kenny Smith added a jump shot, cutting the deficit back to seven.

The partisan Cobden crowd cheered loudly, hoping the Appleknockers would start a rally. Ron Rhoades stemmed the momentum when he canned a 23-footer for the Chinks. Jim Neal scored on a rebound bucket, but Cobden was called for fouls on Pekin's next two possessions, and the Chinks hit four straight free throws to go back on top by 11 points, 25-14, with a little over three and a half minutes left in the quarter.

Coach Ruggles called a timeout. The players gulped water and toweled the sweat off their necks and faces.

"Their shooters are killing us," Ruggles said. "We've got to get more pressure on their shooters and ball handlers. On offense, we need to get the ball inside. That's where we have the advantage."

After the timeout, the Appleknockers inbounded the ball and dribbled through Pekin's full-court press. They got the ball to Jim Neal, and he ducked into the lane for a layup. His shot rimmed off, but he got his own rebound and went back up for another shot. This time he was fouled by Amel Massa. Jim went to the foul line, but both of his free-throw attempts were off the mark, and the Chinks snared the rebound. This time Cobden was back on defense. Jim Neal and Jim Smith trapped Ron Rhoades at half court, and Jim Neal stole the ball. He drove in for a layup, but his shot wouldn't fall. Kenny Smith was there to clean up the miss, and he pulled down the rebound and scored. Jim Couch missed a long jump shot for Pekin, and Cobden got the ball back. Kenny Smith took it the length of the court and dropped in another layup, reducing the Chinks' lead to seven, 25-18, with two and a half minutes remaining before halftime.

Cobden's fans, more than 14,000 people strong, stood and applauded, excited by the Appleknockers' aggressive offensive play. It was the first time in the game that Cobden looked comfortable going to the basket. Sensing an uprising by the Appleknockers, Pekin called a timeout.

"I like what you're doing now," Coach Ruggles said. "Stay aggressive and keep taking the ball inside."

When play continued, the Chinks passed the ball to each other around Cobden's defense. Pekin's hot outside shooting had allowed it to dictate the game's tempo and forced the Appleknockers to spread their 1-2-2 zone. The Appleknockers tried a pressing defense that put a lot of pressure on the Chinks' guards. The tactic was effective against long-range shots, but it left the baseline vulnerable, and Jim Couch got underneath for a layup for Pekin. Kenny Smith hit his third shot in a row, drilling a 15-foot jumper, but the Chinks worked the ball patiently against Cobden's defense until Jim Couch got free for another layup, giving Pekin a 29-20 lead with a minute and a half to play. Chuck drove down the lane for a layup but missed the shot when he was fouled by Amel Massa. The Appleknockers' struggles at the free-throw line continued as Chuck missed both foul shots, but Jim Neal tipped in the second miss to make the score, 29-22.

Cobden employed a pressing defense again and aggressively forced Pekin out away from the basket, but with the Appleknockers' attention focused on the perimeter, Jim Sommer slipped behind the defense and scooped in a layup.

After falling so far behind, the Appleknockers seemed to modify their usual deliberate style of offense. Like Pekin, they took mostly outside shots instead of establishing the inside game where they could generate higher-percentage shots.

Kenny Smith had the hot hand, and he launched a 10-footer. The ball wouldn't go down, but Chuck tapped the rebound back to Kenny and this time his jumper was on the mark. Kenny Flick then stole the ball from the Chinks, giving Cobden the final possession of the first half. Jim Smith tried a long shot just before the buzzer sounded, but it was too strong and bounced off the backboard. The teams entered the intermission with Pekin leading, 31-24.

Pekin had shot a blistering 68.4 percent in the first half, going 13-for-19 from the field. Cobden only managed to hit 11 of its 25 shots, a 44 percent clip.

"They couldn't miss a shot," Ruggles said in the locker room. "Our defense was bad, and we couldn't hit a free throw, and we're still just down by seven. It could be a lot worse."

Keeping his advice short and to the point, he added, "Set it up. Let's play our game and get the ball inside. You've got to move your feet, especially on defense."

The boys listened intently to Coach Ruggles. He drew up some plays he wanted them to run. He had seen some things during the first half that he thought they could take advantage of. A seven-point deficit was something they could overcome. The boys still felt confident in their chance to win the game, but Kenny Flick was uneasy. He was out of sync offensively and had never gotten into a flow in the game. Pekin was defending him aggressively, but he felt he was stronger and faster than the guy guarding him. As he jogged out of the dressing room and back onto the basketball court, he hoped the second half would be better.

Chuck tipped the ball to his brother to open the second half. The Appleknockers immediately went inside as Jim Neal spotted Kenny Flick striding toward the goal and fed him a quick bounce pass that Kenny easily laid in the basket. Jim Couch missed a shot, and Chuck corralled the rebound. Kenny Smith threaded his way through Pekin's press and drained a 15-foot jump shot, and now Cobden was within three points, 31-28, with less than a minute gone in the quarter.

On the bench, Coach Ruggles clapped his hands in approval. This was the kind of start the Appleknockers needed. The crowd rose to its feet, shouting encouragement to the Cinderella team.

The Appleknockers and Chinks traded several scoreless possessions over the next few minutes. Cobden's comeback was slowed by offensive fouls against Kenny Flick and Jim Neal. The foul assessed to Jim was his third so Coach Ruggles took him out and put Jim Smith in the game. Jim Couch broke the scoring dry spell when he hit a 15-foot jumper for the Chinks with three and a half minutes left in the period. It was Pekin's first basket of the second half and put the Chinks up by five points. Kenny Smith was fouled by Dave Golden and made the free throw. Bob was called for a foul on Ron Rhoades, and he connected on his free-throw attempt. Bob hoisted a 10-foot jumper that missed its target, and Pekin got the rebound. Amel Massa missed a shot for the Chinks, and Kenny Smith grabbed the ball, but he was called for an offensive foul, and Pekin regained possession. The Chinks' sizzling first-half shooting had cooled considerably as they missed three consecutive opportunities at the basket before Chuck wrestled away the rebound. The Appleknockers had another chance to cut into the lead, but this time Bob was slapped with a questionable charging foul, and the ball went back to Pekin. Jim Sommer banked in a short shot from the side, and the Chinks had restored their seven-point lead, 36-29. Ron Rhoades was called for a foul when he ran into a pick set by Jim Smith. Jim missed his foul shot, but Chuck was there to tip in the rebound.

Pekin slowed down on its next possession, but with 30 seconds remaining in the quarter, Kenny Smith stole the ball. Chuck was called for traveling and turned the ball back over to the Chinks. Ron Rhoades drove down the lane, colliding with Chuck, and Chuck was called for a blocking foul with 13 seconds on the clock. Rhoades missed the free throw, and Kenny Flick came away with the rebound. Cobden moved quickly up the court. It had one more chance to score before the period ended. Bob pulled up for a jumper, but it wouldn't drop. Chuck grabbed the rebound and put up another shot that rolled all around the rim and fell off the iron as the buzzer sounded. Pekin remained in front by five, 36-31.

The Appleknockers got the first offensive possession of the fourth quarter when Chuck won the jump ball and tipped it to Kenny Smith. Kenny threw the ball to Bob, and he set up the offense. Jim Smith passed the ball to Chuck, and Chuck fired up a turn-around jumper from 10 feet, but it wouldn't fall, and the Chinks got the ball. Amel Massa drove the baseline under Pekin's goal, but Chuck and Kenny Flick cut him off, and Kenny stole the ball. Jim Smith sank an 18-foot jump shot, the first field goal of the period, pulling the Appleknockers within three, 36-33. Ron Rhoades answered with a shot from 15 feet, and the Chinks' margin was five again. Chuck worked into the lane and sent home a little five-footer, making the score, 38-35, with just under six minutes to play. Pekin failed to score, and Chuck seized the rebound. Kenny Smith dropped in a 15-footer, and suddenly Cobden was down by only one point.

The Appleknockers' fans cheered wildly, clapping their hands and stomping their feet. The massive hall rocked as adulation and support for Cobden rained down from the rafters. The Appleknockers' cheerleaders and mascot shouted out pro-Cobden chants and cheers, and the crowd readily yelled with them.

Ron Rhoades missed a shot from the side, but the rebound went to Jim Sommer. He took a shot, but Kenny Flick blocked it, and Kenny Smith got the ball. Cobden now had a chance to take the lead for the first time since the game's opening quarter. Anticipation mounted in the stands as the Appleknockers' fans hoped for the go-ahead bucket.

Kenny Smith missed a 15-foot jump shot, and Jim Sommer gathered the rebound for the Chinks. Kenny Smith fouled Dave Golden as he went in for a shot, and Golden made both free throws for his first points of the second half. The Appleknockers were doing a much better job defensively on Golden, and Pekin as a whole, in the second half. The Chinks poured on their full-court press, but Cobden had no trouble moving the ball safely across the center line. Bob dished a bounce pass to Kenny Flick in the lane, and Kenny scored a layup, bringing the Appleknockers back within one, 40-39, with four minutes left to play.

Once again, the crowd cheered and howled with delight, raising the decibel level in the hall through the roof. Pekin signaled for a timeout. It was a good move by Coach Hawkins as he knew he needed to stifle Cobden's rally.

The Chinks put the ball back in play, looking for a good shot. Dave Golden knifed his way into the lane and made a layup, and Pekin led, 42-39. Jim Smith was off the mark with a jumper from 18 feet, and Amel Massa hauled in the rebound.

Golden drove in for a layup again that missed, but Chuck was called for a blocking foul, sending Golden to the foul line. He made a pair of free throws, giving the Chinks a five-point edge, 44-39, with less than three minutes to go. Kenny Smith missed a 15-footer, and the rebound went through Chuck's hands and into Pekin's possession. The Chinks called for another timeout.

There were two and a half minutes left in the game when play resumed. Coach Ruggles inserted Darrell Crimmins into the lineup, replacing Chuck. Pekin began holding the ball to run time off the clock. With a five-point lead, the Chinks didn't need to take a shot. The Appleknockers tried to steal the ball, but Jim Smith finally had to foul Dave Golden before more valuable time was lost. Golden made both free throws, claiming a seven-point advantage for Pekin with a minute and 40 seconds to play. Cobden wasted no time getting the ball up the floor, and Jim Smith netted a 12-foot jumper from the baseline, to get back within five, 46-41. Pekin attempted to stall again, but Kenny Flick drew an offensive foul from Golden, and the Appleknockers got the ball. Kenny Smith found Darrell inside with a pass, but Darrell missed a five-footer, and Jim Sommer got the rebound. He threw the ball to Golden who ran over Bob as he tried to dribble down the court. Golden was called for another offensive foul. It was his fifth foul, sending him to the bench with less than a minute remaining. He had been a force for Pekin the entire game, scoring 18 points, and he received an appreciative hand from the Chinks' fans as he took a seat.

Cobden got the ball back and had another opportunity to trim its deficit, but Jim Smith missed a shot from the top of the key. Amel Massa grabbed the rebound for Pekin, and Kenny Smith fouled him immediately, knowing every second was precious. Massa failed to connect on his free throw, and Kenny Flick got the rebound. It was the break the Appleknockers were hoping for, and they moved swiftly up the court. Before they could get a shot off, Bob was called for an offensive foul. Boos and groans rang out, expressing the fans' dismay over the questionable call.

The Chinks inbounded the ball, and Bob quickly fouled Jim Couch. Couch stepped to the foul line and sank his first free throw. It felt like a dagger piercing the hearts of Cobden's fans and players. The doubt that had crept into the minds of the Appleknockers' many supporters a few minutes earlier was now taking hold. *Cobden may not win this game*, they thought. The Appleknockers had been in a lot of close games and nearly always managed to win. They had come from behind against Pinckneyville and Galesburg and pulled out victories. They had won so many games that their fans believed they would find a way to win this one, too. Couch made his second free throw, giving Pekin a seven-point lead, 48-41, with 33 seconds on the clock.

Coach Ruggles paced the sidelines. He watched Couch make both free throws, and he felt Cobden may be in too deep of a hole to climb out of in 30 seconds. He never wanted to admit defeat until the final buzzer, but he was a realist. He felt all of the boys on the bench should get a taste of state tournament action. He wanted them all to have the chance to play in a venue like Assembly Hall and to appear on TV.

Before Cobden put the ball in play, Ruggles pulled Kenny Flick, Kenny Smith, and Bob from the game and put in Roy Witthoft, Rodney Clutts, and Roger Garner. As the regulars came to the bench, Ruggles met them with pats on the back, and he told them they had done a good job. Roger Peterman offered them towels and cups of water, which they accepted gratefully, but nothing could ease the disappointment they felt.

Rodney threw the ball inbounds, and the Appleknockers dribbled quickly into their own territory. Darrell missed a shot from 15 feet, but Jim Smith snagged the rebound and scored, pulling Cobden within five, 48-43. Darrell fouled Ron Rhoades, and Rhoades missed his free throw. Roy got the rebound and pushed the ball up the court. Cobden refused to go down quietly as Jim Smith pumped in a 20-foot jumper with just five seconds left. The Chinks put the ball in play with the outcome of the game no longer in question. Rodney bumped into Amel Massa as Massa tried to advance the ball, and with one second showing on the clock, Rodney was called for a foul. Massa went to the foul line, and Pekin's fans began to celebrate. He made both free throws to bring the game to a close with the final score, 50-45. The Chinks won the game and were the IHSA state champions.

Raucous screams and cheers reverberated from Pekin's rooting section as the fans celebrated the exciting victory, but the applause from those not associated with the winning team was half-hearted at best. The Chinks won the title, but before the game had even started, the Appleknockers had won the hearts of the fans.

Pekin's fans and players happily hugged each other and clapped their hands, relishing their triumph. And rightfully so. It was the school's first state basketball championship. But in every other section of the huge hall, a palpable disappointment hung in the air. Cobden's fans were solemn. There were no hugs or handshakes passed around, only shrugged shoulders and conciliatory pats on the back.

The reaction inside Assembly Hall was merely a reflection of the feelings of people throughout the state. Unbeknownst to the team and residents of Cobden, the Appleknockers had been adopted by thousands of basketball enthusiasts in every corner of the state. As Cobden advanced through tournament play, word had spread about the big team from the tiny village in the far southern end of the state. Newspapers from Chicago to Cairo, and from Evansville, Indiana, to St. Louis, Missouri, reported on the exploits of the Appleknockers. Interest in the team grew, especially after the triple-overtime marathon it survived against Pinckneyville. To many, the Appleknockers were a "feel-good" story, an underdog team that had persevered despite the steep odds against it. As each community's local high school basketball team was eliminated from the state competition, its supporters more often than not threw their loyalties behind Cobden. The fan base grew larger with every "Goliath" the "Little David" slew.

All over the state, Appleknocker fans sat glued to their televisions. Families gathered in their living rooms, college students packed into the recreation rooms at their dorms, and those few souls left in Cobden assembled at Fuzzy's Tavern to watch the Appleknockers play for the state championship. The Appleknockers were the darlings of the tournament. When Pekin won the final game, stealing Cinderella's crown and ruining the fairytale ending, it was understandable that Cobden's supporters were saddened by the loss and that the response inside Assembly Hall was something less than enthusiastic.

Cobden's cheerleaders and Roger Burnett had fought back tears and gamely led cheers right to the end. Even when things looked bleak in the waning moments, they had hoped that the boys could somehow find a way to win the game. They had come so close. Now that the game was over, they could no longer contain their emotions. Heartsick over the loss, the girls cried and held each other. Roger stood glumly with them, the sadness registered on his face. He had his hands stuck in the pockets of his baggy jeans, and his stillness was a sharp contrast to the dynamic and entertaining mascot he had portrayed throughout the tournament.

Down in Cobden, there was no victory parade this time. Several fans had gathered at Fuzzy's to watch the Appleknockers play in the finals, and when the game ended with the scoreboard showing: Pekin 50, Cobden 45, they acknowledged the five-point loss with silence. Then, as if on cue, the whole group burst into a long, sincere applause. Tears were shed by some of the boosters, and comments were made by others about how well the boys had done anyway. They were brokenhearted for the boys, but they were still extremely proud of them.

Back at Assembly Hall, the players shook hands, and

the Appleknockers congratulated the Chinks on the hard-fought win. Then Cobden's players and Coach Ruggles moved to the sidelines. The boys put on their warm-up jackets and watched in silence as Pekin's players celebrated on the court. The Chinks raised their head coach, Dawson Hawkins, up on their shoulders, exulting their victory as their fans continued cheering loudly from the stands.

After a few moments, the Appleknockers were told to join Pekin out at center court. It was time to start the trophy presentation. Both teams lined up on opposite sides of the center jump circle. The public address announcer asked the crowd to quiet down and turn its attention to the center of the court where Al Willis, the IHSA executive director, waited with a microphone in his hand. He thanked everyone who helped organize and run the tournament then turned the floor over to Harry L. Fitzhugh, the IHSA president, to present the awards.

"Along with many other things, the State of Illinois is known for its many outstanding high school basketball teams," Fitzhugh said into the microphone. "Many coaches throughout the state are doing fine work in developing hundreds of high school players.

"A few weeks ago, 735 high schools entered the state basketball tournament series. During the past two days, we have seen eight of these finalists perform in this impressive Assembly Hall at the University of Illinois. We congratulate these finalists for their fine display of basketball playing and the fine display of sportsmanship. It is now time to present trophies to the runner-up and to our state champions.

"At this time, we would like for Coach Dick Ruggles of Cobden to please come forward."

The young coach stepped away from his team and stood in the center of the circle beside Fitzhugh.

"Coach Ruggles, we have in this package some miniature silver basketballs for you, your coaching staff, and your fine basketball team," Fitzhugh said. "We congratulate you for bringing this team to the state final runner-up position and for a job well done."

"Thank you, thank you," Ruggles said. He shook hands with Mr. Fitzhugh and accepted the small box containing the basketballs.

"We'd like at this time for team captain Ken Flick to come forward," Fitzhugh said.

Coach Ruggles stepped aside, and Kenny joined Fitzhugh in the center of the circle.

"Captain Flick, just a few weeks ago, I suspect that Cobden was just a dot on the map in the State of Illinois, but that's no longer true. Certainly the basketball playing that you fellows have done, the fame that you've brought to your town and to your community and to our state is tremendous. We know that all the people of this state are behind you people 100 percent."

At that remark, loud applause erupted in the hall, causing Mr. Fitzhugh to pause while the crowd showed its affection and appreciation for the little school and its team.

"It would be the understatement of the day to say that this was the sentimental favorite in this gymnasium tonight with the support that was shown you boys when you came out on the floor to start the basketball game," Fitzhugh continued. "We think you've brought a great honor to high school basketball, and we salute each and every one of you fine people throughout Cobden and the community for a fine school and for a job well done. Congratulations."

"Thank you," Kenny said.

Fitzhugh handed Kenny the large gold second-place trophy, and the spectators gave the Appleknockers another hearty round of applause. Fitzhugh then turned his attention to Pekin to present the championship trophy. For Cobden's players, the ceremony seemed to drag on and on. They put on brave faces, but inside they were crestfallen. They stood with their eyes cast downward, not looking around or at each other. They were ready to get off the floor and out of the spotlight.

When the ceremony was over, the Appleknockers shuf-

fled to their locker room. Unlike after their games with Galesburg and Decatur, this time there were no reporters clamoring
to get in. This was fine with the players. They had just lost the
most important game of their lives, and they were distraught.
They sat on the benches not speaking, unable to put the loss
into words. Tears flowed freely from some of the boys while
others remained stone-faced.

The boys knew everyone considered them underdogs,
but they believed they had the ability to compete with any
basketball team. They had worked so hard all season, and they
had come to the tournament to win. Feelings of disappointment, frustration, and sadness welled up inside them.

Their goal had been within reach, and they had failed
to achieve it. This loss was especially hard for the players to
accept partly because of the magnitude of the game, but also
because they felt they hadn't played well, except perhaps for
Kenny Smith who had a great game offensively. It was one
thing to lose knowing that you gave it your best effort, but
another thing to lose when you know you're capable of playing better. They had come out tentative to start the game, and
Pekin had made them pay. The Chinks' precision marksmanship from long range in the first half had allowed them to build
up a good lead. Although the Appleknockers were much more
aggressive in the second half, they were unable to overcome
their slow start.

The boys wanted to play the game again. They were
convinced they could beat Pekin if they had another chance to
play them.

Coach Ruggles was stopped by a reporter after the
awards ceremony and lingered on the court after the players
had gone. As he made his way to the locker room, it was with
a heavy heart. He knew how disappointed the players were,
and he had no idea what to say to them. He was disappointed,
too, but he was also very proud of the team and everything it
had achieved. When he reached the dressing room, he paused
and put his ear to the door. He heard only silence. The tension

in the room was evident. Deciding he would try to lighten the mood, he dashed into the room and said, "Put grins on your faces, boys, because even though we stunk tonight, we missed being state champions by only five points."

His attempt at humor fell flat. The boys knew he was trying to make them feel better by making a joke, but the loss was too fresh. Coach Ruggles sat down with the players. For a few moments, no one said anything.

"I'm proud of you boys," Ruggles finally said. "You should be proud of yourselves. You accomplished a lot this season and went further than most people thought you would. We gave it our best shot. You are a great team...you just had a bad night."

While the players showered and changed, Coach Ruggles met with the press in the hallway outside Cobden's locker room. He was still reeling with emotion and thoughts of the game, but he did his best to compose himself and answer the questions.

The reporters asked him why the Appleknockers had faltered in the championship game, and so many things went through his mind. The boys had played poorly, especially in the first half, but there wasn't one specific factor he could put his finger on. They had tried their best and for whatever reason, things just hadn't gone their way. The rugged battle with the Reds earlier in the day had taken something out of the boys and left them more tired than they realized or wanted to admit.

"This is the first time the boys had to play twice in the same day, and they all showed it," Ruggles said. "Remember in southern Illinois there are no tournaments, preseason or otherwise, that have the semifinals and finals on the same day."

"How does Pekin compare to other teams you've faced this year?" a reporter asked.

Ruggles thought for a moment and said, "I'd say they're similar to Pinckneyville. Both squads were well coached and had great defenses, but perhaps most important was they both had five men that could beat you."

"Your ace Kenny Flick has been leading you in scoring," another sportswriter said. "Why did he have just four points tonight?"

"They just had him bottled up so he couldn't get position, and my men know not to shoot when they don't have position," Ruggles replied. "Even though Flick had a great early tournament, we don't revolve our offense around him. We're a five-player club and have been all year. We let whichever player who has the best position take the shot."

Some of the other coaches at the tournament had complained about the referees, calling them inconsistent from game to game, and a reporter asked Ruggles his opinion of the officiating. Ruggles may have disagreed with some of the calls the referees made, but he knew the officiating had nothing to do with the Appleknockers losing. He wasn't going to use it as an excuse.

"The officiating was fine," he said, making that his only comment on that topic.

When Coach Ruggles and the players returned to the Paradise Inn, they were met by a small group of well-wishers. A little party had been organized, complete with cake and balloons, to celebrate the Appleknockers' runner-up finish. Some of the players' parents were there, and they told the boys how proud they were of them. Pinckneyville's coaches and players, who continued to conduct themselves with the highest level of sportsmanship were also there, and they congratulated the Appleknockers on a great showing in the tournament.

The boys appreciated the support and accepted the kind words as gracefully as possible, but their disappointment gnawed at them. They ate the cake, of course, because nothing stopped them when it came to food, but they found the party was something more to be endured rather than to be enjoyed.

The adults in the group were taking the loss hard, too, and perhaps no one was more shaken up than Jack Lamer. He had coached the boys in their formative years. He had watched them develop over the seasons, and they had grown into a first-rate squad. Coach Lamer had attended every state basketball tournament since 1951, and he really felt Cobden was going to win the title this year, especially after it beat Decatur. Too down to hang out at the party, he called it a night and retired to his room.

Some of the Cobden supporters who attended the party discussed the game and commiserated in the hotel lounge.

"The boys never gave up," Donald Ballance said. "They fought to the end."

"That's true," Mike Basler agreed. "You can't fault their effort, especially in the second half."

They were all proud of the boys' efforts, but the loss to Pekin was still a letdown. They felt Stephen Decatur was the best team Cobden had played all year. If the Appleknockers were going to lose, it should have been to the Reds. They meant no disrespect to Pekin, which was a good ball club, but they felt certain that Cobden was the better team.

Coach Ruggles hugged Mary and young Randy, who was up well past his bedtime. Mary could see the disappointment in her husband's eyes. No words were necessary. She knew him well enough to know how he was feeling.

"You and the boys did so well, and we had such an exciting season," she told him. "We've had a lot of fun, and I couldn't be more proud of you."

Ruggles knew she was right. The season had been fun and exciting, but tonight's loss was still too close for him to have a clear perspective. Right now he wanted that final game back. He wanted a chance to do it over, but he knew that was impossible. And he felt bad for the boys. He had been in their shoes and understood the pain they were feeling. He also felt bad for the Appleknockers' fans. He knew how important this was to the people of Cobden. They had been on this ride with the Appleknockers all season. He wished he could have taken them across the finish line in first place.

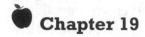 **Chapter 19**

The Trip Home

The next morning, Coach Ruggles and Mary woke up early and decided to attend church before going to the station to catch the train back to Cobden. Jack Lamer had also risen early, and he agreed to watch Randy while the two of them were gone. Ruggles got directions to the nearest Catholic church, and then he and Mary borrowed Mike Basler's car and drove to the church for mass. The peace of the sanctuary gave them the opportunity to reflect on the basketball season. What a whirlwind the year had been. They knew how blessed the Appleknockers were to have accomplished so much and gone so far in the state tournament, but the disappointment of last night's loss still stung. It was a feeling that couldn't simply be prayed away.

When they got back to the Paradise Inn, Doris Garner, the school superintendent, waited for Coach Ruggles in the lobby.

"Good morning," he said. "I just wanted to remind you that we're having a ceremony for the boys in the gym when you get back home this afternoon. I know everything has been really hectic since you've been up here, and you've been on the go every minute so we've taken care of the arrangements down there. It's just going to be a little reception to welcome the team home."

"Thanks," Ruggles said. "That was nice of you. The boys will appreciate that."

"I better get on the road so I don't miss it myself," Garner said, heading to his car to make the drive back to Cobden.

Coach Ruggles roused the rest of the gang. Most of the boys were already up, with sleep having eluded them much of the night. They all went to the hotel's restaurant for breakfast, but not even food could brighten the players' solemn dispositions, and they didn't eat with their normal zeal. Once the meal was over, the whole crew, their luggage, and the large second-place trophy were chauffeured to the train station downtown. Cobden's cheerleaders were riding the train home with the players, and they arrived shortly after the team.

Conspicuous in their letter jackets and possessing the large trophy, the players were recognized instantly when the station's porter came out to the platform to help them with their bags.

"Hey," he said enthusiastically. "You're the Apple-knockers! You put on quite a show up here."

"Thank you," Coach Ruggles said.

"You made this tournament really exciting," the porter continued. "You have a lot of fans here."

"Thank you," Ruggles said again. He understood the man's interest. The crowds at Assembly Hall had been almost overwhelming in their support of Cobden, and he appreciated that. In his head he knew that his team had done well, but his heart just wasn't ready for a discussion about the tournament yet.

"Your train is scheduled to leave on time," the porter said, rounding up the bags. "You can start boarding. I hope you folks have a good trip home."

They all found seats in the passenger car, and they decided to keep the trophy with them. This was the first time the cheerleaders had the chance to hold the prize so they passed it around to get a better look. It was an impressive award. It just wasn't the one they had hoped to win. After everyone got a look, Coach Ruggles asked Roger Peterman to take care of the trophy during the ride home.

As the Illinois Central train called the "City of New Orleans" steamed out of Champaign and headed south toward Cobden, the atmosphere was much different than it had been on the trip up a few days prior. A somber mood emanated from the dejected passengers. It was unlike the immense sorrow they had felt when Tom Crowell had died, but more like a deep regret over an opportunity lost and a goal unattained. The boys felt down about their loss and said little to each other. They were full of thoughts about the game, analyzing the plays and wondering what they could have done differently. They rarely had to deal with loss, and this loss – the state championship – was extremely tough to take.

Coach Ruggles looked around the train car and could see the disappointment written all over the faces of the players and cheerleaders. *It's like a morgue in here*, he thought. Everyone was so quiet. He wished he could think of something to say to make the kids feel better. He thought of the reception and ceremony for the team that the school superintendent had planned, and he hoped the boys would feel like going.

Like the players, Coach Ruggles kept thinking about the loss to Pekin. He knew it was futile to second guess the decisions he had made in the game, but he couldn't help but wonder if a few key adjustments could have made a difference in the outcome. Last night his team hadn't played well but had still come within five points of winning the state title, and it was impossible for him to just shrug off an event of that enormity. *We were tired*, he thought. He wished they could play Pekin again when the boys were rested.

Mary sat next to him, talking to Randy and trying to keep the small boy entertained. Even he, at less than three years old, was more subdued than usual. He was worn out from the tournament and being out of his routine. She knew how her husband was feeling, and she squeezed his hand. He gave her a wan smile to let her know how grateful he was that she and Randy were there with him.

The miles loomed before them, and the ride seemed longer this time. The players had been so excited on the way up to Champaign that the trip had practically flown by. Exhausted by the emotions of the tournament and a lack of rest, some of the boys slept. Others gazed blankly out the windows. Outside the corn and soybean fields glistened green and gold under a cloudless blue sky, but the sunny day did nothing to raise the gloomy spirits of the passengers inside. They just wanted the trip to be over.

The train made its usual stops, picking up people and dropping them off, but the boys paid no attention to the comings and goings of the other passengers.

Kenny Flick and Evalena sat together, holding hands. They hadn't seen much of each other while in Champaign and now they were anxious to get home to see their son.

Jim Neal had kept to himself since boarding the train, not speaking to anyone. He was filled with emotion and regret. Coach Ruggles had taken him out of the championship game late in the third quarter and never put him back in. Jim had no idea why. He hadn't fouled out, and he believed he could have helped the team if he had been on the floor. Jim lived and breathed basketball, and he was discouraged that while the Appleknockers played the biggest game of their lives, he had watched the end unfold from the bench. He had tremendous respect for Coach Ruggles and wasn't about to ask him why. But he knew the question would nag at him forever.

The train rolled on southward, and the boys began feeling apprehensive as they got closer to home. Everyone in Cobden had been so supportive all season, and the players felt bad that they had let them down.

Well, this is it, Kenny Smith thought. *We got as close as we could, and we blew it. We've disappointed everyone.*

He looked out the window as the train approached the cemetery north of Cobden and saw cars lined up on both sides of the road. *That's odd,* he thought. *It's Sunday. They're having a funeral on a Sunday? Somebody important must've died.* He found it strange that his mom and dad or anyone else for that matter had failed to mention anyone dying. In Cobden, news traveled fast, especially news of a birth or death, and he hadn't heard anything.

Then he saw more cars. They were parked everywhere, and a long line of them extended into town as far as he could see.

"Look at all the cars," he said to his teammates. What's going on?!"

The other boys all jumped up and pressed their faces to the windows to get a better look. Coach Ruggles was sitting on the opposite side of the train and turned his head when he heard all the commotion. All he could see was the backs of the players and cheerleaders as they peered out the windows. He stood up and craned his neck to get a better view. A grin broke out over his face as he realized what was happening.

"Looks like we've got a welcoming committee," he declared.

An estimated 4,000 to 5,000 people had descended on the village of 900 to welcome the Appleknockers home and celebrate their trip to the state tournament. Welcome signs hung everywhere. Rows of American flags lined the sidewalks and flapped in the spring breeze. An hour before the train was due, cars carrying people from counties throughout southern Illinois and the surrounding region were already backed up on U.S. Route 51 around the curve from Carbondale to the north and down the highway from Anna to the south.

Coach Ruggles and the team saw a giant "welcome home" banner strung across the bridge that spanned U.S. Rt. 51 as the train chugged underneath it and then eased to a stop at Cobden's small depot. They all stared wide-eyed out the windows in surprise and amazement at throngs of people. They had never seen so many people in their town. *We lost*, they thought. *Are they all really here for us?* The sinking feeling they had carried with them since last night's game started to lift. The sheer volume of people that had shown up seemed to say, "You didn't lose. You won." and "We're proud of you."

Crowds crammed both sides of the tracks, screaming, clapping, and waving. People stood on the hoods of their cars, and some had climbed to the roofs of the post office and clinic so they could see the Appleknockers when they alighted from the train. They were proud of the Appleknockers, and they wanted them to know it.

"Look at all the people," Mary said to her husband, incredulous and happy. "This is so wonderful."

Still a little dazed himself, Ruggles hugged her and Randy to him. Then he noticed the boys were just standing in the train. They appeared transfixed and unsure of what to do.

"This is no time to be camera shy," he said to them. "They're all waiting for you."

He took a hold of Mary's and Randy's hands and stepped out onto the platform. The crowd roared with delight. Photographers snapped pictures, and a young girl, Patti Emery, handed Mary a beautiful bouquet of flowers.

Inside the passenger car, the players hesitated. Then Kenny Smith picked up the trophy, lifting it high, he took a deep breath and stepped off the train. The mass of people cheered loudly. Marching bands from Cobden, Anna-Jonesboro, and Dongola high schools began to play as the boys emerged from the train one by one, wearing smiles of disbelief. They squinted into the bright sunshine, trying to locate their friends and family members as the crowd gathered around them. They saw some familiar faces, but most of the people were strangers. Community rivalries had been set aside, and it seemed that all of southern Illinois had united behind Cobden during its tournament run. The Appleknockers had become southern Illinois' team, not just Cobden's, and sports fans and non-sports fans alike had come from all over to show their support and share in the team's success.

Photographers took pictures as cameramen and reporters from the local television stations documented the scene. After everyone had exited the train, Coach Ruggles, the players, and the cheerleaders were escorted through the crowd to the street where several convertibles sat waiting.

Kenny Smith still had the trophy and he, Chuck, Kenny Flick, and Coach Ruggles climbed into the back of one of the cars while Mary got in the front passenger seat. The other players and cheerleaders hopped into the remaining cars and a parade began, with state police cars leading the procession.

Cobden's shiny red fire engine, siren blaring and sporting a big sign that read "Welcome Home Champs," fell in line next, and was followed by the convertibles carrying the team. The crepe-paper-strung vehicles cruised slowly around the downtown loop of Cobden's business district. As they passed the small shops, people waved, shouted their names, and yelled, "Go Appleknockers!"

The boys couldn't stop smiling as they rode past the cheering onlookers. They held the trophy high and with true affection, feeling real pride in their accomplishments for the first time. They were being treated like heroes. It was a greater homecoming than any of them could have ever imagined. Even Jim Neal's melancholy was eased as he got swept up in the fanfare.

After circling the loop three times, the motorcade headed to the high school for the reception in the gymnasium. Spectators packed the bleachers and filled the floor all the way to the free-throw line at the west side of the gym where a 15-foot cake was displayed. It was shaped and frosted to look like a basketball court and an inscription in icing stated: "We love our Appleknockers." Cobden's band played the school's fight song, Illinois Loyalty, and everyone sang at the top of their lungs.

The gym stage was decorated with colored streamers and large floral arrangements. Wallace Rich, the president of Cobden's bank, was the master of ceremonies for the reception. He stepped to the podium in the center of the stage and tapped the microphone. It was turned on and let out a high-pitched squeal at his touch. He steadied the microphone, silencing the squeal and then asked for the crowd's attention. The gym was wall-to-wall people. They were sandwiched into every crevice and overflowed into the lobby. He had never seen the gym so full. There were hundreds more people in attendance than anyone anticipated.

"I want to thank everyone for coming," he said. "We're here to celebrate and honor the accomplishments of an exceptional group of young men. I'd like you to please give the Appleknockers a round of applause."

The people readily obliged with a deafening ovation. When the gym quieted, Rich called Cobden's mayor, Frank Petty, to the stage to speak on behalf of the town.

"Cobden sure got a lot more residents while I was up in Champaign for a few days," Mayor Petty said, joking with the crowd. "I'd like to welcome all of you to Cobden for this fine celebration. We are proud of the biggest crop we have ever grown – the Appleknockers – and the greatest import Cobden has ever had – Coach Ruggles."

Another thunderous ovation followed. Rich introduced Doris Garner and handed him the microphone. The superintendent told everyone about the many telegrams the school had received from people all over, with one coming all the way from Texas. He also said that schools from throughout the state had sent messages of good luck and good wishes to the team, and he knew how much the boys had appreciated all the encouragement. Then he summoned Coach Ruggles and the players to the stage.

Coach Ruggles had been as surprised as the players at the size of the crowd that had been waiting to greet them when they got to Cobden. He knew there was going to be a reception, but he had never expected such a large celebration, and he was enjoying every minute. Mayor Petty had referred to him as an "import," but the residents of Cobden had been so welcoming to him and his family from the day they arrived that he almost felt like a native. Mary's parents had brought Kathy to meet the team at the depot, and he and Mary were happy to be reunited with their little girl. Ruggles now took Mary, Randy, and Kathy with him and joined the superintendent on the stage.

It took the boys much longer to get there. As they worked their way through the mob, they kept getting stopped by their friends and neighbors who wanted to speak to them or shake their hands. Many of the players found their parents and girlfriends among the horde and stopped to hug them, wanting to share this special occasion with those they cared about most.

"This is the greatest thing that ever happened to Cobden," Roy Witthoft remarked to a reporter as he ascended the steps to the stage.

Once all the players made it to the stage, Coach Ruggles introduced each one individually. He spoke fondly of each young man and what he contributed to the team. The boys stepped forward, smiling and waving when their names were announced. They were overcome with feelings of joy and gratitude for the support they received from the jubilant crowd. The reception had lifted them from the doldrums and turned this day into one of the best days of their lives.

Ruggles told the crowd that Kenny Flick had been chosen first team all-tournament by an Associated Press poll of sportswriters and broadcasters. He had received more votes than any other player, earning the distinction of best performer in the state tournament. Ruggles said Kenny Smith was chosen second team all-tournament. Ruggles conveyed what an honor this was by saying only 10 players in the whole event were selected to the two teams.

"We had a great year," Coach Ruggles said. "We had a lot of fun, and we want to thank you for coming to all the games and supporting us all season. You were a big help to us, and we truly appreciated it.

"The tournament was very exciting. The boys worked hard and played well. We caught a few breaks along the way and made a nice run at the title. I'm so proud of these boys." Ruggles paused and looked at his players. "I could not have asked for a better group of young men to work with. They have conducted themselves as perfect gentlemen on and off the basketball court."

With the speeches complete, the cake was cut and served, and the party continued as people talked and laughed and shared stories of the Appleknockers' incredible season. The pep band played, and all the trophies and plaques the team had won during the year were exhibited for everyone to see.

Several bushels of plastic apples were placed on the stage, and the players were asked to autograph them and toss them to the people on the floor.

"Over here! Over here!" the people shouted, clamoring for the souvenir apples.

The boys signed apple after apple and began throwing them to their eager fans. Soon apples were flying everywhere, and it looked like it was raining apples in the gym. The shower of apples was a fitting end to the celebration since the Appleknockers had been showered with support by their fans all season.

Epilogue

Some defeats are more triumphant than victories
~ Michel de Montaigne

There's an old sports adage that says, "It's not whether you win or lose. It's how you play the game." That phrase, modified slightly to say, "It's not whether they won or lost. It's that they played the game," fits the Cobden Appleknockers of 1964. The amazing season that they put together was not diminished by their loss in the championship game of the Illinois state high school basketball tournament. The basketball experts never expected Cobden to even make it to the state tournament, as evidenced by their ranking of 13 in the field of 16 teams. But by the end of the tournament, one sportswriter observed, "While Pekin was a fine champion, there wasn't a team at Champaign that could beat the Appleknockers when they were at their best." Cobden may have arrived at the tournament as a curiosity or conversation piece, but the Appleknockers left with the respect of everyone who had watched them play. Their accomplishments that year transcended basketball and are a testament to perseverance and what people can do when they don't let others set limits for them.

As the years passed, a curious phenomenon occurred. Many people in Illinois and elsewhere think the Appleknockers won the state championship in 1964. The reason for this revisionist history is unclear, but members of the team and residents of Cobden often run into people who refer to the Appleknockers as the "tiny team who won the state tournament."

"I used to correct people," said Chuck Neal. "But not anymore."

Where Did They Go?

Coach Dick Ruggles guided the Appleknockers to the best record ever in Cobden High School's history. The team compiled a 59-5 record in his two seasons. He left the Appleknockers after the 1964 season and moved to Nashville, Illinois. He taught at Nashville High School for 29 years and coached boys' basketball, football, track, baseball, and golf. He retired in 1993 but then went back and coached girls' volleyball for three years. He and his wife, Mary, still live in Nashville. In addition to Randy and Kathy, they had another son, Kevin, who is deceased, and two more daughters, Kim and Kristi.

Kenny Flick earned all-state honors and was a first team all-tournament selection at the 1964 state tournament. After graduating as salutatorian of his high school class, he played basketball for two years at Mineral Area College in Missouri. He still lives in Cobden and is happily married to Evalena. They had two more children after Kevin, Bruce and Kenny Kay.

Chuck Neal graduated as the valedictorian of the class of 1964. He attended Memphis State University and played basketball there for four years. After graduating, he joined the U.S. Air Force, becoming a pilot and serving 21 years. After completing his service in the Air Force, he flew for Northwest Airlines. He married his high school sweetheart, Judy, and they had three boys: Ryan, Robin, and Nathan. He lives in Anna, Illinois.

Jim Neal played basketball for the University of Dayton before serving in the U.S. Air Force for three years where he played on the base's basketball team. He subsequently played basketball for the University of Georgia and Carson-Newman College in Jefferson City, Tennessee. He coached high school basketball, worked in the insurance business, earned a bachelor's degree in biblical studies, and served as pastor of two Baptist churches. He and his wife, Patti, had four children: Jamia, James, Staci, and Joshua (deceased). He operates an insurance brokerage firm in Bakersfield, California.

Kenny Smith was designated second team all-tournament at the state tournament in 1964. He was recruited to play basketball at Southern Illinois University but was drafted into the U.S. Army and served a tour of duty in Vietnam. He met his wife, Rosie, while in the Army, and they had two children: Tammy and Tim. He worked for the Department of Justice for many years and lived in Cobden. He and his wife tour the country in an RV and still own property in Cobden.

Jim Smith was drafted after graduation and served in the U.S. Army for two years. He worked for the Sparta Printing Company for 27 years and then for the State of Illinois. He and his wife, Joan, had three sons: Joe, Jimmie, and Jason. He is retired and lives in Carterville, Illinois, but continues to work as a basketball referee, something he has done for more than 30 years.

Darrell Crimmins attended the University of Missouri-Rolla where he earned both bachelor's and master's degrees in mechanical engineering. He played intramural basketball, and his team lost only one game in five years while he played there. He and his wife, Marty, had three children: Blaine, Darren, and Kelly. He lives in Carrollton, Texas, and retired in November of 2009 after 30 years with Frito-Lay and started his own engineering company.

Bob Smith graduated from high school in 1965 and worked as a correctional officer in the prison system. He lived in Cobden for many years and died in 2008. He had one daughter, Christi.

Roy Witthoft joined the U.S. Air Force after high school and served for four years. He played basketball on the base's team.

After he was discharged, he attended Southern Illinois University Edwardsville where he played basketball for four years. He and his wife, Jackie, had one son, Tim. Roy lives in East Alton, Illinois.

Ralph Rich got a bachelor's degree in education from Southern Illinois University. He taught and coached at the junior high and high school levels in Waverly, Illinois. He and his wife, Deanne, had one daughter, Jennifer. He is retired and lives in Waverly.

Roger Garner was a sophomore in 1964. He worked as the industrial arts teacher at Cobden High School for many years and had one daughter, Tammy, and a son, Rick. He lives in Buncombe, Illinois.

Rodney Clutts was a sophomore in 1964. He became a lawyer and served as an associate circuit judge for many years. He had five children: Erin, Tyler, Emily, Stephanie, and Rachel. Now retired, he lives in Anna.

Dan Marsh lives in Murphysboro, Illinois, with his wife Mary Sullivan. He works as a counselor at Mulberry Center, the psychiatric unit at Harrisburg Medical Center.

Jack Lamer and his wife, Jean, lived in Cobden for many years, and he continued to coach the boys' junior high school basketball team. From 1965 to 1967, Lamer's teams won 37 consecutive games and compiled a 37-1 record. Lamer never missed a basketball game for sickness or any other reason. During his three decades of coaching at Cobden, his teams won 81 trophies with 31 championships and 21 second-place finishes. The Illinois Basketball Coaches Association inducted him into its Hall of Fame in 1989, a rare achievement for a junior high coach. He is retired from his job as Cobden Elementary School principal.

About the Authors

Teri Campbell and Anne Ryman both grew up in Cobden and graduated from Cobden High School. Teri still lives in Cobden. Anne lives in Phoenix, Arizona, with her husband, Scott Cancelosi, and daughter, Maria. In 2003, they began documenting the history of the Amazing Appleknockers to preserve the story for generations of Appleknockers to come.